Art and craft in

africa

Laure Meyer

**EVERYDAY LIFE,
RITUAL,
COURT ART**

· TERRAIL ·

Cover illustration

Marionette
Bambara. Mali.
Private collection.

Previous page

Top of messenger staff
Akan, Ashanti, Ghana.
Carved wood covered
with gold leaf.
H.: 30.7 cm.
Barbier-Mueller Museum,
Geneva.

Opposite

Beadwork tunic
Oba costume (détail).
Yoruba. Nigeria.
L.: 133 cm.
National Museum, Lagos.

© FINEST S.A. / ÉDITIONS PIERRE TERRAIL, PARIS, 2001
25, rue Ginoux - 75015 Paris - FRANCE
ISBN 2-87939-098-2
Printed in Italy

Published with the assistance of the French Ministry responsible for culture
Centre National du Livre (The National Book Centre)

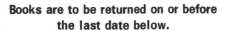

Art and craft in

rica

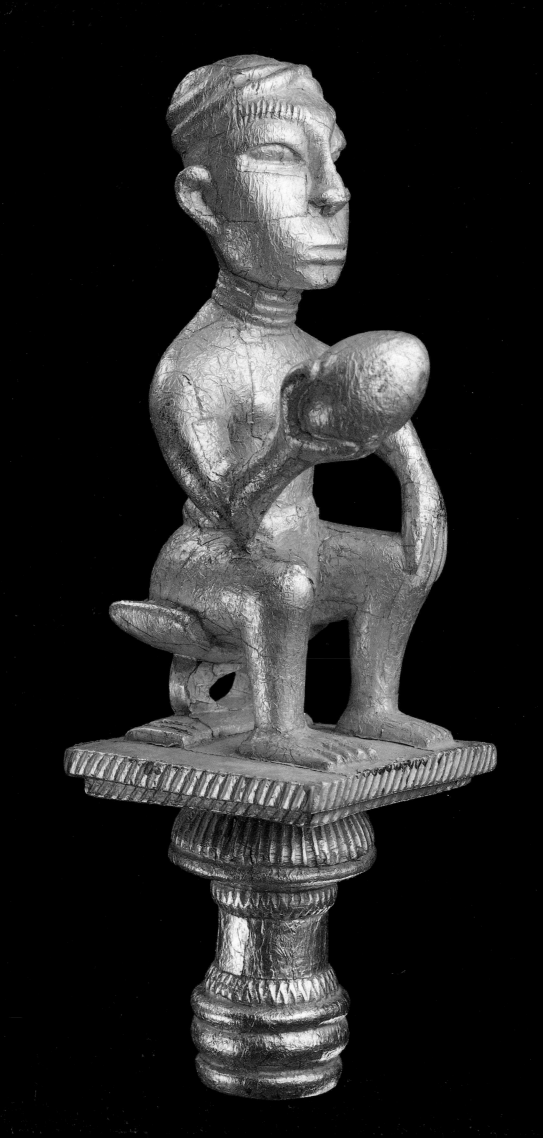

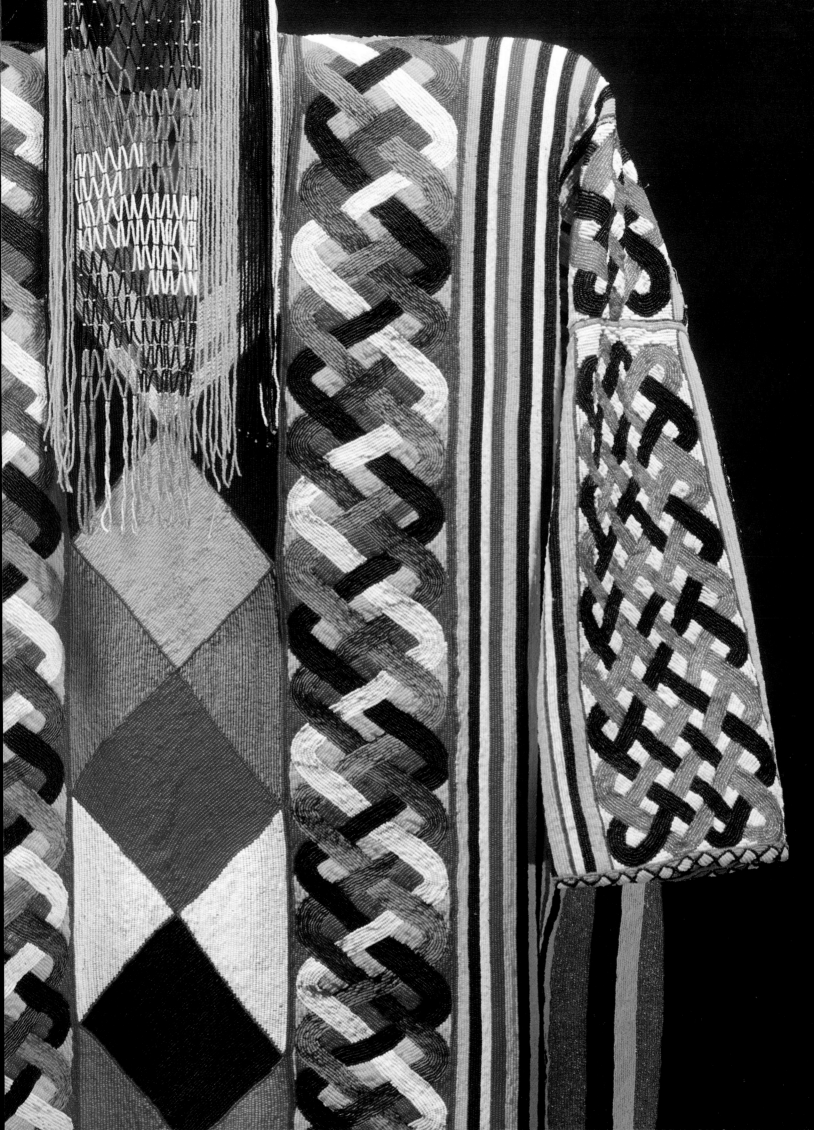

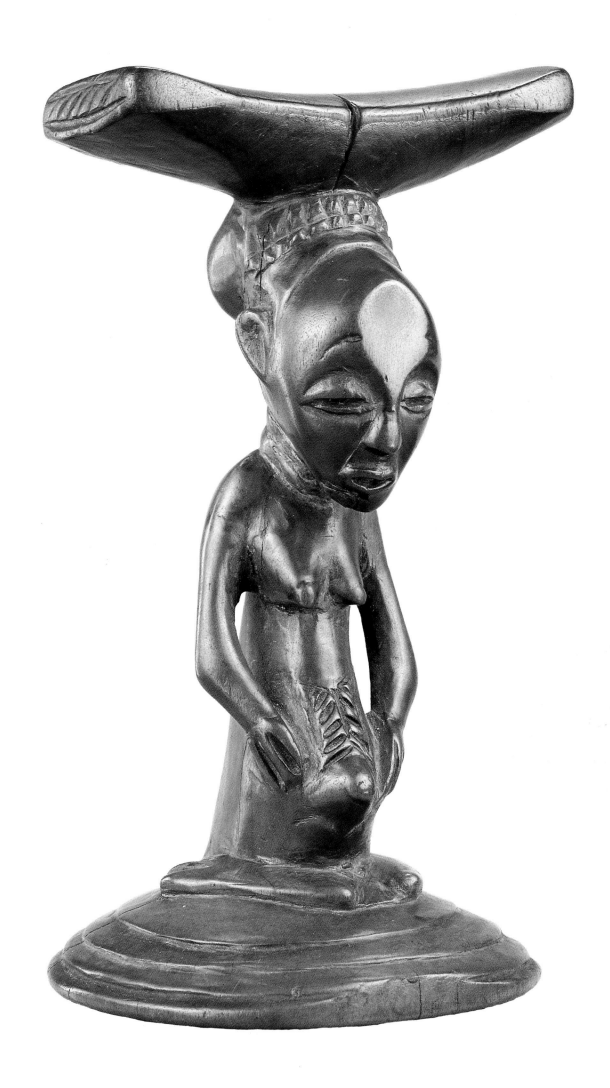

Contents

Head-rest
Luba. Wood. H.: 17.5 cm.
Private collection.

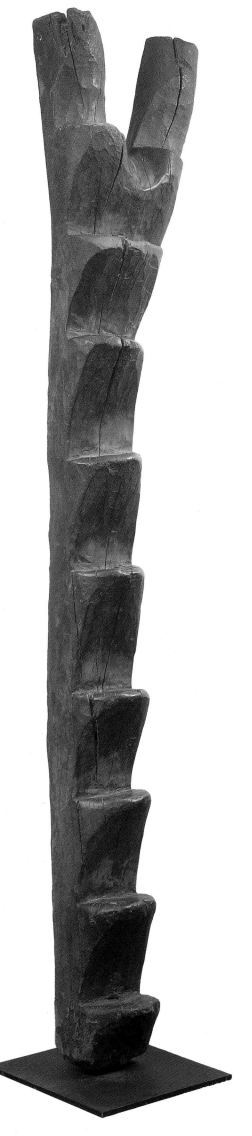

Dogon ladder
Mali. H.: 240 cm.
Monbrison Archives.

Page 11

2. Door of millet granary.
Dogon. Mali. Archives of the Barbier-Mueller Museum, Geneva.

Presents the usual motifs found on Dogon doors: rows of elongated human figures symbolizing ancestors, a reptile, and, below, scenes of daily life.

Introduction

The art of the object in Black Africa

It has often been said that the 'objet d'art' in the European sense – that is, an object created more for the sake of its beauty than its utility – does not exist in Africa. Yet perhaps nowhere is the art of the object and the love of aesthetic form so present in daily life as it is in Africa.

An aesthetic sense is evident in every area of African cultural activity, and not just in the ritual objects and sculptures which first caught the attention and interest of European art-lovers. Linked to ancestor worship and inspired by high religious feeling, these statues and masks have naturally made a great impression on Western artists, who although unaware of the deeper significance of these objects, were sensitive to their psychological dimension and grasped the artistic solutions which they displayed. Understandably enough, sculptures and masks became the 'star' objects of African culture.

But all the other artifacts – those used in everyday life, the handy and discrete objects which enlivened the more prosaic sides of life, the textiles, ornaments, weapons, the artifacts used in feasts and celebrations – these countless objects demonstrate an aesthetic sensibility all the more remarkable for serving the humblest of purposes. Compared with the 'stars', they play much more than the role of being mere 'extras'. A pervasive aesthetic sense manifested in so much of African culture has been noted by most ethnologists and should not be overlooked, despite the low living standards among some populations.

Aesthetic sensibility in the case of utilitarian objects can appear on two levels. It shows itself first in the elegance or fitness of the forms, which, in and of themselves, provide simple visual pleasure without recourse to ornamentation. This elegance, however, is never an end in itself, but emphasizes the functionality of the object by subordinating and adapting itself to it. Simple, pure forms are designed with an unerring sense of line.

This first level, or dimension, of aesthetic sensation is often heightened by a second level, in which ornamentation is applied to the basic design to complete and enhance it. All the features which transcend the merely functional and which serve no practical purpose, are evidently intended to satisfy a need for aesthetic pleasure. In this sense, art may be defined as the transcendence of craft.

This formal and ornamental beauty is often meant to advertise the status of the owner. No wonder, therefore, that no effort was spared in furnishing chiefs, kings and their courts with prestigious attributes. Handmade by master craftsmen or professional artists working with valuable materials like metal, ivory and beads, their primary purpose was to display conspicuously the owner's wealth and rank. On the other hand, these regal objects often served as models for the arts and crafts of the common people and certainly stimulated their development.

The objects of the court and the objects of the people both have their place in this survey. They will be studied mainly in the light of their aesthetic qualities; ethnological details, although necessary in some cases, will be reduced to a minimum. Our task has been above all to define the everyday needs which these objects answered, and the kinds of solutions – technical, formal, or decorative – that were found for their design.

The simple, fundamental realities of everyday life are what provided the thread for this book. Each chapter presents a group of objects designed to satisfy the basic needs of human beings in a natural environment: domestic furnishings, serving meals for large families, clothing, adornments, defence of the right to life and assertion of strength, the pleasures of society, and the symbolic confirmation of the authority governing the group.

Those objects created to satisfy these needs will be presented in the human context which brought them into being and the living conditions which influenced their development. Accounts from early travellers, old picture postcards and recent photographs will help bring these objects and their original setting back to life.

By using this approach – portraying the objects in their original context – we may also note that the style indigenous to each culture in the realm of masks and sculptures is paralleled by stylistic features in the design of functional objects. Style, here, was not the product of theory, as is the case with Western art, but derived from a certain vision of the world which was shared by all the members of the social group. The various craftsmen and artists never strove to distinguish themselves personally by the originality of their creations. They worked within the context of customs observed by everyone else. In turn, their imagination was nourished by the myths, artistic traditions, and specific history of the culture and world in which they lived.

It should be kept in mind, moreover, that there was a clear distinction between the tasks with which the craftsmen were presented. In the case of ritual objects – the statue of an ancestor or a mask – sculptors enjoyed only a relative amount of freedom of invention. They had to work within the narrow confines of a veritable programme defined by mythology and the magic efficacity sought by their 'client'. Under the circumstances, artisans were by no means free to follow their own inspiration. But in the case of objects made for daily use, artisans' margins of invention were much greater, and they were free to work according to the dictates of their own taste. Where the design was fixed by tradition or function, they could exercise their creativity and show how they treated forms and ornamentation, being free to combine or juxtapose traditional motifs as they saw fit.

The craftsman's freedom was restricted, of course, by the technical constraints of the materials. Metals like bronze, copper or brass could be melted and cast. Very different results were obtained depending on whether open moulds or the lost-wax process was used. Where steel and iron were concerned, the necessary fusion temperatures required industrial conditions that were technically beyond the reach of pre-colonial Africans. All steel and iron objects were forged and hammered into shape.

The rudimentary tools available also set unavoidable limits. Great variations in textiles were obtained depending on the range of weaving and ornamentation techniques which the weavers could employ on their looms.

Yet despite technical limitations and primitive tools, the objects produced were often remarkably well-executed. Working at their own pace, artisans could attend to the slightest details and polish the surfaces to a smooth finish. Michel Leiris spoke of 'a group of arts in which beauty, far from being relegated to a sphere of its own, appears inextricably mixed with the facts of life'.

This beauty was produced by adapting ornamentation precisely to the form of the object. Ornamental motifs were not afterthoughts, but an integral part of the design. Thus they seem to surge out of or merge with the basic forms, simplifying the curves of the weapons, articulating the surfaces of the vessels and pots with patterns and colours, enlivening the beadwork and jewellery.

The materials used, however humble, corresponded to the function of the crafted object and endowed it with an unerring fitness. The materials were not camouflaged, but left to speak for themselves, often enriched with a patina which enhanced their colour and lustre. The work of the artist, however, also transformed the object by giving it forms which addressed the imagination: spoons were given the shape of a woman's body, the strong and graceful caryatids supporting a head-rest watched over the dreams of the sleeper. Jewels and adornments transfigure the body, while decorated fabrics dazzle the eye with an incomparable *joie de vivre*. Different forms of musical instruments give expression to the musicians' unconscious minds, allowing them to transcend themselves. The sanza (thumb-piano) and harp are female, drums resonate like the bellowing of cattle, the royal megaphone represents the jaws of a crocodile. Examples of such associations may be found everywhere in Africa.

What makes for such wealth of associations is the foundation of all of these objects in time. They spring out of the depths of a remote past, enriched by tradition, and, unlike so many products of the Western world, they are not infected by the fast pace of modern life. They are characterized by sincerity, purity, authenticity, and not a little naïveté. Polished by innumerable hands and by generation upon generation of human contact, the inevitable effects of age become visible and tangible qualities, and stand as the surest guarantee of their value.

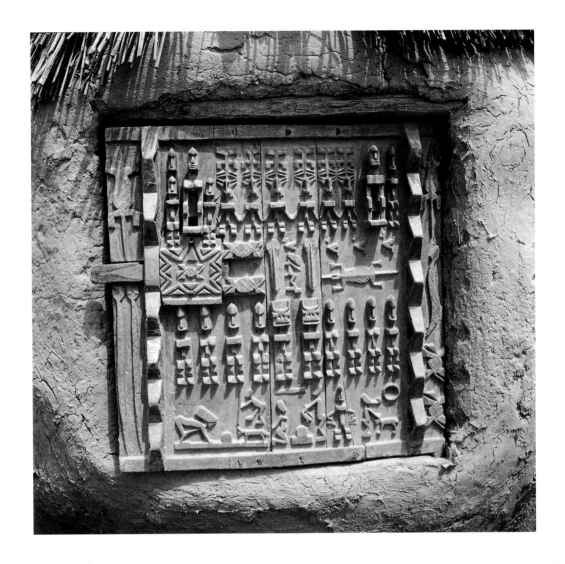

African art, rooted in time, the past and tradition, presents the image of a continuity which is lacking in our own culture.

Most of the objects discussed in this book were made in the nineteenth or first half of the twentieth century. Some are much older, but none dates from later than 1960. This date marks the beginning of a period of intense change, whereby the traditional arts and crafts were brutally replaced by objects, materials and manufacturing processes imported or copied from those of Western countries.

It should not be necessary to point out, finally, that Africa is an enormous continent and that its arts vary greatly from one region to another. It is impossible to generalize about such a vast area and for every example, a counter-example may be found. The commentaries given for the objects in the course of this book should never be taken as general statements, but rather as descriptions of what could be found at a given place and at a given moment in time.

Within these limits, and given the attention they deserve, these African objects – like the ritual masks and statues – can offer something to our culture which goes far beyond aesthetic pleasure. Although created for everyday use, they are charged with a spirituality that only awaits a receptive beholder to reveal itself. With African objects, one may truly say that there is always more than meets the eye.

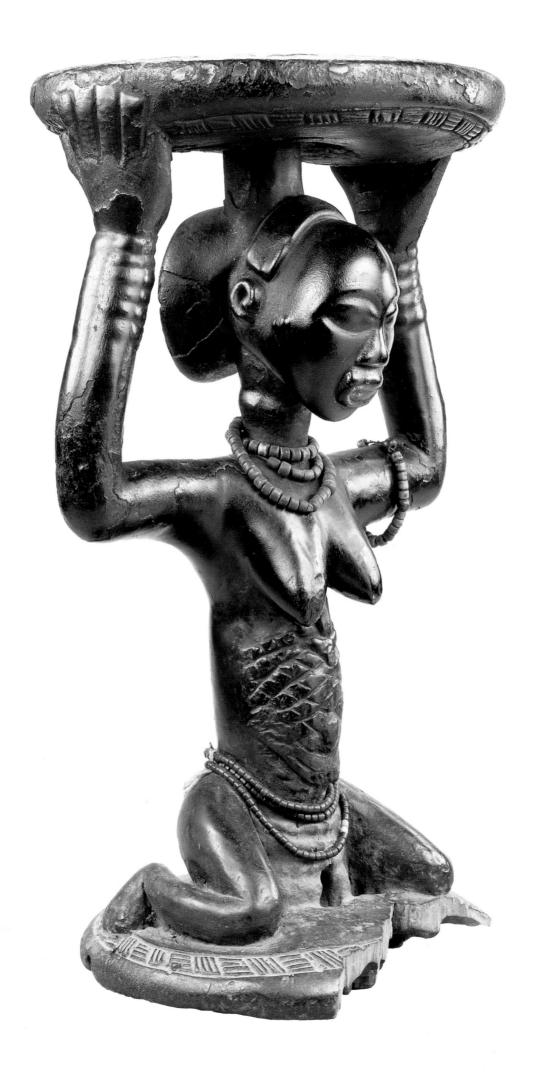

Furnishings
for the hut
and palace

All of the fine African objects described in this book came into being in a living context. Whether they were modest or luxurious, they were made to be used in an everyday setting which included women's domestic activities, children's cries and games, men's work and discussions and chieftains' ceremonials.

For a continent as vast as Africa, it is of course impossible to describe a typical village. Until the beginning of this century, each region, and sometimes each tribe, had its own type of dwellings which had developed through the experience of countless generations. The explorer Günter Tessmann,[1] writing around 1913, gave this description of a Fang village in Gabon, at the heart of the equatorial jungle: there was a central lane with, on either side, rows of long and squat huts with wooden frameworks and covered with overlapping raffia mats like rooftiles. The head of each family had two houses: a house for domestic life, ruled by his wife, and a house for a social gatherings in which he both worked and received visitors.

Nothing of the sort among the Dogon of Mali: even today, their small earthen dwellings nestle in crevices and gorges, or at the foot of the Bandiagara cliffs, the Dogon's ultimate refuge from Mossi raids. The ethnologist Marcel Griaule,[2] who made many trips there between 1931 and 1946, left us this description:

Opposite

Stool with caryatid
Luba. Zaire. Kiambi workshop. Wood, glass beads. H.: 53 cm. Private collection.

1. House entrance at Kabanpe.
Ghana. Imprinted wall decoration. Photo Library of the Barbier-Mueller Museum, Geneva.

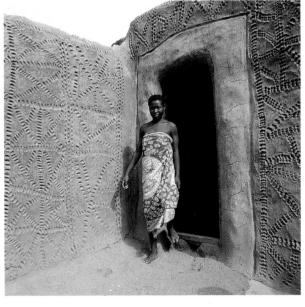

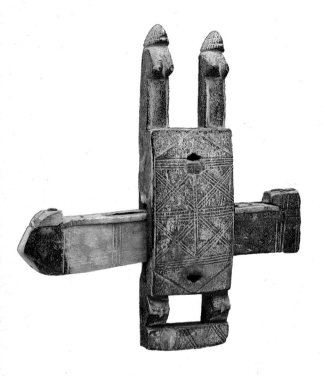

3. Carved lock
Dogon. Mali. Wood
and metal. H.: 41 cm.
Private collection.

This is not just a simple
bolt, but a lock with
an internal mechanism
and key.

Opposite

4. Lock
Mauretania. Various types
of metal. Ethnographic
Museum, Neuchâtel.

'Lower-Ogol, like all Dogon villages, was a group of tiered houses and granaries, earthen terraces alternating with thatched huts. Walking through the small, narrow streets, alternately shot with sunlight or sunk in shadow, in between the truncated pyramids, the prism-shaped, cubic or cylindrical huts and granaries, the rectangular doorways .... one felt like a dwarf lost in some kind of a maze. Everywhere one looked, the earth was cracked from the rains and heat.'

In Ghana, the setting changes once again (fig. 1). The woman in the photograph greets us at the threshhold of a dwelling whose outer walls are completely covered with patterns scratched into the moist mud, a common practice in this land.

In these towns and villages (for example, Timbuktu and Gao in Mali, or Kano in Nigeria), or on their outskirts, could be found the houses of the chiefs or wealthy notables, and sometimes royal palaces (those of Benin or Ife in Nigeria, for example), which drew the best craftsmen, who were always assured of finding suitable work there. Out of their hands came objects made of precious materials like gold, bronze or ivory whose refinement and splendour loudly proclaimed the rulers' prestige.

Although often reduced to mere ruins today, a great many grandiose and mysterious palaces played an important role in the history of Africa. During the fifeteenth century, the Emperor of Mali, whose court was literally ablaze with gold, was considered to be of equal rank with the Christian sovereigns. Archaeological excavations at Kumbi Saleh have recently brought to light the vestiges of his buried capital.

The only feature common to all the old African palaces was their enormous size: veritable labyrinths of countless rooms and dependencies intended to accommodate the king's wives, his descendants, his servants and guards, and all the dignitaries of his court. When he arrived at Niangara, among the Mangbetu in northern Zaïre, the American ethnologist Herbert Lang[3] was astonished and fascinated to discover the court of King Okondo, with his 180 wives. Since the Audience Hall of the previous ruler had been destroyed, and to impress his white visitor, Okondo summoned his architects and ordered it to be reconstructed.

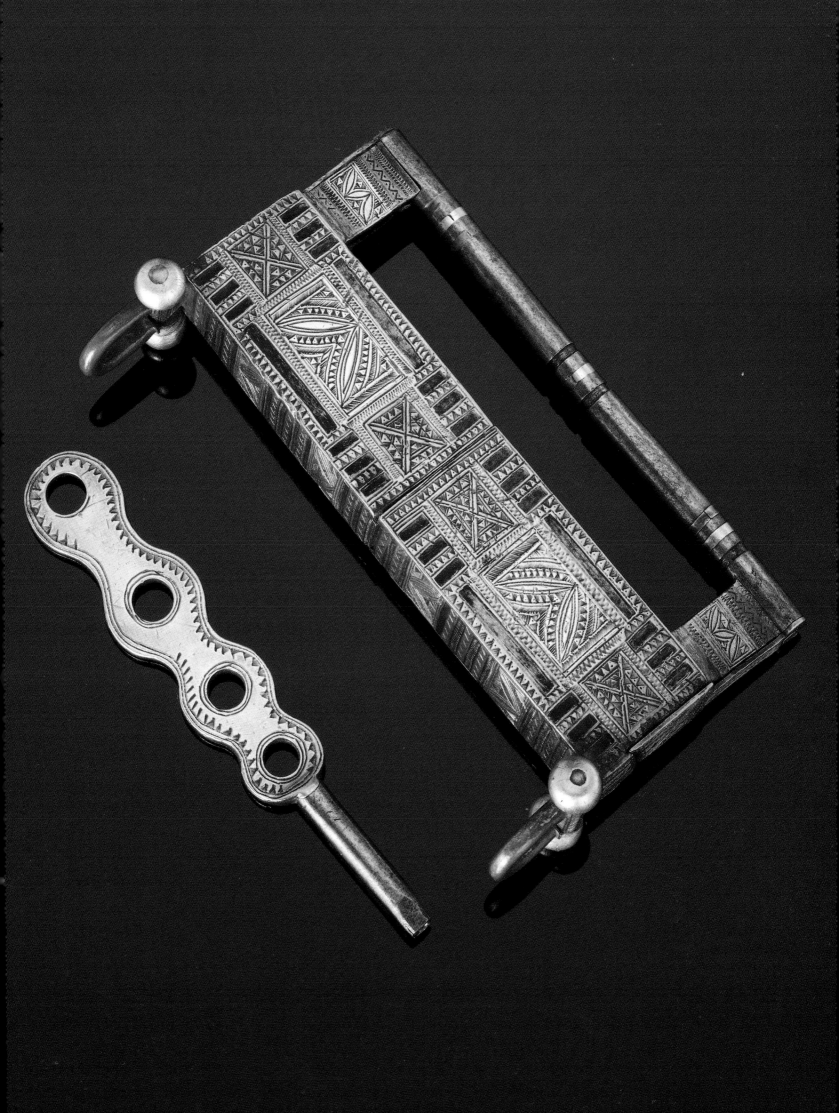

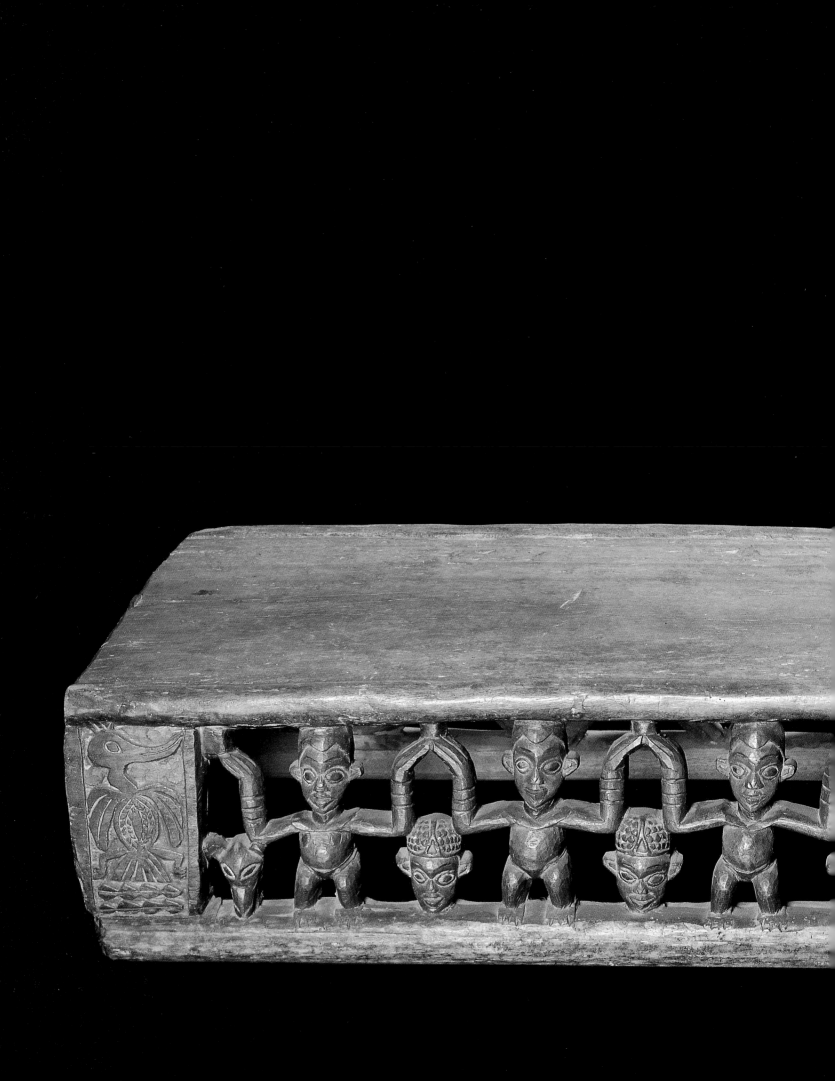

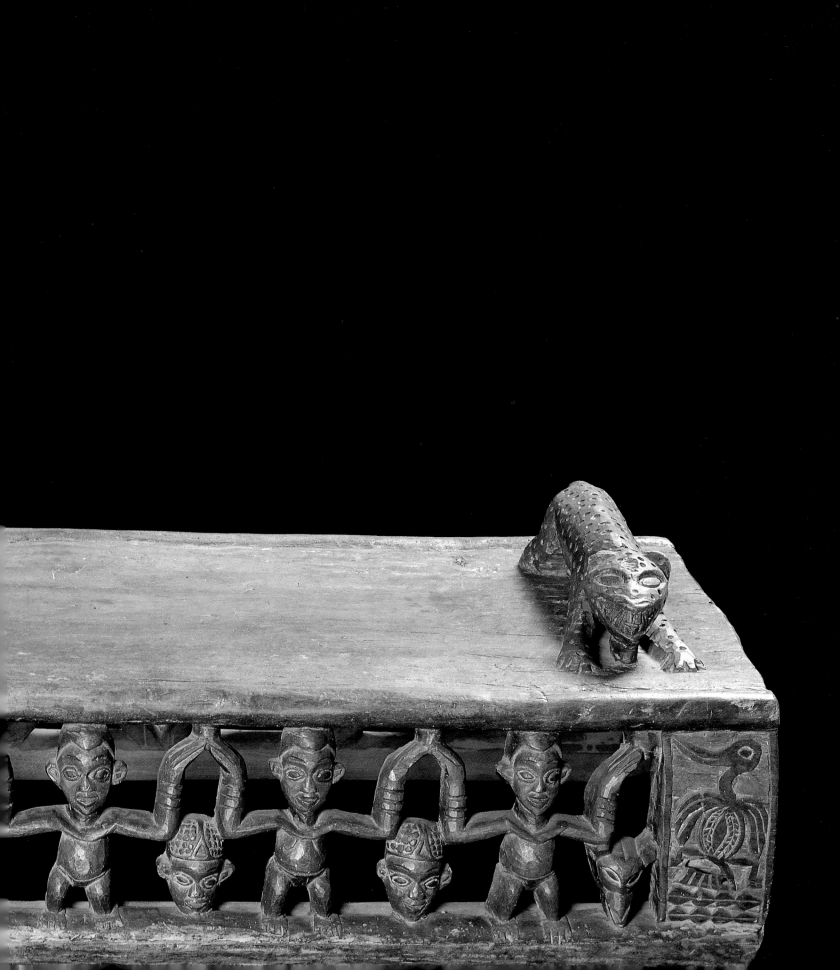

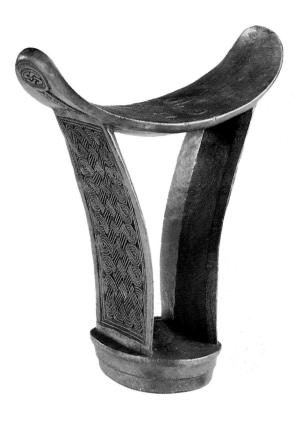

6. Head-rest
Boni. Somalia. Wood.
H. (support): 14 cm.
National Museum
of African Art,
Washington D.C.

Overleaf

**5. Ceremonial bed
for a chief.**
Bamileke. Cameroon.
Single piece of carved
wood, decorated with
figures of servants and
heads in the Babanki style.
H.: 36 cm. L.: 181 cm.
Barbier-Mueller Museum,
Geneva. Formerly in the
Joseph Mueller Collection
(acquired before 1942).

After one year, and the relentless labour of 500 men, Lang was able to admire an imposing wooden structure 55 metres long, 27 metres broad, and 9 metres high. Inside and outside, the walls were covered with magnificently-tressed reed surfaces, and the roof was supported on a forest of wooden pillars. This hall was used for royal audiences and for feasts with music and dancing, which included frenzied dances performed by the king himself before his admiring wives.

Regardless of the living standards of their inhabitants, whether modest or regal, these dwellings displayed, and still display, the same concern for aesthetic beauty. Each object they made – be it a chair, a bowl, a weapon, or a fabric – reveals the artisans' particular care to create an appearance that pleased the eye. They would choose fine colours, and paint or carve ornaments, no matter how simple. The craftsmen were not content to produce a functional object, it also had to be beautiful: to satisfy their pride as craftsmen, to please their client, and, of course, to attract future business. The results were very often nothing short of remarkable, considering the limited means at their disposal.

This is often visible in the forms and outer surfaces of the buildings. There are, for example, the magnificent doorways to the houses of the Bamileke notables in Cameroon,* which are framed by posts and a carved lintel, or, on a more modest scale, the Senufo* and Baule* doorways of the Ivory Coast, which are very often decorated with mythological scenes carved in low relief. As for the millet granaries of the Dogon tribe mentioned by Griaule, a modern carved door (fig. 2) shows that the traditional techniques and designs have not been lost. The rows of stylized figures refer to Dogon mythology or to ancestor worship.

In the past, these doors had carved wooden bolts or locks (fig. 3) which were also decorated with mythological figures. Similar types of locking devices may be found among other agricultural tribes, like the Senufo of the Ivory Coast* or the Bambara of Mali, who were all understandably concerned with the safekeeping of their grain supplies.

Note: an asterisk (*) in the text indicates that a comparable object is illustrated in *Black Africa: Masks, Sculpture, Jewelry*, by the same author and publisher (1991).

In other regions, like Mauretania, theft and plundering were such common practices that travellers and merchants in caravans had to use metal locks. These were often decorated with engraved designs and metals of different colours (fig. 4).

The interiors of these mysterious African homes aroused the curiosity of the European travellers of the past. In his *Voyage à Tombouctou* [4] (1825–1830), René Caillié gave a detailed account of what he saw. During his stay in the camp of King Lam-Khate in Senegal, he noted:

'The king's bed is made in the Negro manner: a sort of platform covered with reed mats, held by crossboards and stakes, about one foot off the ground. A reed mat on the floor fills the rest of the space under the tent and provides a bed for the king's suite. The common people sleep on the floor on reed mats, which are occasionally covered with some straw.'

What he saw upon his arrival in Timbuktu was not much different:

'The only furniture they have are reed mats to sit on. Their beds are made of four stakes planted in one corner of the room upon which they stretch reed mats or an ox-skin. The rich have cotton mattresses and a cover made by the local Moors out of camel hair and wool from their sheep.'

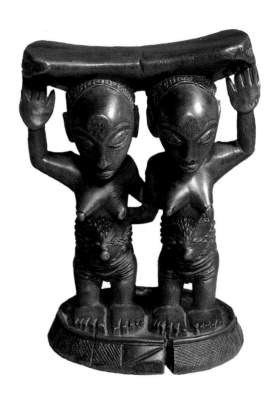

7. Head-rest with twin caryatids.
Luba. Zaïre. Wood.
H. 16.5 cm.
British Museum, London.

Bedding

The reed mats mentioned by René Caillié were found throughout Africa and could be considered as basic furnishing. Used variously as beds, covers, seats, rugs, or even wall-hangings, they were made of plant fibres and were pleasantly cool despite the heat. Differences of colouring often made for interesting weaving patterns, many of which represented a stylized animal.

Beds were generally simple affairs and, in some cases, fashioned from dried mud. They took the form of raised platforms long enough to accommodate an adult. Less frequently, they were constructed out of masonry and decorated with geometric motifs. Others were made of wooden boards clad on a wooden frame supported by

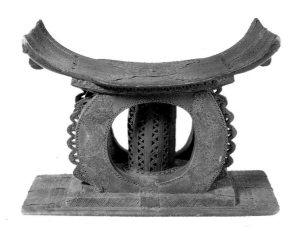

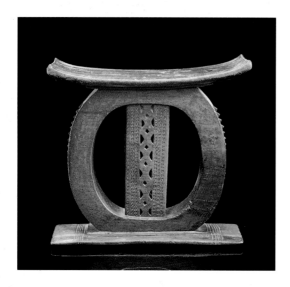

**8. Stool
of a queen mother**
Ashanti. Ghana. Wood
covered with silver leaf.
H.: 53 cm.
British Museum, London.

9. Stool
Ashanti. Ghana. Wood.
H.: 49 cm. L. 50.7 cm.
Barbier-Mueller Museum,
Geneva.

Opposite

**10. Stool
with antelope**
Anyi or Akye. Ivory Coast.
Wood. H.: 50 cm.
Barbier-Mueller Museum,
Geneva.

stakes, like those described by René Caillié in Timbuktu. In some cases they were equipped with mosquito netting made of fine and tightly woven plant fibres or cloth. In 1915, among the Mangbetu of Zaïre, Herbert Lang noted the use of a wooden framework which, depending on its length, could do service both as a bed or as a seat.

The true monoxylous beds (that is, beds made out of a single piece of wood) were luxury objects which only the wealthy could afford. The largest of these were used as funerary beds.

Beds of carved wood were an exception, but could be found in the grasslands of Cameroon, where they were the privilege of chieftains. The Babanki-Tungo workshops, where the kings themselves sometimes tried their hand at wood-work, produced such famous pieces as this magnificent bed (fig. 5) with an openwork frieze of figures as a base, and a carved panther, symbol of royalty, as a head-rest.

Sophisticated head-rests

Not infrequently, indeed, the refinement of the head-rests compensated for the simplicity of the bedding. These objects were designed to preserve certain very elaborate hairstyles. Already used in Ancient Egypt, they maintained the head at the same level as the shoulders during sleep, but their function went beyond the strictly utilitarian. Being associated with sleep and dreams, the head-rest was believed by Africans to be a recipient for occult forces. It was an eminently personal object and was never lent to another. The men of the Karamojong tribe in Uganda walk about in daytime with their head-rests hanging from their arms. In such cases, the head-rests have become indispensable for their sleep because their hair is mixed with wet clay to create complex structures which are meant to last for several months.

A number of very old head-rests have been found in Mali and attributed, not to the Dogon who live there today, but to the Tellem,* their predecessors. The Dogon believe that the head of the village's spiritual leader should never touch the ground, lest disaster strike. And so, for him, a head-rest was also an indispensable item.

The simplest head-rests I have ever seen – and which

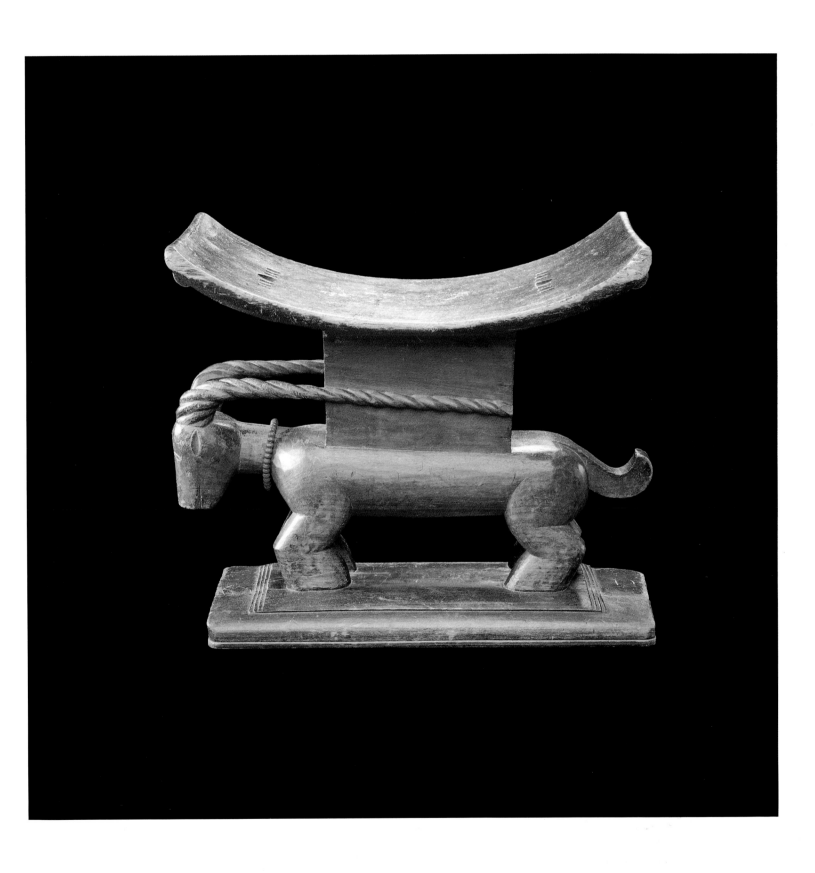

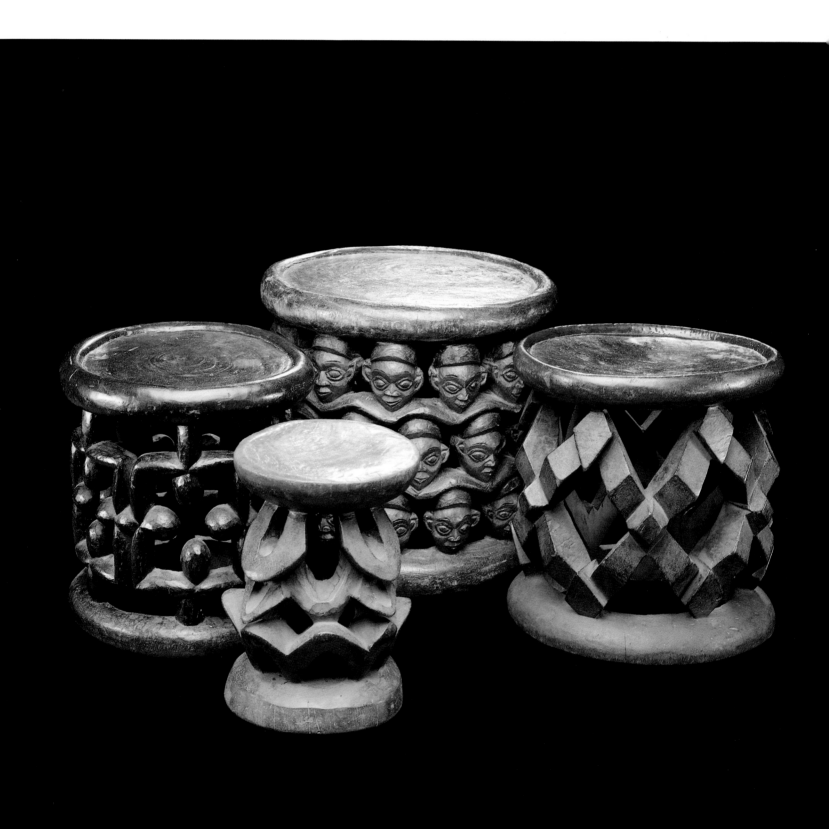

have been produced recently – are used by shepherds of the Upper-Nile Valley and the consist of a triple-forked branch. Other models display much more complex designs, although in most cases they involve abstract shapes of striking simplicity, with smooth sides, as among the Karamojong. One of the finest head-rests is attributed to the Boni tribe of Somalia (fig. 6), which is characterized by supremely harmonious curves and exquisitely carved braided-knot motifs on the sides. The whole object seems to bloom like a flowerbud.

When figurative motifs are used, they are carved on the middle part of the head-rest. The figures may be zoo-morphic – quadrupeds being an evident choice – but the finest pieces show human figures. These are found especially in Zaïre. The proportions of the bodies are never realistically represented; because of technical constraints, the feet, and in certain cases the hands as well, are over-proportioned, and the legs shortened or depicted in a squatting position. Some of the female figures display the powerful forms of atlantes.

The outstanding feature of the head-rests made by the Luba tribe in Zaïre is their elegance. A prime example of this is the head-rest formed by twin caryatids (fig. 7). The care taken in the rendition of the hair and ritual scars attests to a high level of skill.

The stool, indispensable for prestige

By far the most important piece of furniture in Africa, however, is the seat, usually in the form of a stool or a chair.

This piece of furniture serves as a sort of social insignia, for each subgroup is entitled to use a specific type of seat corresponding to its rank in the tribal hierarchy. The less-privileged members of the group are alloted their own appropriate types of stool, and the higher ranking or wealthier members have their own prestigious models – typically opulent and showy. A native of Benin is reported to have said in 1966: [5] 'In the old days, a man was judged and respected according to the kind of stool he had; now it's by his car.' The Zaïreans say: 'A man without a stool is a man without dignity.'

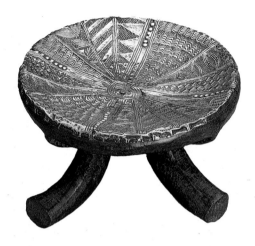

13. Stool
Kota. Gabon. Wood and copper with repoussé decoration. Diam.: 36 cm. Barbier-Mueller Museum, Geneva.

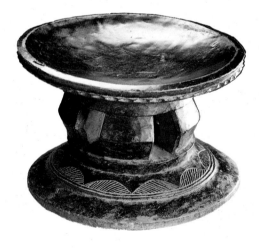

11. Stool
Yohure. Ivory Coast. Wood. Diam.: 36 cm. Barbier-Mueller Museum, Geneva.

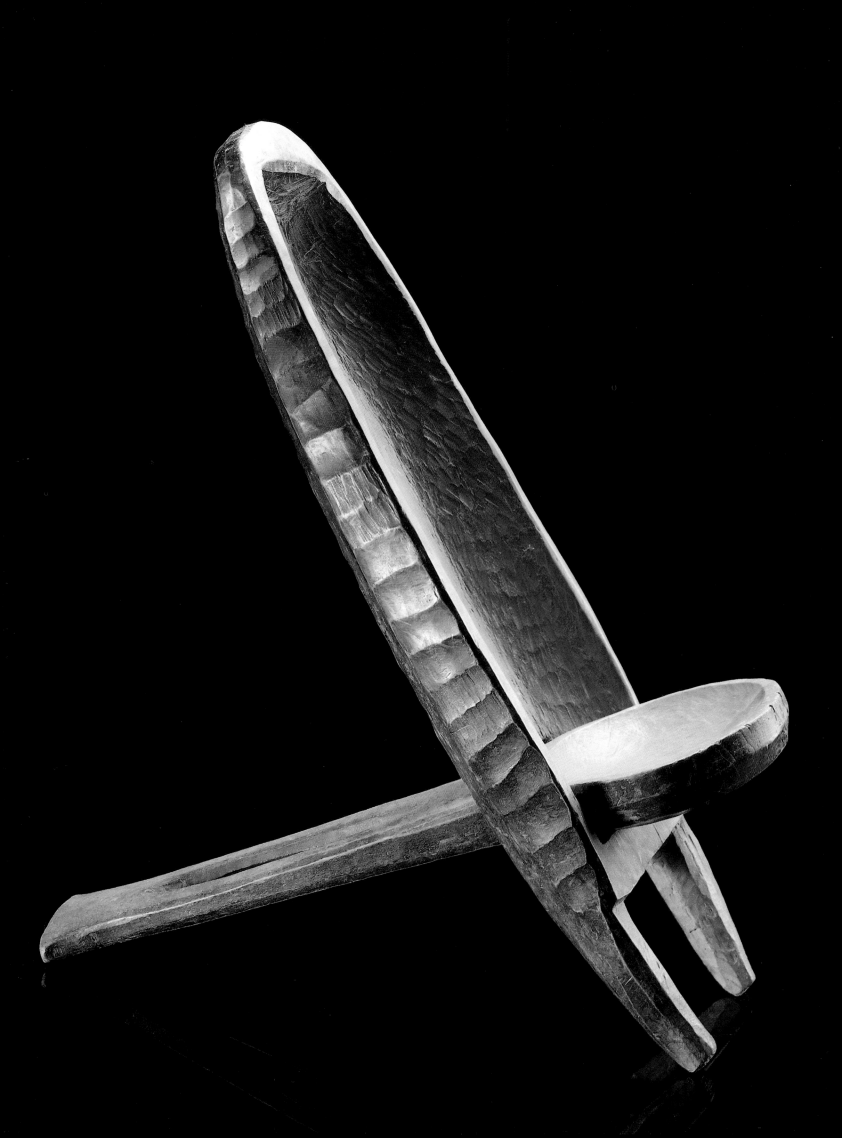

The social significance of the stool has its origin in religious beliefs. Like the head-rest, the stool was a strictly personal item. Among the Ashanti of Ghana it was believed to be the 'seat' of its owner's soul. When it was not needed, it was tipped to one side so that it could not be used by anyone else.

This accounts for the importance of the royal stool of the Ashanti and why it was always the object of great veneration. Legend has it that a gold-covered stool was sent from heaven to the first Ashanti king, Osei Tutu, at the beginning of the eighteenth century. It was displayed only on rare occasions. Even the king was forbidden to use it, but had to sit on another seat behind it. In 1900, the British governor ordered the famous stool to be brought to him, a gesture which led to war. The Ashanti lost the war, but saved the stool. In 1920, workers discovered the stool near Kumasi and stripped off the gold. When the theft was discovered, the Ashanti went into mourning. The British authorities, having finally grasped the significance of the object, arrested and imprisoned the desecrators.

The fate of an Ashanti chief's stool is a good index of his authority. If the chief is not equal to his duties, his stool will be taken away from him, and his prestige with it. If, however, he distinguishes himself in his functions, then upon his death his stool may be 'blackened' and enshrined in a special room reserved for stools; these are worshipped like ancestral idols in other tribes.

The Ashanti stool in the British Museum (fig. 8) made for the Queen Mother is covered with finely tooled silver plate, for her symbol is the Moon and its corresponding metal is silver.

As for the stools made for the common run of mortals, the midsection is the part which changes the most as to form and decoration. A stool can be bought by anyone, as long as the model is appropriate to their social rank (fig. 9).

Among other tribes of the Akan group – to which the Ashanti belong – the stools are variations on the Ashanti theme. Among the Akye, or Anyi, the four corner-supports could represent human figures; but animals, like the antelope in fig. 10, were more frequently represented in this function. Writing in *Arts de la Côte-d'Ivoire,*[6] T.F. Garrard reports that this last motif originated in a legend:

Page 22

12. Four stools
Bamileke. Cameroon.
Wood. Barbier-Mueller
Museum, Geneva.

These seats were used by nobles from the royal court. The one on the left is decorated with stylized spiders. The one in the back shows cut heads (the king's enemies). The decoration of the others probably contains stylized human or animal figures.

Opposite

14. Articulated chair
Senufo. Ivory Coast.
Wood. L.: 94 cm. Barbier-Mueller Museum, Geneva.

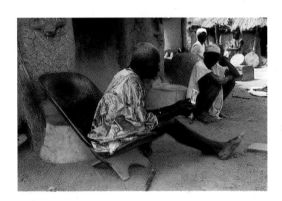

15. Man seated in an articulated chair
Senufo. Ivory Coast.
Photo Library of the Barbier-Mueller Museum, Geneva.

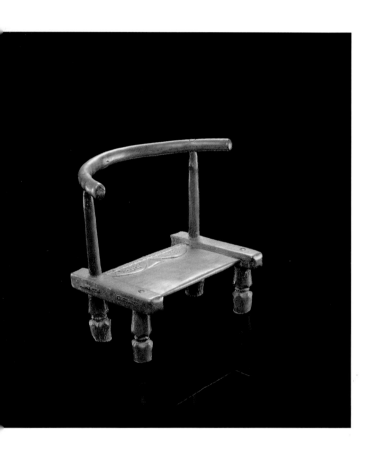

16. Chair
Baule. Guro or Yohure.
Ivory Coast. Wood.
H.: 37.5 cm.
Barbier-Mueller Museum,
Geneva.

'The antelope used to have such long horns that the other animals had to keep at a distance to avoid injury .... The antelope decided to shorten them and asked the other animals to push them back into its head; which they did, until all that showed were the tiniest bits of horn. The antelope then remembered that it needed horns to defend itself against predators, but it was too late. The moral of the story is that it is useless to harbour regrets.'

Outside of the Akan group, stools do not have a ritual function, but still serve as distinctive signs of social rank. Many reports by seventeenth- and eighteenth-century travellers tell us that when a chief went on a journey, he was always followed by a servant carrying his stool. They also tell us that, for women, the stools were lower and less ornate than those for men of the same rank. Those for children were lower still. Most stools were carved out of a single piece of wood and often equipped with a wooden or plant-fibre handle for transport. In some cases, they were round, in others rectangular – like the sacred golden stool of the Ashanti.

Among the Mossi tribe in Burkina Faso, the rectangular stools sometimes have handles in the shape of a human head. Among the Bambara in Mali, these anthropomorphic features are even more pronounced, and two of the legs are actually shaped as human legs; suggesting that the owner of the stool is sitting on the back of a crouching slave – which may very well have been the case in the past.

The round-shape, derived from the Tree of Origins, is also very common. The median section is carved and emerges out of a round base which is also carved. The Yohure are masters at making this type of object (fig. 11), deploying great skill to create powerful forms in space, although on a relatively small scale.

The craftsmen of the great Bamileke group in Cameroon, famed for their skill in woodcarving, created a remarkable variety of round stools (fig. 12) with round, openwork supports composed of tiered motifs. One can find zig-zag patterns, or openwork, but there is no lack of figurative motifs; often stacked-up rows of animal or cut-off human heads.

All sorts of variations on the low stool with four legs, often intended for women, were made by the Kota of Gabon. An exceptionally luxurious model covered with copper plates worked in *repoussé*, probably destined for a chief, is shown in figure 13.

Back-rests and chairs

The back-rest, a piece of wood set at a 45° angle to the ground, is unknown in Europe. There are many different kinds to be found in Africa, ranging from the simplest constructions made of forked branches, to the most sumptuous, entirely covered with pewter wire, as are the back-rests of the Mangbetu chiefs in Zaïre.

While the back-rest is often just set directly on the ground, articulated chairs have legs. The latter may be found in many areas of the Ivory Coast (figs. 14 and 15). They are constructed out of two crossed pieces of wood, and, even when undecorated, the balanced and harmonious design make it a very inviting piece of furniture. Because of its high price it became a luxury item for the rich, but it was intended for everyday use.

Still in the Ivory Coast, and in addition to the articulated chair, there is a completely different and typical chair design: low, with a vertical back, and decorated with carvings (fig. 16). It was reserved for the members of a secret society, called the *poro*, and was offered by wives or female relatives after the initiation. The austere rigidity of the straight back was a sign of the new social standing and dignity of these men.

The Ashanti chairs of Ghana (fig. 17), which were exclusively reserved for chiefs, may well have been inspired by similar models brought by European travellers, even if the brass nail decoration on the baroquish curves and countercurves give it a style of its own. The Tshokwe chairs from Zaïre were also prestige objects inspired by European furniture; in this case Portuguese, for a part of Zaïre was colonized by Portugal as early as the sixteenth century.

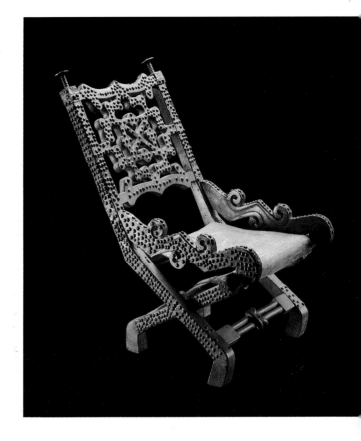

17. Chair
Ashanti. Ghana.
Wood and brass nails.
H.: 78 cm.
Barbier-Mueller Museum,
Geneva.

Overleaf

18. Ceremonial chair
Gurunsi. Burkina Faso.
Wood. Barbier-Mueller,
Museum, Geneva.

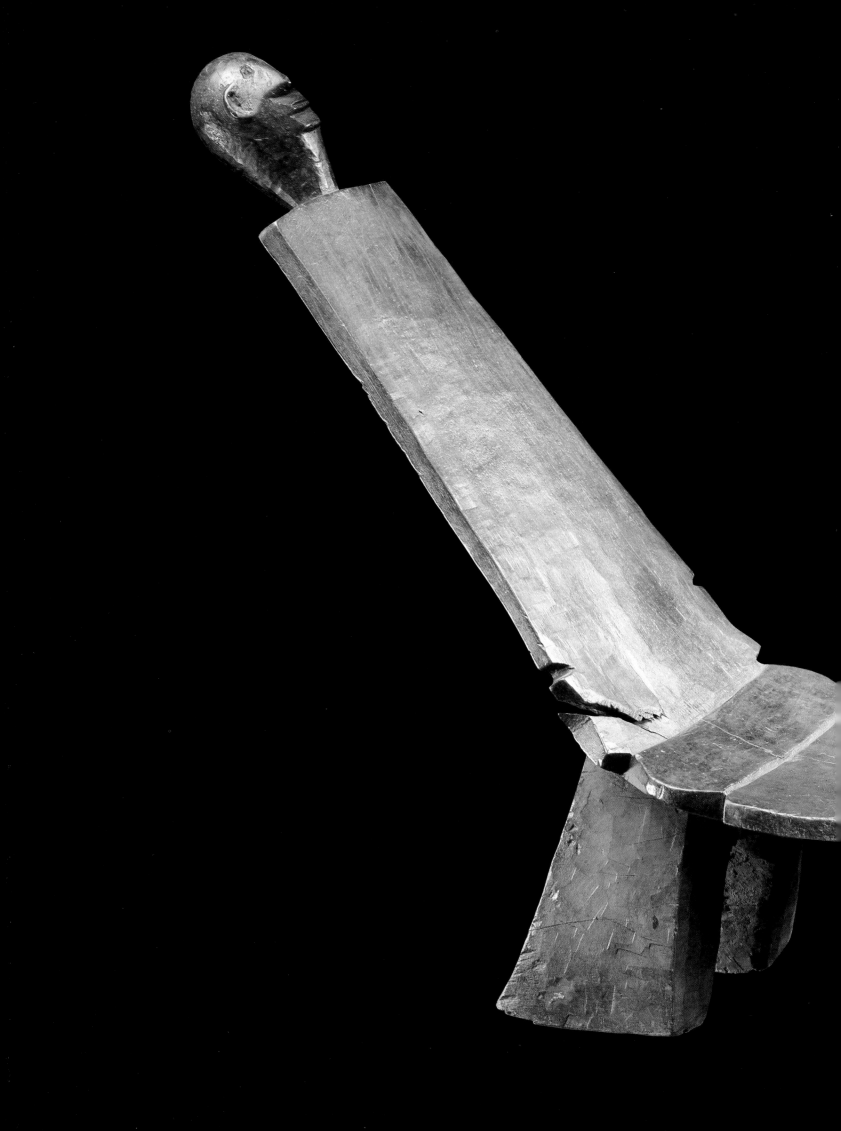

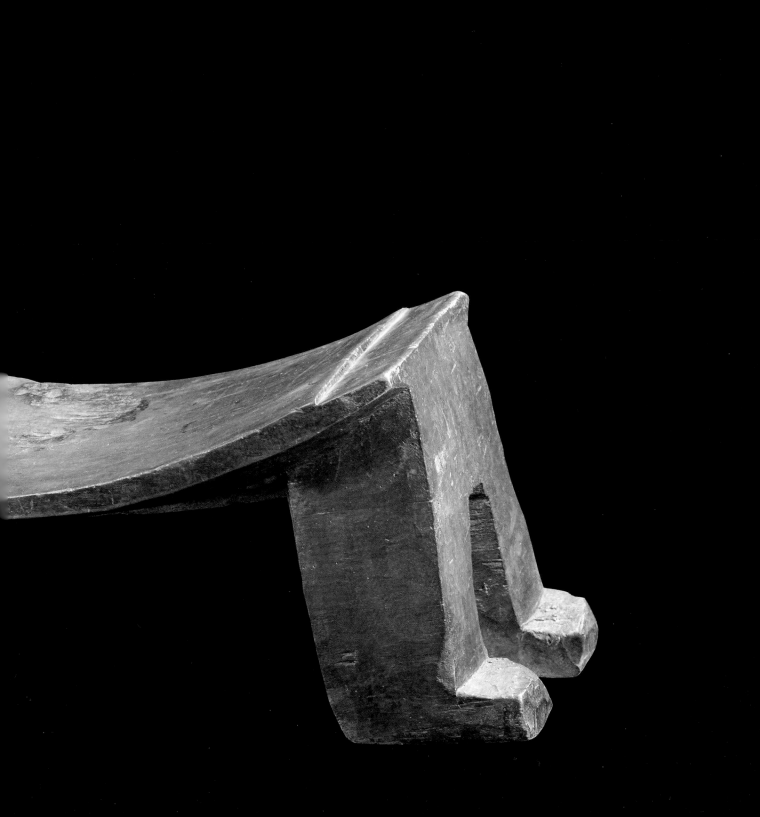

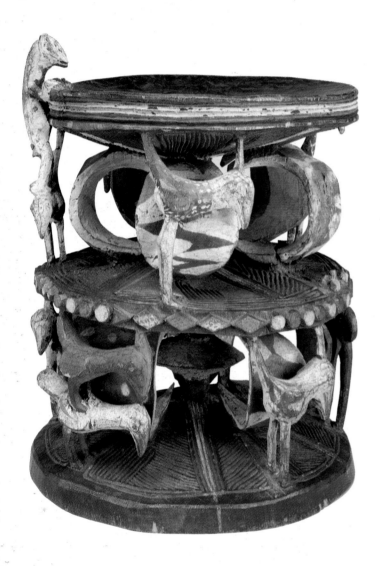

Chairs of great prestige

Royal courts have always attracted the best sculptors. Not surprisingly, the royal seats display the peak of skill achieved by each tribe and the maximum development of the designs, many of which are priceless one-of-a-kind pieces.

The artists based their decorations on symbolic motifs expressing the link between the living chief and his ancestors. Thus the anthropomorphic seats belonging to the *fon* (king) of Kom in Cameroon, and known as Afo-a-kom,* have backs decorated with figures, one of which may be a likeness to Nkwain Nindu, who ruled from 1825 to 1840. In other cases, the seat is carried by anthropomorphic or zoomorphic representations that symbolize the sovereign's power, which extends over the human as well as the animal realm.

On the large beadwork thrones made by the Bamum* under the patronage of King Njoya, the seat is borne by a base decorated with squatting figures of slaves. These same pieces also feature ornamental motifs in the shape of mythic animals like two-headed serpents or panthers, all symbols of the king's power.

These two themes – reference to the founding royal ancestors and symbolic representations of the chief's omnipresent authority – are common features of all the seats of the great chiefs which will be described below.

The overall design of the Gurunsi chair from Burkina-Faso (fig. 18) recalls the articulated chairs from the Ivory Coast already mentioned above (figs. 14 and 15). The purity of its forms amply qualifies it as the chair of a tribal chief. The carved head which tops the back, a quite beautiful sculpture in its own right (fig. 177), would seem to allude to the ancestral lineage which justifies the chief's prominent position.

The zoomorphic elements carved in openwork on the mid-section of the large Ibo stool from Nigeria (fig. 19) can be interpreted as symbolizing the extent of the chief's power. Among the many animals represented are birds and quadrupeds, perhaps dogs. A strange animal even seems to be trying to climb onto the seat. The exact significance of this scene, which surely involves myth, remains unknown.

The base of the Duala chair from Cameroon (fig. 20) is

19. Ceremonial stool
Ibo. Nigeria. Wood.
H. 46.4 cm. The
Metropolitan Museum
of Art, New York.

Opposite

20. Ceremonial throne, with symbols of royal power
Duala. Cameroon.
Wood. L.: 43.5 cm.
Barbier-Mueller Museum,
Geneva.

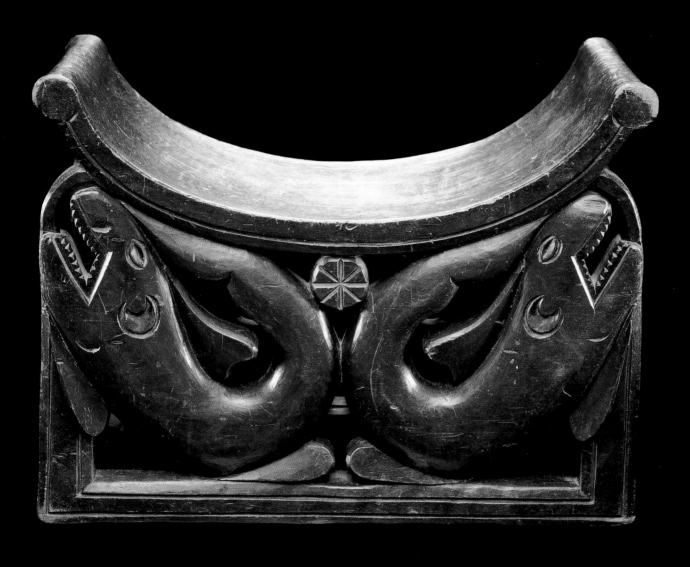

**21. Royal throne
with
anthropomorphic back**
Bamileke. Cameroon.
Kingdom of Bafoussam.
20th cent. Wood, cloth
and cowries. H.: 160 cm.
Collection of Njitack
Ngompe Pele, Head Chief
of Bafoussam.

A panther (leopard?)
in striking position
carries the seat.
This is one of the most
venerated animals
of the African bush,
and symbolizes
royal might. The figure
represents the chief
minister of the royal
ancestor cult.

Opposite

**23. Stool
with two caryatids**
Luba. Zaïre. Wood.
H.: 54 cm. !9th cent.
Museum für Völkerkunde,
Berlin.

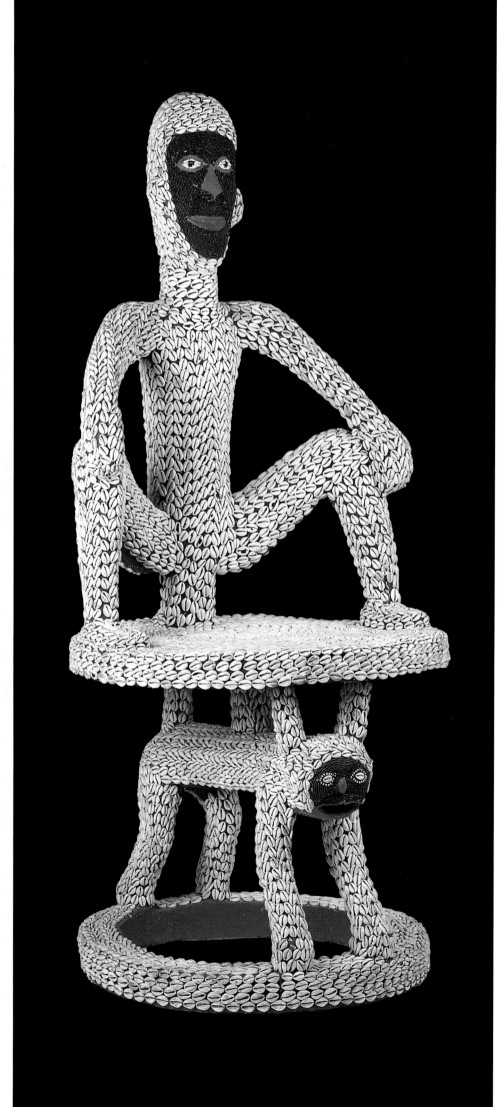

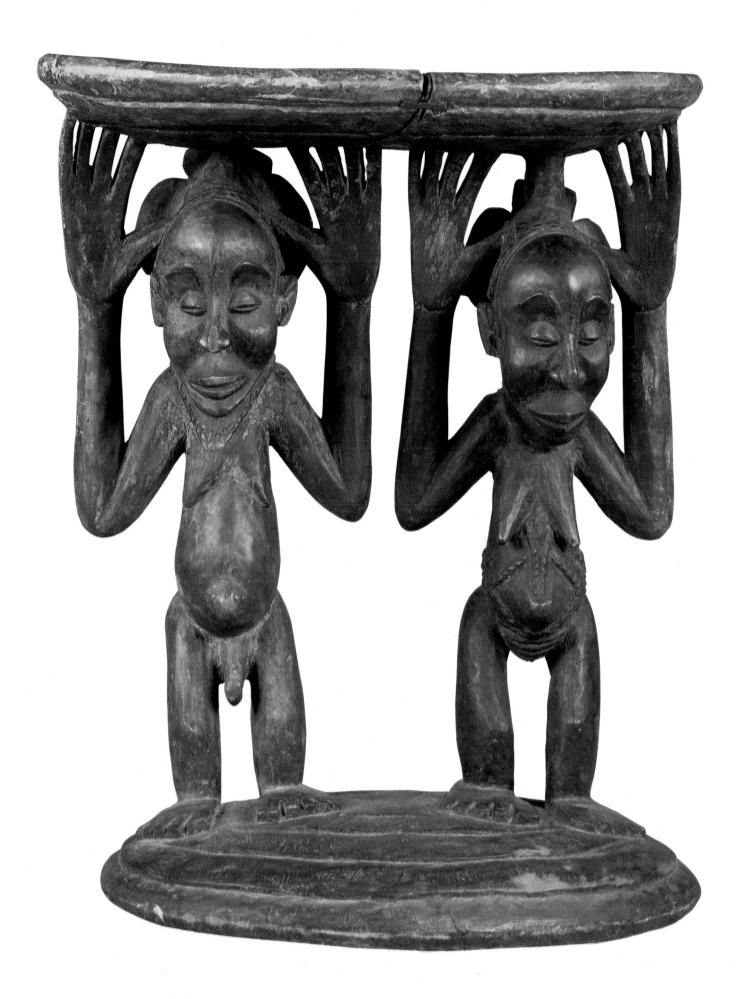

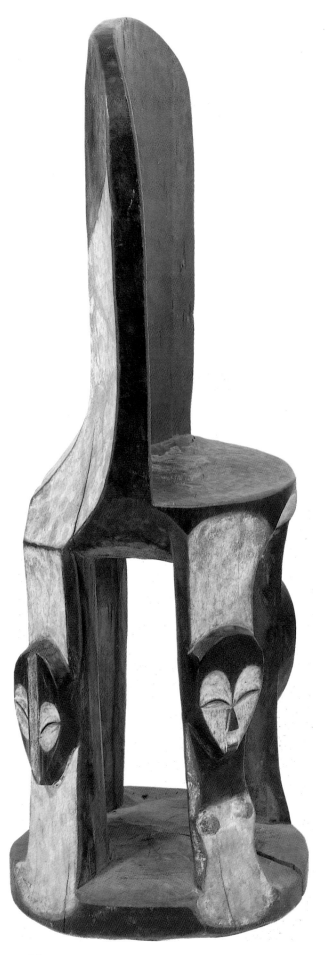

adorned with magnificent figures of fish. Their presence is easily explained by the fact that the Duala, who lived on the coast, were great fishermen and canoe racers. The fish, surging like waves, completely harmonize with the curves of this ceremonial chair, a fitting seat of royal power. By the richness and fullness of its dimensions, the beauty of its surfaces and the balance of its curves and counter-curves, such a chair was able to reinforce the authority of the chief for whom it was designed.

In the grasslands of Cameroon, the ceremonial chairs were quite different, being entirely covered with beadwork. Remarkable examples of these were made by the Bamum and Bamileke. A royal Bamileke throne with a human figure for a back-rest (fig. 21) may still be seen in the kingdom of Bafussam. Covered with cowrie shells and beads, it has a grandiose and almost surrealistic presence. The seat is carried by the figure of a panther, one of the most venerated animals in the bush. The Bamileke king, called *fon*, was claimed to be able to transform himself into a wild beast. With his first wife, he was a member of the fearsome society of panther-men who maintained order throughout the kingdom and guaranteed respect for royal authority. These attributes are all represented by the figure of the panther. The seated figure at the top is the minister of the cult of royal ancestors, guarantor of the king's lineage, and so of his legitimacy. Chairs of this kind were publicly displayed only twice a year for the major religious feasts.

The chair of the Kwele chief from the People's Republic of the Congo (fig. 22) presents elements of its own form of ancestor worship. The legs bear carvings of four human faces, two of which are female. The faces are stylized into heart shapes characteristic of Kwele masks. The small mouths refer to the dead ancestors and the Netherworld, where no one speaks. The straightness of the forms emphasizes the king's authority and dignity, and perhaps also his religious function.

From the Luba of Zaïre, the creators of remarkable sculptures, comes this double caryatid chair (fig. 23) attributed to the Master of Buli (or his workshop), so called because he is supposed to have lived in the Luba village of Buli. Twenty pieces have been attributed to this master-carver, who is said to have been active at the turn of the century. These unforgettable sculptures are characterized by their great expressivity; the bodies are gaunt, the faces taut with contained stress – wistful mouths, blank gazes – framed by hands made disproportionately large in order to carry the seat. The two figures here are ancestors of royal lineage. The Luba chief customarily sat on this kind of throne for his investiture and sported the other regalia that symbolized his legitimacy and authority. This prestigious chair was brought out in public only on special occasions. The rest of the time, custom dictated that it be entrusted to the care of the king's first wife.

These great thrones, the crowning achievement of all African chairs, were of course to be found only in the homes of chiefs and kings. We will now turn again to more modest dwellings to discuss other aspects of everyday life and the objects that went with them.

Heating, lighting, and tools

Houses and huts in villages were usually heated by an open fire indoors; because there was no chimney, the smoke escaped through the roof – a system which had the advantage of keeping mosquitoes away.

Lighting in houses away from towns and cities is a recent feature. What little lighting existed was provided by oil burned in cup-shaped lamps. The oil came from the karité tree of Sudan, whose grains yield a fatty substance. The wick was made of cotton. For the Bambara of Mali who created some superb designs, the cup was meant to be a mouth and the wick a tongue. When the light went out, the mouth no longer spoke – as in death. According to the research of the ethnologist André Blandin,[7] the wrought-iron lamps decorated with stylized anthropomorphic figures and having only one cup were used by the Bambara in a domestic context: those with several cups seem to have been intended for ritual use in nocturnal ceremonies. Among the Senufo of the Ivory Coast, not far away, the structure is similar (fig. 24), but the lamps are topped with figures of antelopes or birds. All of these lamps were made by blacksmiths. Different kinds are found elsewhere, some made of terracotta by potters, and with or without small human figures.

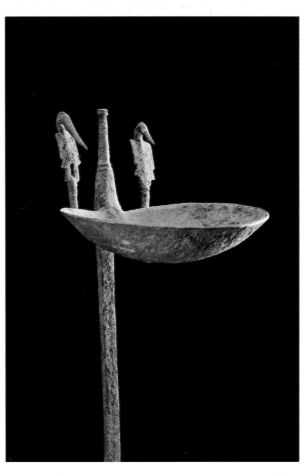

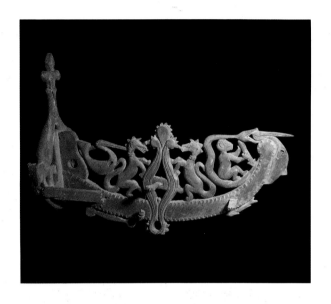

In the houses or in their vicinity could be found tools for agriculture or crafts, but these were rarely decorated. Among these types of object, the only ones that seem to have benefitted from any aesthetic attention are the pulleys of the looms which were in constant view of the weaver during the long hours of monotonous work. These were often decorated with figurines of highly refined design (fig. 51, p. 63 and fig. 52, p. 64) executed in the same styles as the sculptures of the respective tribes. These particular objects never served any ritual purposes.

Since many villages were located on the sea coast or along a river, a few words about water-related activities are in order.

Life on the water

Africans generally travel on rivers and are not overly tempted to venture out onto the high seas. Their dugout canoes are simply designed, but devoid of ornamentation. The notable exception under that respect is to be found among the Duala of Cameroon, who participate in annual canoe races in boats with ornate carved bows featuring interwoven human and animal figures (fig. 25)

Fishing along the innumerable rivers, lakes and swamplands is anything but a regular activity, and in some areas it is even forbidden. Those tribes which do practise fishing use all sorts of nets and baskets made of plant fibres or cotton. They are also lacking in ornamentation, but their functional forms are invariably elegant (fig. 26).

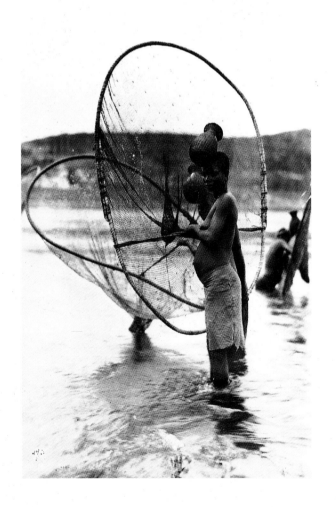

Above and opposite

**25. Carved bow
of a dugout canoe**
Duala. Cameroon, Wood.
L.: 162.5 cm. Museum
of African and Oceanian
Arts, Paris.

26. Fisherwomen
Banzyville. Congo.
Postcard.

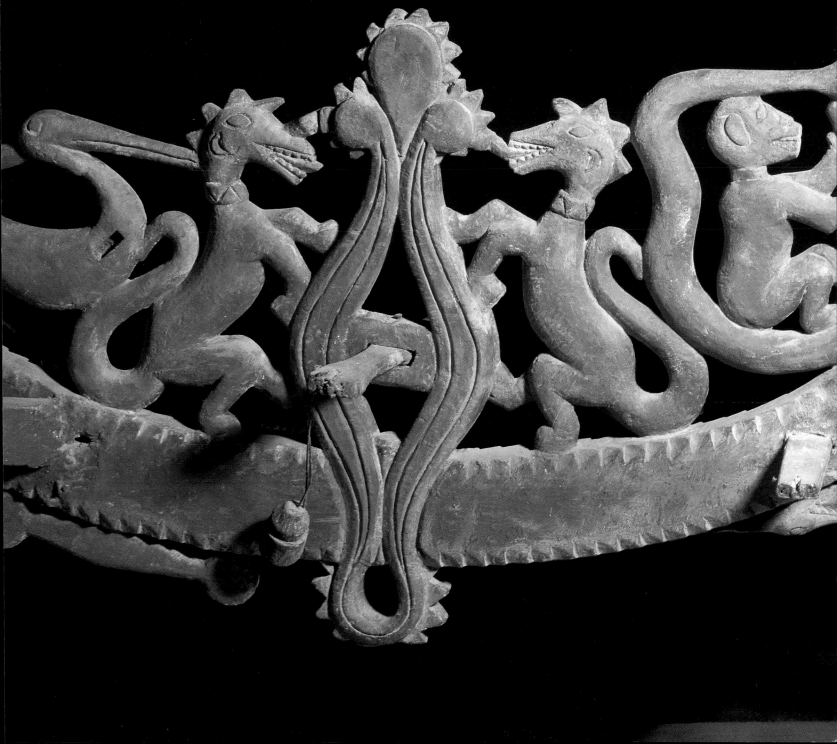

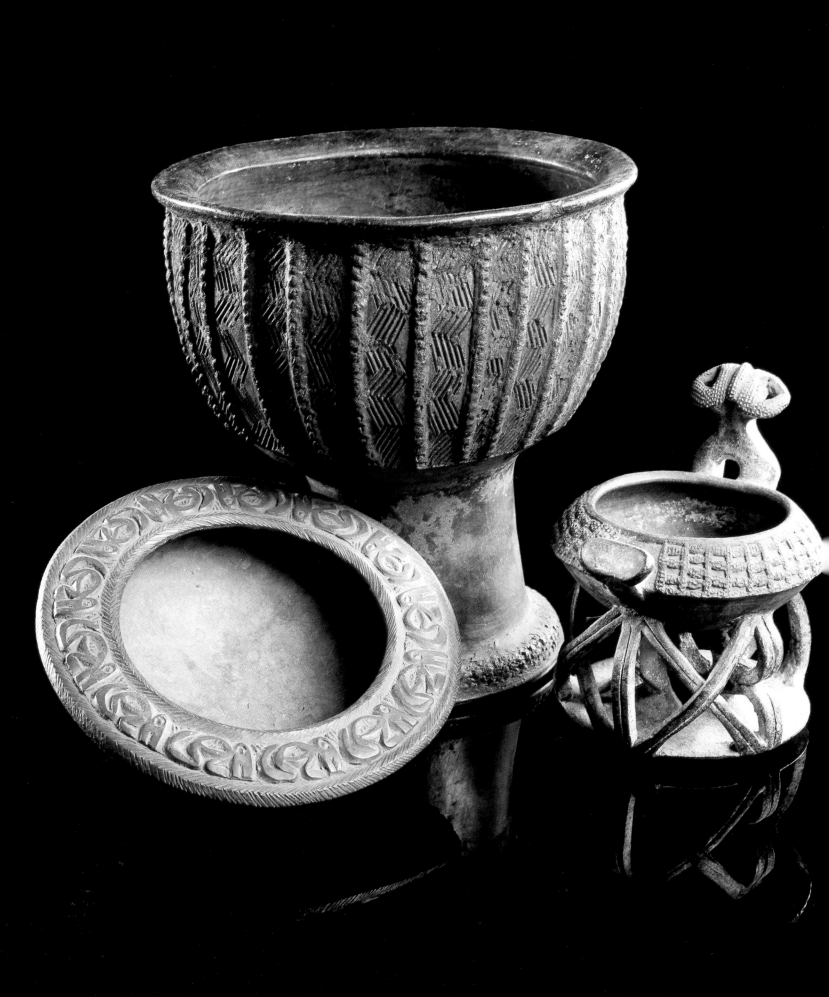

The culinary arts:
bowls, bottles
and spoons

As a rule, the hospitality of the Africans is always generous and warm, conviviality being more developed there than in Europe. Mealtimes, even for a single family, can involve quite a large number of people, to say nothing of the great celebrations in which the entire population of a village will assemble together for a feast.

In his autobiography, the Peul writer, Amadou Hampâté Bâ, tells of his childhood at the beginning of the century in the family of a well-to-do and respected chief: [8]

'We would take our meals in two separate groups: one for the men and one for the women. Special guests were served separately, unless they expressed the desire to eat with the others. Dishes were regularly saved for people from the outside, whether relatives, friends, or persons to be honoured. According to tradition, a well-to-do family always put a dish aside for poor people.'

Hampâté Bâ then goes on to describe the meal presided over by his father seated on a sheepskin. A servant would come with a large bowl filled with water, some soap and a towel for him to wash his hands, after which those present would do the same. The father was the first to serve himself, by reaching with his hand and taking a fistful of food from the dish. Children received their share after the adults. At the

Opposite

28. Three terracotta vessels
Cameroon grasslands.
Barbier-Mueller Museum, Geneva
(acquired before 1942).

27. Women carrying pottery jars
Sirigu. Ghana. Photo Library of the Barbier-Mueller Museum, Geneva.

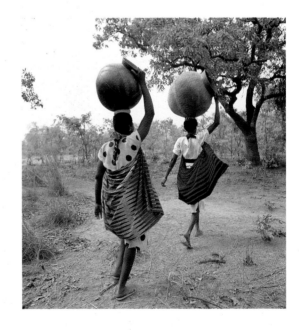

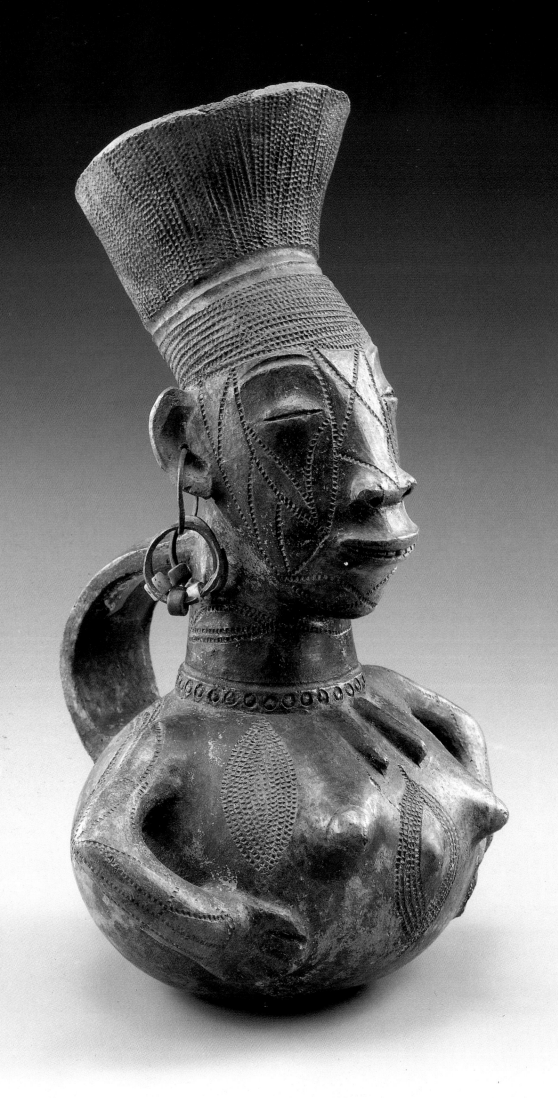

end of the meal, his father would be the last to rise, 'so that the others would have time to eat their fill.'

This account indicates that eating practices have not changed much over the centuries, for they tally with the descriptions of many European travellers before. More often than not, we see the same habits reappearing, regardless of the tribe. The main meal, taken in the evening, consisted of a single dish of cooked cereal, vegetables and tubers, served hot and with an assortment of sauces. The contemporary anthropologist, Georges Balandier, gives us a summary of what travellers to the Kongo kingdom in Zaïre saw in the eighteenth century: [9]

'Adult males and boys of the same clan ate together, served by the women, asserting their solidarity by eating the same food and drinking water out of the same large calabash. The women, girls, and small boys ate their meal next to the domestic fireplace. There were codified gestures to be observed by all: the balls of food were to be picked up with the first three fingers of the right hand, and the sauce was drunk with a banana leaf rolled up into a cone.'

The king's meal was also ruled by etiquette: 'At mealtimes he was presented with a large cauldron .... filled with boiled or roasted meat. This he would eat with his fingers and then distribute a portion to each of his servants.'

To meet the demands of preparing food daily for large numbers of people, reserves had to be collected and stored, which meant making and using all kinds of vessels and containers. Currently, metal enamelware is the most popular item on the marketplaces, but it has not completely eliminated the 'old-fashioned' types of vessels. These may be grouped into three types: pottery, gourd bowls (calabashes) and baskets. These three types were used all across the social scale. More prestigious – and generally older – wares, made of carved wood, bronze, ivory, or covered with beadwork, were used at the courts of certain kings.

Despite the appeal of these costly materials, pottery has

Opposite

29. Vase
Mangbetu. Zaïre.
Ceramic. H.: 30.5 cm.
Private collection.

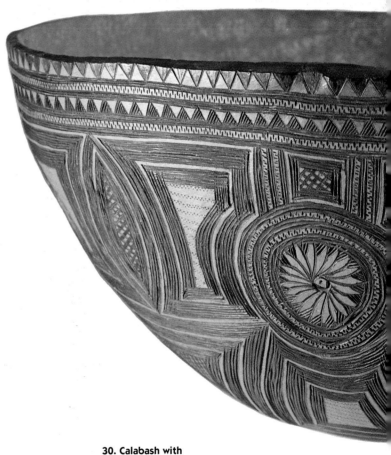

30. Calabash with pyrographic designs
Fulbe (Peul). Cameroon,
H.: 27 cm. Diam. 48 cm.
Musée de l'Homme, Paris.

41

31. Bottle
Thonga. Mozambique.
Gourd and beads.
H.: 20.9 cm. Museum of
Cultural History, University
of California, Los Angeles.

32. Set
of royal vessels
Bamileke. Cameroon.
Barbier-Mueller Museum,
Geneva.

Left: carved wooden
drinking cup. Right: bottle
made of gourd covered
with beadwork on cloth.
Front: carved drinking
horns. The round
stool-like object is
a stand for the bottle
behind.

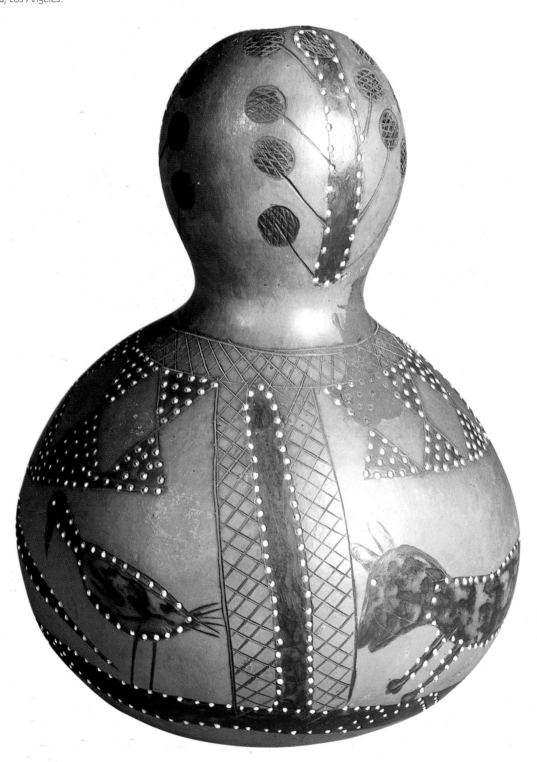

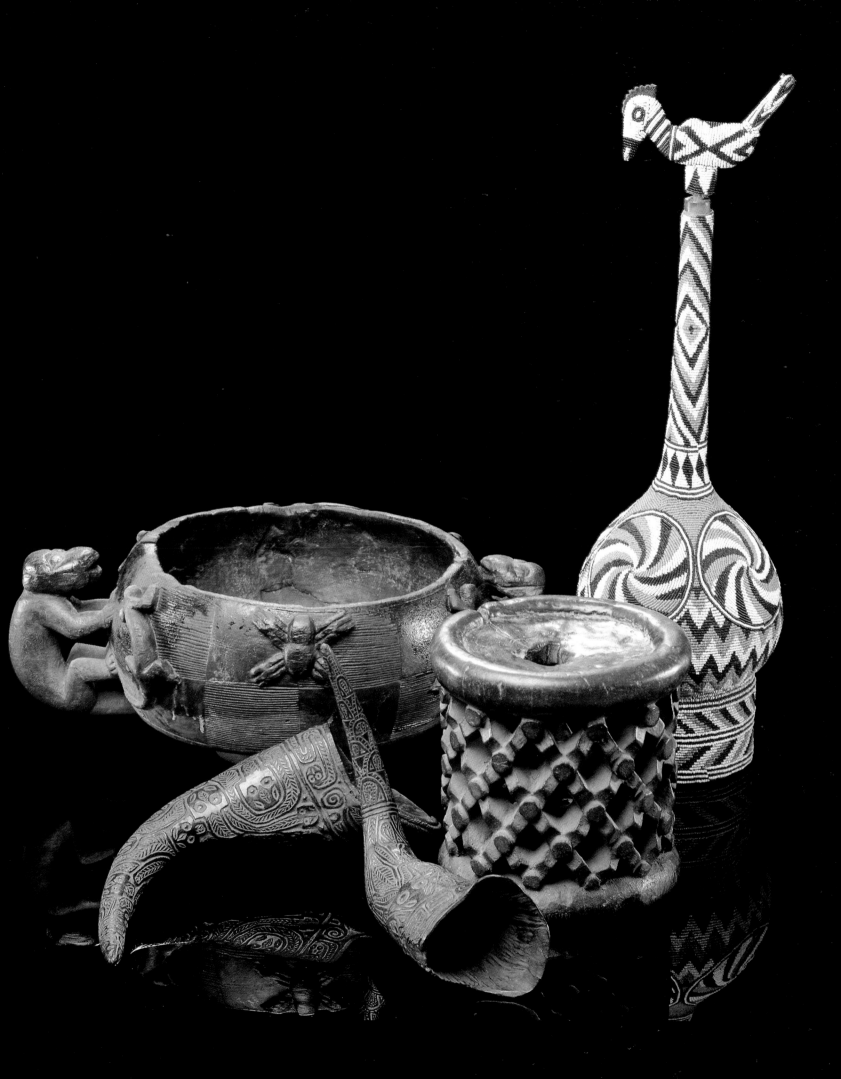

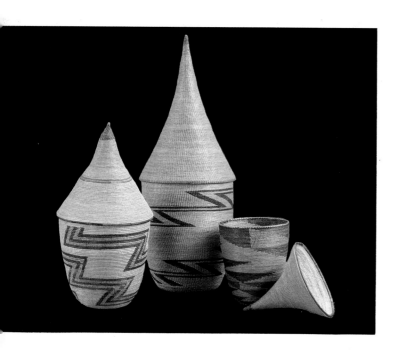

33. Three basket-work containers
Tutsi. Rwanda.
Private collection.

prevailed, if nothing else, because it has the advantage of permitting a longer cooking time.

Pottery, a millennial art

The making of pottery in the Sahara began in the 7th millennium BC and continues to thrive today (fig. 27). In all the known cultures, the so-called Neolithic Revolution, that is, the transition from the nomadic hunting-gathering way of life, to the more or less sedentary agrarian lifestyle, was accompanied by the development of pottery.

In the vast majority of cases, pottery was made by women, and more specifically by the blacksmith's wife. She did not work the clay on a wheel, but modelled it entirely by hand, starting with a ball of clay which she gradually hollowed and fashioned into the desired shape. In other cases, she cast the clay in a simple concave mould made of pottery, wood or a calabash. She used the colombin technique – clay rolled into strips between the palms – only adding handles or a lip to the finished vase at the final stage.

After the clay has been left to dry, the pots are gathered in a pile and covered with a combustible material (wood, bark or dried dung), and baked outdoors in an open fire. In Mali and Nigeria, the pots are baked in real kilns.

Countless types of vessels were made in this way, some without any decoration at all, but the taste for ornamental surfaces was widespread, as a visit to any market will show. The polishing of pottery is a common practice; or alternating bands of polished and matt or incised surfaces permits an almost infinite play of geometric patterns. A deep and lustrous patina obtained by the firing process is particularly appreciated in Central Africa.

As far as colour was concerned, plant dyes were used more often than not to create geometric motifs, or were randomly splashed on after the firing, a practice that was particularly popular among the Congolese people in what is now Zaïre.

Simplicity and balance of form was what the potters worked for in most cases, but certain objects benefitted from a supplementary ornamental treatment. Effects of relief or depth were obtained by scratching the wet clay with a blade or comb, or making impressions with a piece of rope, stamp or roulette (tracing wheel). One large cup (fig. 28) displays incised zig-zag patterns alternating with rope-like bands standing out in relief. In other regions, human or animal figures were added to enliven the surfaces (fig. 28), or to serve as handles or pouring beaks. The clay could be carved out before it had dried completely to make open-work designs, the practical aspect of which was to permit sauces to be warmed on the coals without burning them (fig. 28). The Mangbetu were masters at combining intaglio geometric designs with modelling in the round to create remarkable anthropomorphic vases (fig. 29). Our example displays the traditional hairstyle for Mangbetu women at the turn of the century.*

Other materials could also be added to the pots for utilitarian or ornamental purposes. In another practice common to the Mangbetu, the vessels could be fitted with basketwork covers, making them both more functional (for a better grip) and more elegant. Herbert Lang [10] reports simply that 'the Mangbetu make these kind of covers because they find them beautiful'.

Yet despite its beauty, pottery had two drawbacks: it was both heavy and fragile. This is why food that needed no cooking was more often than not served in a calabash.

The ubiquity of the calabash

Gourds are used in Africa to produce a great variety of containers called calabashes. The gourds come from a tree of the same name or from vines. The ripe fruit is picked and left to decompose in water. The bark-like peel is then either pierced or cut in half, and the pulp removed. The original shape of the calabash is like a pumpkin, but it can be altered by binding it while it is still growing.

Calabashes of different sizes are used as containers for all different kinds of things: cereal, liquids, butter, or even snuff. They are also used for the storage of clothes or as jewel boxes. Cut lengthwise, they make good spoons or ladles. They can be used to make masks, musical instruments, and even penile sheaths (fig. 102, p. 115). When a calabash is so damaged as to be no longer useable as a container, the

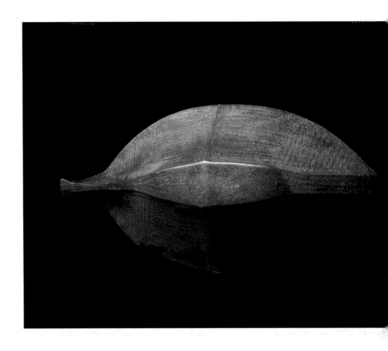

34. Oval dish
Wongo. Zaïre.
Wood. L.: 68 cm.
Private collection.

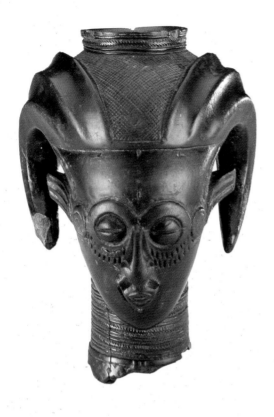

**36. Ceremonial
drinking cup**
Human head
with ram-horn design.
Kuba. Zaïre. Wood.
H.: 21 cm. National
Museum of African Art,
Washington, D.C.

Opposite

**33. Anthropomorphic
drinking cup**
Wongo. Kuba. Zaïre.
Wood. H.: 18 cm.
British Museum, London.

broken pieces are hard enough to be used as tools to incise designs in clay or even to work the soil. If the calabash is only cracked, it is repaired with painstaking care, and the result can take on the aspect of embroidery. Africans are very attached to their calabashes, some of which are handed down from generation to generation. The great emotive value of the calabash is most clearly demonstrated by the role it plays in certain myths. The Fon tribe of Dahomey believed that the universe was a sphere made of two calabash halves, one on top of the other, like the sky vaulting the land and the seas.

In their natural state, calabashes have colours that range from ochre to honey, and can be polished to a brilliant finish. It is the ideal support for all kinds of decorations. Calabashes can also be dyed to a uniform colour by being dipped in baths of red-ochre (very often), and sometimes in white or indigo pigment. With the help of an oily paste, they can be decorated by using resist techniques as in textiles. More often than not, however, the decoration was incised with a red-hot metal tip. Calabashes lend themselves to an infinite variety of curvilinear designs that cover the forms with an uninterrupted play of geometric patterns of unfailing harmony and originality (fig. 30). Very often, too, they are decorated with naïvely represented scenes of everyday life executed in a graffiti-like style.

A calabash pierced simply with a hole at the top makes an excellent container for liquids. Bottles and flasks of this kind, adorned with remarkably effective black motifs outlined in white beads, were found at the beginning of this century among the Thonga of Mozambique (fig. 31).

If the calabash 'skin' was thick enough, it could be carved with intaglio patterns, as the Yoruba of Nigeria were fond of doing. But more frequently, the calabash was covered on the outside with leather or basketwork. In the grasslands of Cameroon, strikingly colourful ornaments were made with beadwork to cover bottles elegantly tipped with animal figures and mounted on round bases (fig. 32).

The horns of cattle, hollowed out and carved with designs, could also be used as drinking vessels, but the calabash remained by far the preferred recipient. In the western or north-western provinces of Cameroon, these ox or water-buffalo horns (fig. 32), like the beadwork bottles,

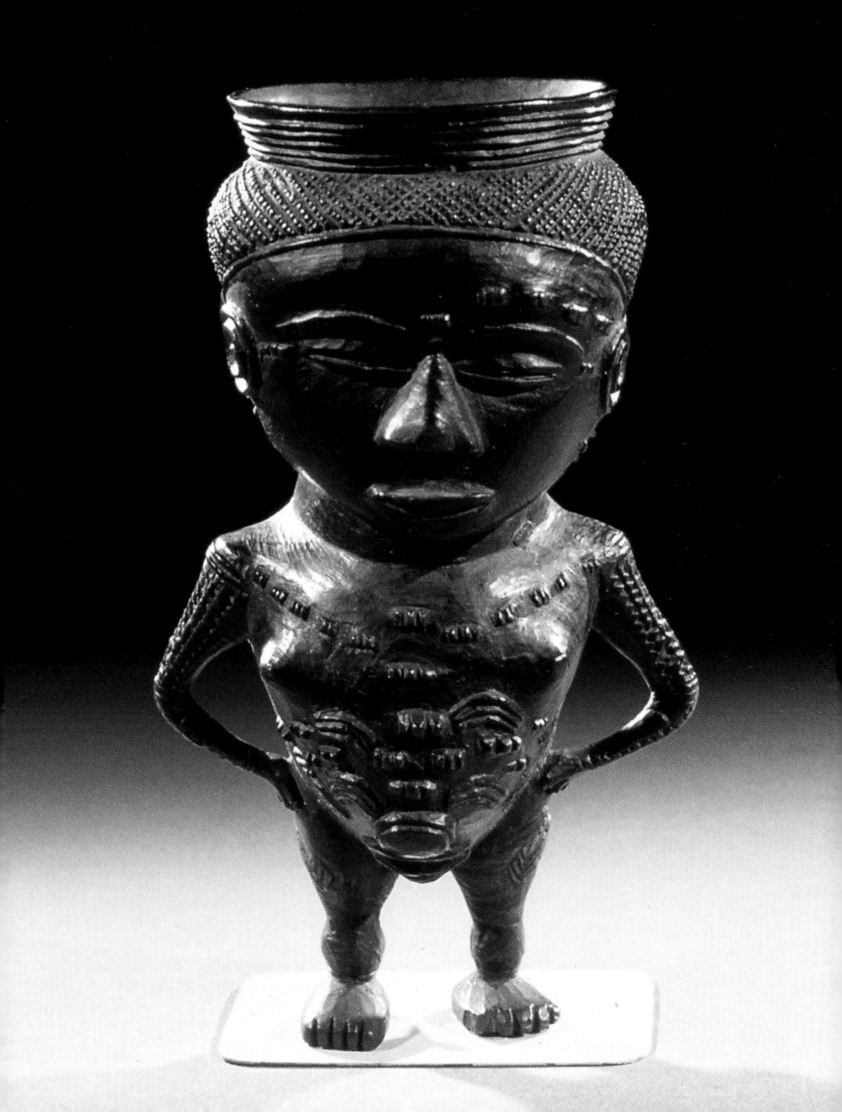

were reserved for chiefs, and could also serve as ritual objects.

Along with calabashes and cattle horns, whose forms were dictated by nature, a large variety of vessels were made out of woven plant fibres.

Basketwork: simplicity and variety

The technique of basketweaving, which permits the production of durable, lightweight and inexpensive objects, is perfectly suited to the African way of life. It is widely practised and, depending on the region, considered variously as work for men or for women.

Once again, the material is found in nature – in different types of grasses: vines, raffia, leaf parts, date palms, papyrus, sorghum, etc. The various braiding techniques, often quite complex, have similarities with textile weaving. Crossed or checked weaving is preferred in West Africa as a rule, while coiling techniques are more often found in the central and southern regions of the continent.

Basketry is used to make countless types of objects: baskets and other containers, of course, but also mats (previously discussed) and shields. Basketweaving in some cases even serves as a substitute for pottery, for a very close weave can make watertight containers, like those used in Ethiopia to keep milk fresh. A looser weave is used to make filters and sieves.

Decorative effects may be obtained by using fibres of different natural or dyed colours.

In the hands of certain craftsmen, basketweaving can be an art. The Tutsi of Rwanda create very refined containers with a spiral structure, elongated conical covers, and geometric patterns (fig. 33). A similar technique used by the Lozi of Zambia also permitted the representation of animal figures.

The Mangbetu women of Zaïre often practised basketweaving in the past. They made baskets to store their personal effects, everything from jewellery to remedies. Using tressed leaves, they displayed endless ingenuity in making their characteristically oval-shaped buttock screens (fig. 103, p. 114).

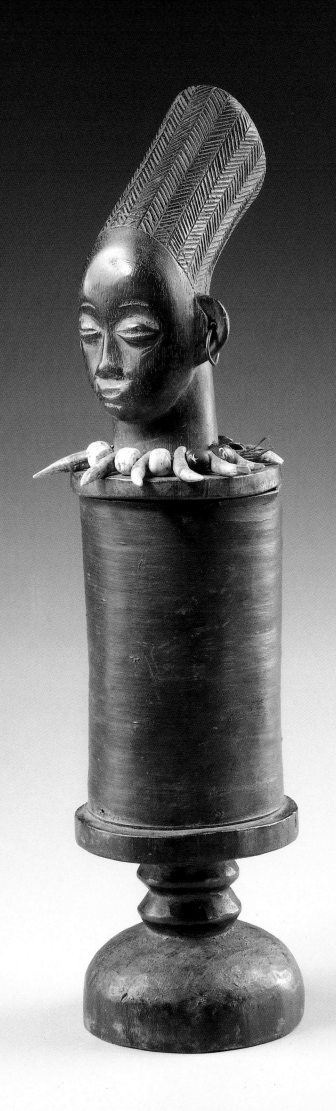

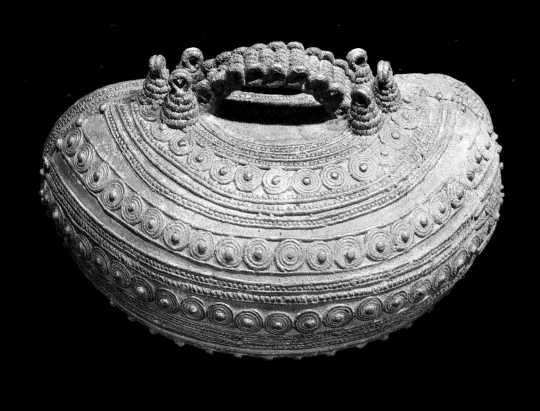

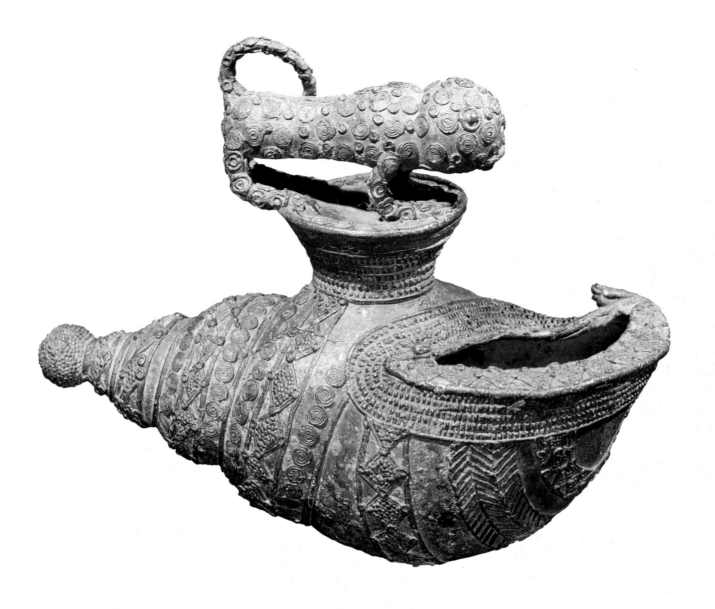

**39. Shell-shaped
vessel topped
with animal figure**
Igbo-Ukwu. Nigeria.
9th–10th cent. Bronze
with lead content.
L.: 20.6 cm. National
Museum, Lagos.

Opposite

**38. Crescent-
shaped bowl**
Igbo-Ukwu. Nigeria.
9th–10th cent. Bronze
with lead content.
L.: 13.9 cm.
National Museum, Lagos.

In Zaïre again, the Bwaka made boxes covered with geometric designs of great intricacy that recalls embroidery. These were not unrelated to the patterns traced on velvet by the Kasaï and to the sculpture of the Kuba.

Wooden containers

The Kuba tribe, and some of their neighbours, like the Wongo, produced scores of wooden objects of high aesthetic quality: chairs, head-rests, pipes, drums, and above all a great variety of containers.

These objects, often intended for the kings and chiefs belonging to the aristocratic lineage, were made by professional artists who spent long periods of time at Mushenge, the capital, where they were treated like dignitaries. The consummate style of their work set an example which the common people sought to imitate with the more modest means at their disposal.

All of these artisans working with wood shared a deep sensitivity to and respect for the beauty of this material. Certain oval-shaped Wongo bowls (fig. 34) used for storing palm oil were not carved, but their regular and harmonious curves, and their surface, often still bearing the marks of the adze or various dotted-line motifs, display the care and love which presided over their creation.

Countless Wongo and Kuba palm-wine cups, on the other hand, are characterized by their prolific carved ornamentation, which saturates all the surfaces. These are often geometric patterns in low relief and interwoven designs imitating basketry, the knots of fishing nets, or braids. Each of the designs had a specific name and they were combined in an unflagging rhythm. They were carved freehand, yet adapted to the round forms of the objects – like the Kuba cups, for example – with the kind of precision that goes into jewellery.

In other cases, these ornamental designs were artfully associated with anthropomorphic motifs. The head was hollowed out into a cup. In the one illustrated here (fig. 35), the vertical progression of the forms is so regular and perfect that it recalls a blooming flower. Certain faces have such stunning features that some have called them portraits.

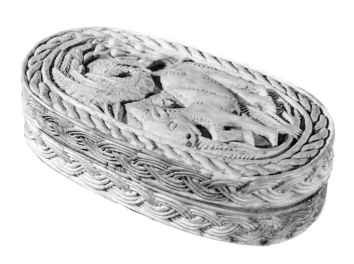

40. Box with cover
Kingdom of Benin.
Nigeria. Late 19th-cent.
Carved ivory. L.: 15 cm.
National Museum, Lagos.

The culmination of this series are the cups which solely represent the form of the human head, and in which the high, elongated temples are topped by ram's horns (fig. 36), which in some cases prolong the lines of ritual scars and stylized – and clearly detached – ears. The effect is sometimes very beautiful and the face seems to be infused with a deep spirituality.

The decoration of carved boxes among the Kuba is as elaborate as that of their drinking cups. Made exclusively for the Bushoong clan, they were intended to hold, not food, but cosmetic products and accessories, like razors and the red *tukula* powder used for body care. These were in effect very luxurious toilet kits, with surprising forms: round, oval, a human face, a boat, or the roof of a hut.

Intended for purely profane purposes, and not for ritual use, these Kuba objects existed mainly to satisfy an elitist pleasure and pride in the ownership of beautiful things. As Joseph Cornet, an ethnologist specializing in the arts of Zaïre, pointedly remarked: [11] 'The art of the Kuba is centred on Man, the glorification of power and the beautification of life.'

In north-east Zaïre, the Mangbetu population was also ruled by an aristocratic class that developed a court art. It was a much more realistic art than that of the Kuba, but it also succeeded in integrating the human figure in a decorative scheme. We have already seen an example of this in the anthropomorphic pottery, and the same goes for the boxes made of wood or bark by the Mangbetu. These boxes were intended for all manner of personal effects and treasures: jewellery, charms, and even articles of clothing, but also *tukula* powder and honey. The covers and round bases of these boxes were of wood, occasionally carved, while the cylindrical body was made of bark held together by finely sewn plant fibres. At the beginning of this century, the cover was often topped by a sculpture representing a human head (fig. 37). Later, the boxes took on the form of a statuette,* as the representational aspect took precedence over the utiliarian function of the container.

Many fine nineteenth-century wooden boxes from Benin have come down to us. Long and narrow, they were carved in low relief with representations of court figures holding swords. They were intended primarily to contain sacrificial offerings, medicine, or kola nuts. They were made not by

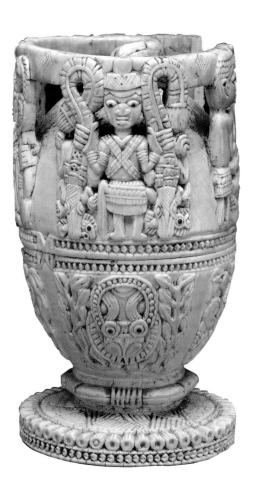

41. Covered cup
Yoruba. Owo. Nigeria.
17th–18th cent. Ivory,
wood or coconut bark.
H.: 21 cm. Metropolitan
Museum of Art, N.Y.

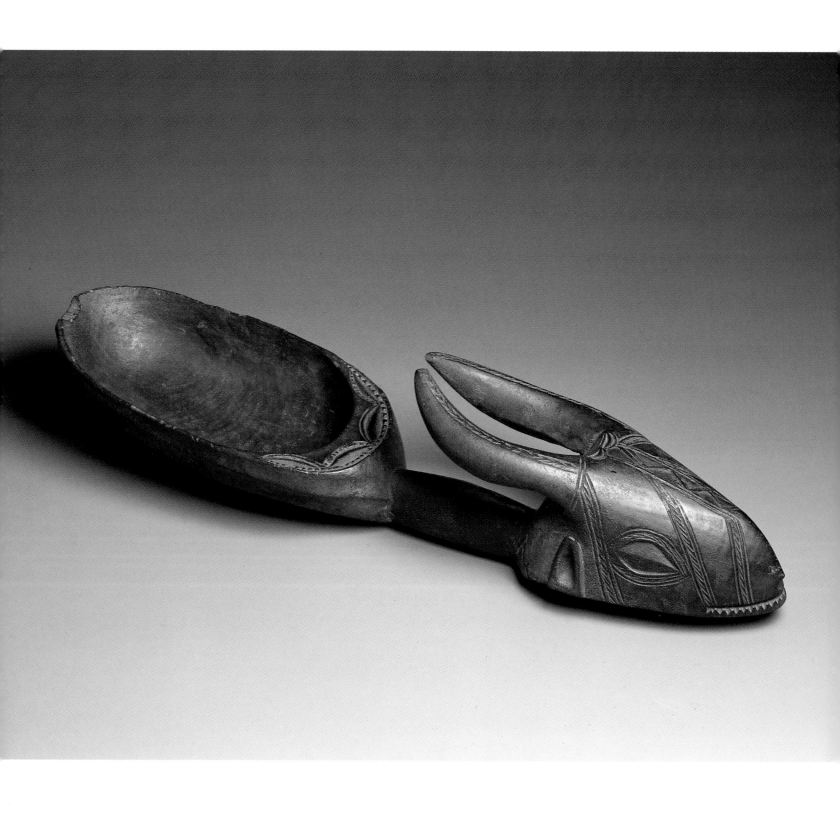

the ivory-carvers, but by pages of the king who belonged to an association called *omada*, a group of boys between the ages of six and twenty who were apprentice-sculptors. They enjoyed a wider range of freedom than the other artisans working for the court.

Prestigious bronze and ivory

While objects made of wood – which easily fall prey to the elements and termites – rarely date from before the nineteenth century, those made of more resistant materials, like bronze and ivory, are often many centuries old.

The Igbo Ukwu culture, one of the most mysterious and bewitching of Nigeria, distinguished itself particularly by its use of bronze. Analyses of certain bronze containers with Carbon 14 have yielded dates going back to the ninth century. These are the oldest bronze objects made with the lost-wax process in Africa, and they display an extraordinary mastery on the part of the craftsmen who made them. The entire surface is covered with intricate designs, a veritable metal embroidery composed of tiny figures, often insects. Even the slightest defects in casting are covered by little round patches.

These containers are often bowls in the form of a calabash or other fruit that has been cut in two. Some of them were given the shape of seashells represented with great art (fig. 39). Because they were so rare, these objects were very likely to have played a role in court ceremonies or religious rituals, but this has not yet been proven. Their superb workmanship and their thousand-year-old patina, with its green and purple lustre, are a wonder to behold.

In Benin, many brass objects were made for the court of the king, or *oba*, between the sixteenth and nineteenth centuries. These were mainly boxes with variously shaped covers designed to hold personal effects or to be used in official ceremonies. Other boxes, used for storing kola nuts and other foodstuffs, were made of ivory carved with great skill (fig. 40).

The activities of the bronzesmiths and ivory-carvers of Benin were strictly regulated, and the craftsmen were organized into guilds established in the vicinity of the

**42. Ceremonial
Wakemia spoon**
Dan. Ivory Coast.
Wood, metal and fibres.
L.: 60 cm. Barbier-Mueller
Museum, Geneva
(acquired before 1939).

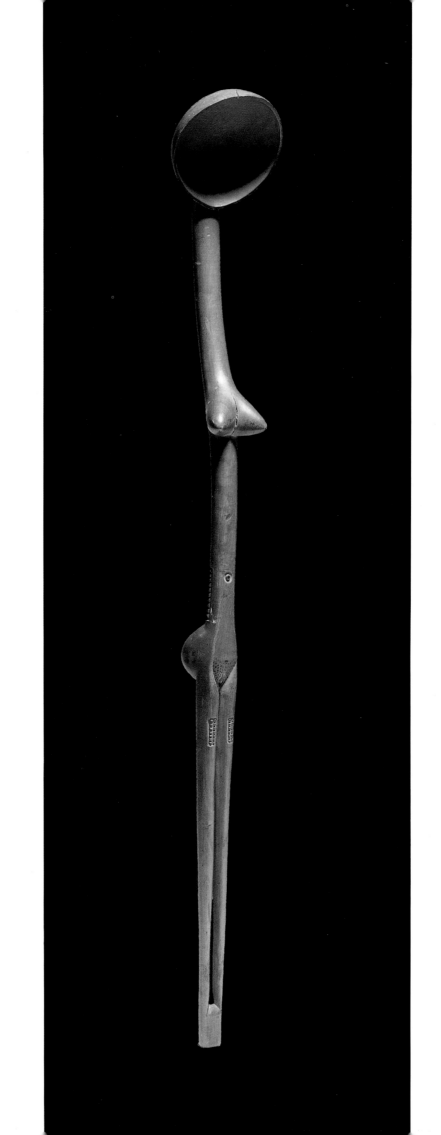

palace for more effective control. The privilege of owning bronze objects was reserved for the *oba* himself, but the use of ivory was less restricted. Dignitaries of the court had to apply to the king for permission to buy it.

The city of Owo, about one hundred kilometres away from Benin, was a major centre of ivory production. Its ties with the royal court must have been very close, for many objects in the Owo style have been found in the palace in Benin. Among the ivory vessels carved at Owo, the most remarkable are doubtless the covered drinking cups. One of these is today in the Metropolitan Museum of Art (fig. 41). It is a deep, oval-shape cup whose sides are covered with human and animal figures carved in high relief, set side by side or intertwined. The general significance of these figures remains unknown, but they seem to symbolize the awesome might of the kings of divine lineage. The cups in this series were probably gifts presented by the king of Owo to high-ranking visitors.

What were the spoons used for?

Accounts by ethnologists of meals in traditional African cultures indicate that people generally ate with the fingers of the right hand. Confirming the description given of the Congo by Balandier in the eighteenth century, René Caillié wrote of the Mande around 1827: [12] 'I saw a large calabash filled with boiled rice, on top of which a rather large quantity of meat had been added. We sat around it, and each ate out of it with the hand, as was the custom.' One century earlier, the Scotsman Mungo Park had observed that, even in the case of couscous, the Africans used only their fingers to eat. Even today, European guests of nomads should not be too surprised if a hospitable host reaches into the common dish and offers them a handful of couscous.

These reports notwithstanding, it is a fact that spoons are often found in Africa, and many of them are decorated with fine carvings. Their use corresponded to specific situations and not to the everyday use to which we are accustomed. The first models known, small round bronze spoons used in Mali for gold dust, go back to the fourteenth century (fig. 85, p. 96).

Opposite

44. Spoon
Zulu. South Africa.
Wood. L.: 57 cm.
Musée de l'Homme, Paris.

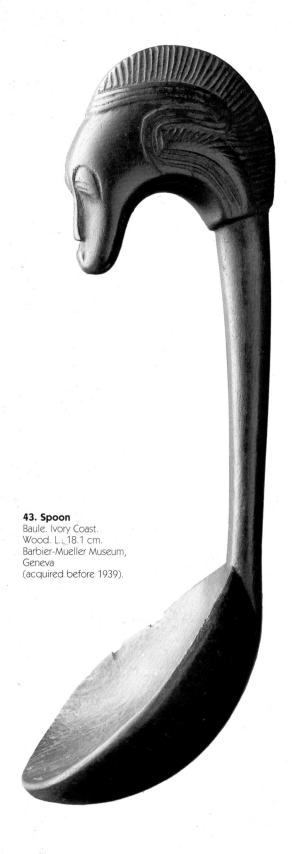

43. Spoon
Baule. Ivory Coast.
Wood. L.: 18.1 cm.
Barbier-Mueller Museum,
Geneva
(acquired before 1939).

Of more recent date are the spatulas and ladles used in cooking or to serve food. Writing again about meals among the Mande, René Caillié noted: [13] 'Meals were cooked in the open; the women each held a large spatula to stir the rice and meat.'

Among the Dan and We tribes of the Ivory Coast, large carved spoons were – and still are – used during feasts. They are the attribute of a woman known in the village for her signal generosity and hospitality. At the behest of the chief, she has the reponsibility of organizing banquets for large numbers of guests. She is given a large spoon called a *wakemia* as a sign of her special status and a token of the village's appreciation. She uses it to serve the meat and rice, exhibits it, and, accompanied by her assistants, brandishes it in the 'dance of the hospitable woman'.

The form and carved decoration of the *wakemia* is subject to great variation. The containing element itself has the gentle curves of the female body. Filled with rice, it is associated with fertility and the promise of childbearing. Sometimes the spoon is doubled and explicitly takes on the form of breasts. The handle often becomes a piece of sculpture in itself. When the figure is zoomorphic, it is often the head of a sheep or goat (fig. 42); if it is anthropomorphic, it takes on the shape of a woman's head or legs.*

A relationship between carved spoons and ritual is also to be observed among the Senufo, who use round ladles to serve millet beer to the newly-initiated members of the secret poro fraternity.

In many other tribes, the spoon has different uses. Spoons of smaller size are not ritual implements, but, like all finely-made objects, conspicuous signs of the owner's status. Among the Baule (fig. 43), who had a highly developed sensitivity to sculpture, this dimension was perfectly well understood. The sinuous forms and soft surfaces of this object lent themselves to a perfect harmony of overall design and decoration.

The Baule woodcarvers also produced a type of object that was an exceptional rarity in Africa: the fork. This is proof that, among the Baule themselves, there was an art form that was practised outside of any religious context and appreciated for its own sake.

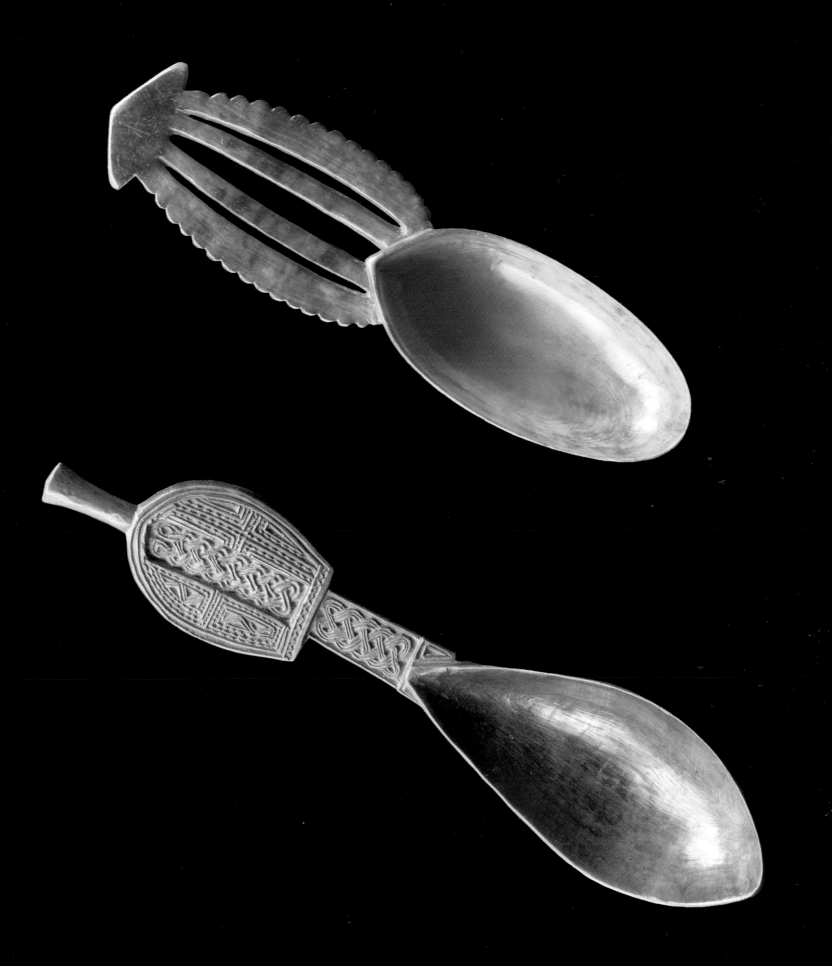

46. Spoon
Lega. Zaïre. Ivory.
L.: 20 cm.
Private collection.

Below

45. Spoon
Boni. Somalia. Wood.
L.: 26 cm.
Private collection.

Opposite

47. Spoon
Sapi. Sierra-Leone.
16th cent. L.: 25 cm.
Museum für Völkerkunde,
Vienna.

Another example,
among many others, of
'these miniature works
of art, both superb and
unique, eminently
worthy of adorning the
aristocratic tables for
which they were made'
(E. Bassani).

The Zulu of South Africa gave to certain spoons the form of a highly-stylized woman's body (fig. 44), an artistic treatment which did not prevent these objects from having a practical utility. A young woman having given birth to her first child acquired her first spoon as a sign of entry into the new domestic phase of her life: running a household and cooking for her husband. The large size of these particular spoons suggests that they were intended for the preparation and serving of food, rather than for personal use.

From the extreme stylization of Zulu spoons to pure abstraction was only a step away. This step was often taken by carvers who liked to create intricate geometric decoration, as exemplified in the endless knot patterns of the Boni spoon from Somalia (fig. 45) in which aesthetic style, form and function retain a perfect balance.

The vast majority of spoons were made of wood, but other materials were also used. Spoons made of brass or ivory were used in Mali and by the Akan in Ghana to handle gold dust. The spoons of the Lega tribe are justly famous (fig. 46): the forms, often geometric, are superbly brought out by the orange colour of the ivory. They are flatter than wooden spoons and the handle is decorated with openwork designs and graced with small circular patterns. When human or animal heads were represented, these were greatly stylized. Associated with ideas of life forces, ivory spoons seem to have been used in a ritual context.

Whether figurative or geometric in design, all of these spoons were crafted with as much care as statuettes, and reflected the styles of the sculptures and masks of the respective tribes. The craftsman's task – to unite a functional form and what was in effect a sculpture into a harmonious design – was not an easy one. This was often achieved by using the handle as a transitional element to preserve the overall balance and the flow of the form, without detracting attention from the sculptural motif.

There exists also a particular class of objects which does not reflect the traditional African style. These are the ivory spoons made in the sixteenth century in Sierra Leone and Nigeria for Portuguese merchants who sold them at the princely courts of Europe. Very elegant despite a busy and overabundant decoration, they display a perfect purity of line and, like their wooden counterparts, effortlessly combine decorativeness and functionality (fig. 47). They are graced with realistically represented animals and have been fashioned with such delicacy that the spoon lip seems translucid.

According to Ezio Bassani, an ethnologist specializing in the study of ivory objects produced for the European market, these spoons were the work of Sapi craftsmen, the ancient inhabitants of Sierra Leone. They also made salt-cellars of very intricate design intended for the Renaissance courts. Although not the product of a purely indigenous art, the elegance and technical mastery displayed by these objects is a lasting testimonial to the skill of the native ivory-carvers.

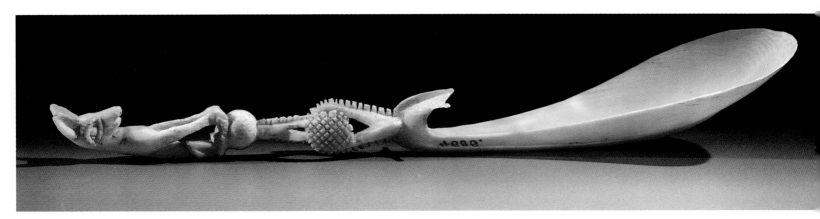

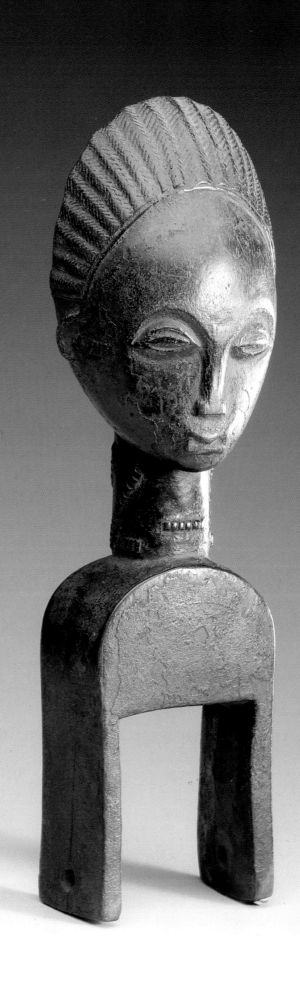

The colourful world
of woodbark
and textiles

Until relatively recent times, textiles in Africa were made not to protect the body against the climate or inclement weather, but rather to provide pleasure and to satisfy the aesthetic sense. The textiles were intended above all to be seen, to adorn and to assert the wearer's presence with brio. Even today, and despite the influence of European fashions, the fabrics explode with colour and a profusion of ornamental patterns. Textiles of very different colour and design are unabashedly mixed. This is especially visible during public feasts, where clothing combines with jewels and other insignia of rank to proclaim in no uncertain terms the prestige of the dignitaries or of those who want to stand out from the crowd.

Clothing practices differ traditionally according to the country. In Islamic areas, the tendency is to wear lots of clothes, ample boubous with tunics and pants for the men, and equally ample dresses for the women. The men cover their heads with a cap or turban. In countries with an animist tradition, the spectacle is entirely different, and partial nudity is still practised. This is the case for the Kirdi women in the northern regions of Chad who often wear only a *cache-sexe* made of tubes of metal. The Mangbetu women of Zaïre reduced clothing to the minimum, but prided themselves on their woven-leaf *cache-fesses*, or

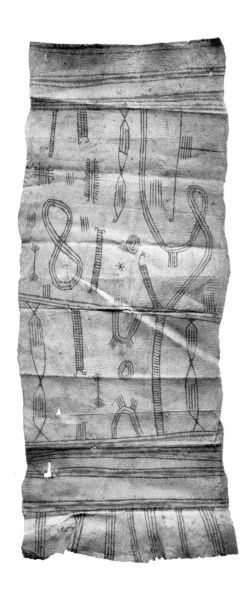

Opposite

51. Pulley from a loom
Baule. Ivory Coast. Wood. H.: 23.2 cm. Barbier-Mueller Museum, Geneva.

48. Woodbark cloth
Pygmy. Zaïre. L.: 86 cm. W.: 36 cm. Barbier-Mueller Museum, Geneva.

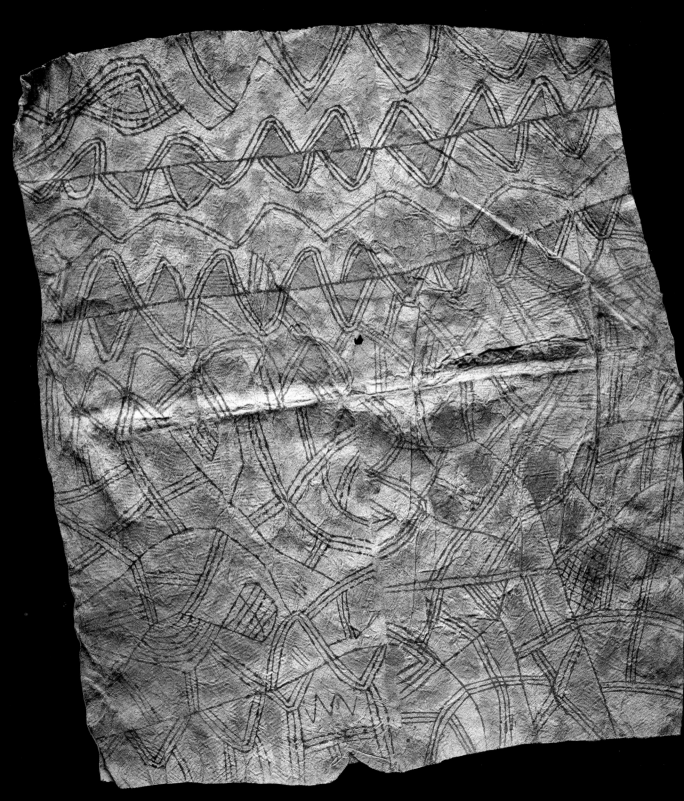

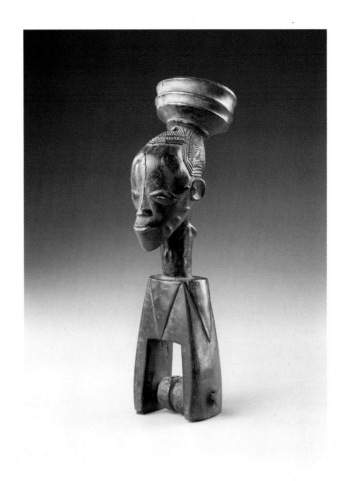

52. Pulley from a loom
Guro. Ivory Coast.
Private collection.

Opposite

49. Woodbark cloth
Pygmy. Zaïre. L.: 77.5 cm.
W.: 67.5 cm. Barbier-
Mueller Museum, Geneva.

buttock-screens (fig. 103, p. 114) and very elaborate hairstyles.

Apart from these exceptions, there was nothing out of the ordinary about the raw materials used to make the textiles.

Simple means and surprising results

Silk, a very rare item, was used in the past only by the Akan tribes of Ghana and the Ivory Coast to make fabrics for kings and high-ranking dignitaries. Other fibres like cotton, raffia – but less often wool – were commonly used and not expensive.

The equipment used to make textiles, even today, is very primitive. The looms are made of rough-hewn wood, and only the pulleys are decorated. Fabrics are coloured either with dyes extracted from plants or in mud baths. Soaking and washing are done in large calabashes. Most sewing needs are met with a needle and small knife.

Although using such rudimentary, slow and inconvenient techniques, the Africans produce remarkably beautiful fabrics. Everything is handmade, and the slight irregularities that differentiate them from industrially made textiles bear witness to the tremendous amounts of time, patience and care given to the production of these fabrics, not to mention the unfailing aesthetic sensibility common to all of the African crafts.

This is visible everywhere, but most particularly among the Pygmies of Zaïre.

Pygmies and woodbark

Although one of the most primitive forms of textile, pounded woodbark fabrics are not lacking in variety of form or decoration. They are used by the Pygmies, the Mangbetu, and other neighbouring tribes for ritual ceremonies, including circumcisions, funerals and feasts with singing and dancing. They are made in rectangles and worn around the loins, hanging in front and behind, or passed between the legs and held in place with a belt.

These are not strictly speaking textiles, for the fibres are not woven but compacted. The material used is the inner lining of the bark (phloem) from different types of trees which is cut in long strips, soaked in water, then pounded with a mallet (generally made of ivory) for hours on end, before being dried in a shaded place. Traditionally, this is men's work.

The decoration, on the other hand, is the work of the women. They use soot from the bottom of cooking pots fixed with different plant extracts, which also provide red and yellow pigments. For the actual painting, the pieces of bark are folded in four and each side is decorated separately.

The decorative styles are anything but uniform. The Efe, a tribe of Pygmies, are known for making patterns of fingerprints. The Mbuti, another Pygmy tribe, use lines to make patterns analogous to those painted on their bodies.

Among the ornaments, there are a great number of pictogrames which probably constitute a code. These designs are currently being researched by Professor Farris Thompson, who has established a connection between certain linear and geometric designs and the drawings traced on the ground by Pygmies to give directions for hunting. Other pictogrames, again according to Thompson, have a more representational function and are related to natural forms: stars, butterflies, spider webs and saplings represented as small, tightly grouped lines. The figures of snakes, crocodiles and leopard are stylized to the extreme, but remain recognizable.

The vocabulary of signs used by the neighbouring Mangbetu on their woodbark loincloths is quite different. Certain designs are definitely representational: human figures and the characteristically shaped Mangbetu knives.

The overall impression given by these accumulations of signs organized in different, contrasting rhythmic patterns, is one of incoherence (figs. 48 and 49). Could they be expressions of the mysterious world of the jungle, or transcriptions of the choral chants for which the Pygmies are so famous? In any case, the women take great pride in their decorative work, saying, 'We make these designs because they are beautiful.' While being attached to traditional motifs, they are especially fond of invention and variety.

The use of woodbark for fabrics in Africa is restricted to a relatively small region in north-east Zaïre. In other regions, weaving is the preferred technique.

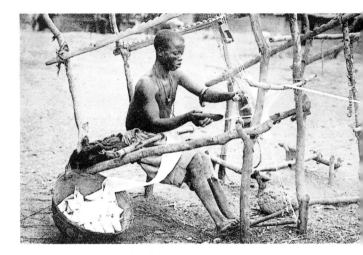

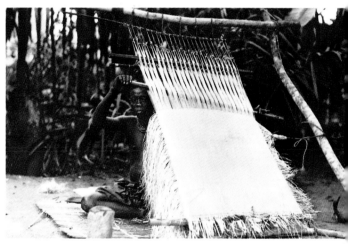

Weaving, a millennia-old craft

The most common textile fibre in Black Africa is cotton. Wool is also used, but infrequently, in regions on the fringes of the Sahara. Raffia is sometimes used in West Africa, but much more often in Central Africa and the Congo basin.

Although it is not found in the southernmost parts of the continent, weaving is a very ancient practice. Traces of woven plant fibres have been uncovered at Igbo-Ukwu (Nigeria), at sites believed to be a thousand years old. These remains of textiles had finished edges, which means that looms were used.

The Bambara of Mali believed that weaving had a divine origin: it was introduced by Faro, the Sun and Water God who also transmitted metalworking techniques to humans. The Bambara have remained master-weavers down to this day. In Benin, it is supposed that weavers were grouped into corporations in the fifteenth century by an *oba* (king) who wanted to hide his paralysed legs under decorated fabrics made by these specialized craftsmen.

In more recent times, it may be observed that cotton and wool are spun by women, and that weaving is – traditionally, but not exclusively – the work of men. Different types of looms were used according to the region and the kinds of effects sought. There are three main types, with numerous variations in each case.

In West Africa, one finds a fixed, vertical loom without pedals and a single heddle, which is used to make a relatively large fabric, but of limited length. This type of weaving is the province of women, who are expected to possess the necessary skills when they marry. The cloth so made is intended for use within the family, and is worn draped around the body without being tailored or sewn.

It is a different matter for the male weaver: he is a master-craftsman who has undergone an apprenticeship and often travels to offer his services (fig. 50). He works on a vertical-frame loom with two heddles activated by pedals, and the whole can be disassembled, if necessary. The cloth produced on this loom is very long and narrow, so that several strips must be sewn together to make a piece of sufficient width. This fabric is always made to be sold.

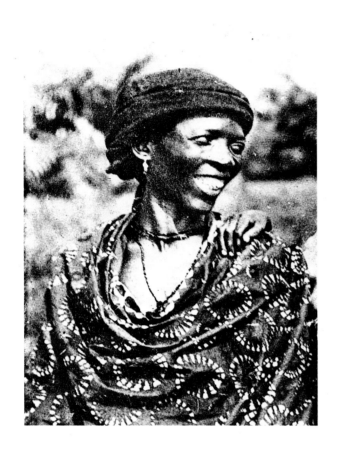

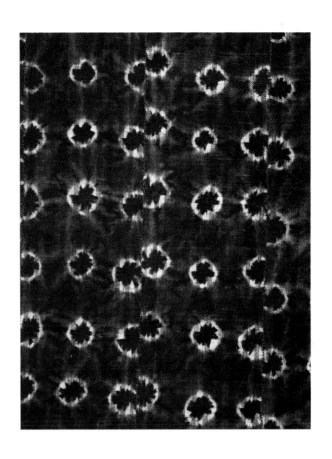

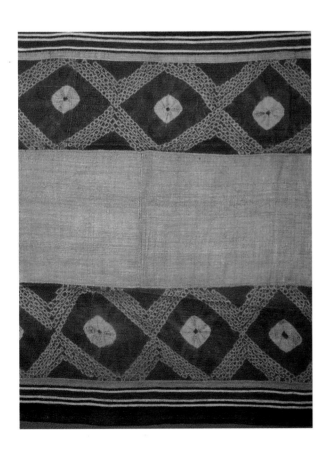

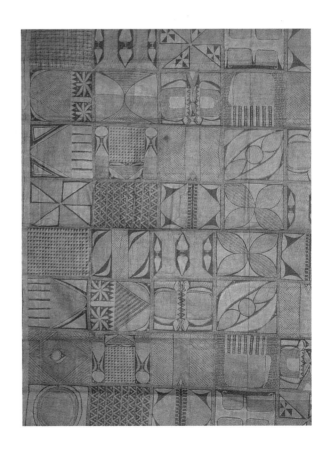

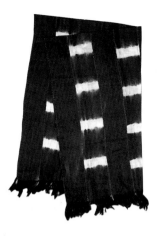

62. Guinea formerly used in commercial transactions
Senegal. Hôtel des Monnaies (Mint), Paris.

Below

70. Women from the village of Farako
Mali. Barbier-Mueller Archives, Geneva.

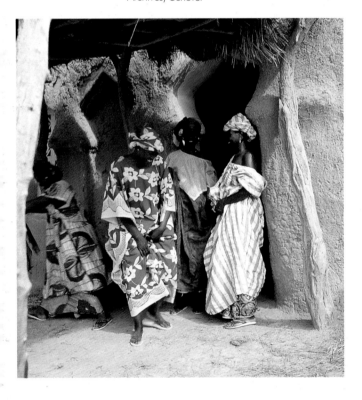

Opposite

59. Detail of cotton fabric
Composed of narrow bands sewn together. Cameroon. Indigo dye, reserves made with raffia thread to create the patterns. Private collection.

Wooden pullies control the tension of the thread on the double-heddle loom, and while the rest of the loom is rough-hewn, these pullies are often decorated with carvings* of high artistic quality, in accordance with the aesthetic requirements of these craftsmen (figs. 51 and 52).

There is a third, and much simpler, type of loom which is used for the weaving of raffia. Because it is not spun like cotton, the fibre lengths are not very long. The loom has a single heddle, and the ends of the fibres are left loose along the edges of the fabric (fig. 53).

Very often the fabric is unadorned and owes its beauty only to the brilliance of the natural colours. But in many cases, it is decorated according to a variety of techniques: the fibres can be dyed in different colours and woven in patterns, or brocades can be added. Decorative designs can also be obtained after weaving through the use of dyes. More precise designs can be achieved by painting or printing techniques. These various techniques, along with embroidery and appliqué, will be discussed separately.

Woven decoration

In the simplest cases, the colours of the horizontal and vertical threads can be changed or alternated to produce stripes and checkerboard patterns. This technique, among others, was used by the Hausa craftsmen of Kano (Nigeria) to make fabrics with white and indigo stripes.

In the past, European travellers often remarked on the drawbacks and impracticality of the narrow strips of cloth manufactured by double-warp looms. The Africans, however, turned these limitations to good advantage, joining the strips to create very effective compositions and patterns ranging from checks to more complex designs. Some patterns were produced by a regular treatment, others by chance.

To compensate for the monotony of stripes and checks, designs in brocade were inserted. Different kinds of weaving techniques were used to create shiny patterns on a matt ground, for an infinite variety of complex designs and sumptuous effects, which can be seen in the finery worn by the King of Indenia of the Ivory Coast (fig. 169, p. 181).

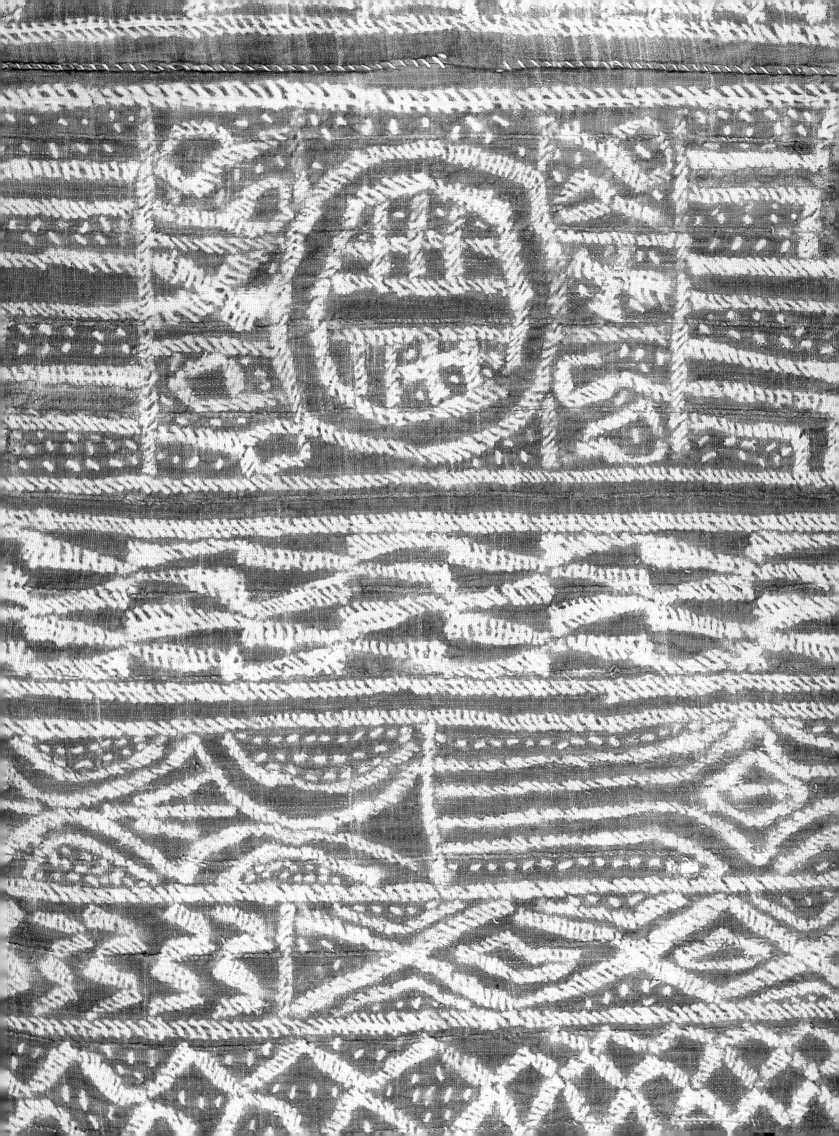

The brocade technique can be used on looms with single or double heddles. The latter type of loom was used by the Yoruba in the city of Oyo to make fabrics called *asoke*, in which stripes were alternated in an irregular pattern with brocade designs on strips that were then sewn together.

The famous *kente* fabrics of Ghana (fig. 54) also played on compositions of lines and geometric patterns combined with strong colour contrasts. All of these designs had a symbolic value, being associated with an idea, a saying or a historical event. They were intended to provide more than just a visual pleasure, but also to transmit a precise meaning. These luxurious fabrics were worn by the political and religious dignitaries of the Akan hierarchy. In the nineteenth century, the *kente* made exclusively for the Ashanti king fetched extravagant prices because they were made entirely of silk. The silk was specially imported from Europe in skeins, but another source came from Dutch fabrics that were taken apart, so that the threads could be re-used for materials with colours and patterns more suited to African taste. The results were fabulous.

Decoration with dyes

Dyeing is an inexpensive way to decorate fabrics and provides an ideal alternative to the necessarily rectilinear patterns produced by weaving. Plain cotton is normally used and the most common dye is indigo

The use of this dye was described by Jean Barbot, who travelled to the Gold Coast (today's Ghana) at the end of the seventeenth century. According to his description, the women gathered the leaves of a bush called *tinto*, which they crushed in large mortars, then rolled the pulp into balls to be dried in the sun. These balls were then broken apart and mixed with water and ash. The resulting mixture was again dried, and only the outer crust was used for the dye. This process is more or less the same as what is still being practised in Ghana and many other parts of Africa.

In addition to indigo, other pigments were made to yield black, yellow and red dyes. Brown was obtained from kola nuts.

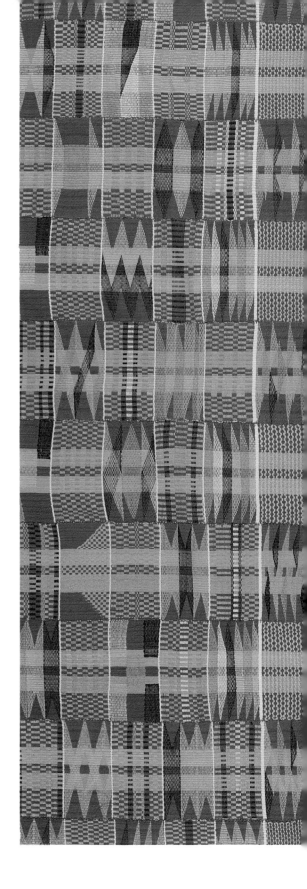

Overleaf

66. Raffia fabric with appliqué
Kuba. Zaïre. Barbier-Mueller Museum, Geneva.

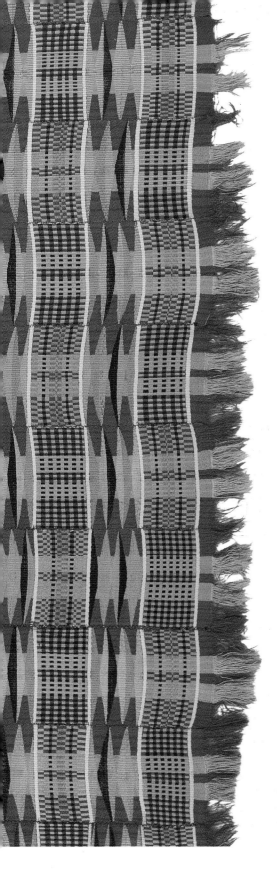

54. Kente fabric
Ashanti, Akan. Ghana.
Cotton and silk (detail).
Private collection.

To create two-colour patterns, the artisans needed only to alternate areas of dye with areas of undyed cloth. To preserve the original colour of the fabric, the dyer could tie knots – as in tie-dyeing – or establish reserves ('resist' technique) by using any number of dye-resistant substances.

In tie-dyeing, as the term indicates, the cloth is bound very tightly with string so that the dye cannot penetrate to the centre of the knot (in which a pebble can be inserted), then dipped into a bath of indigo dye. After rinsing and drying, the knots are unravelled, and in their place, circles or rings in the original colour appear against a blue ground (figs. 55 and 56). The cloth can also be delicately folded lengthwise and bound with string to create rectilinear patterns. The two methods can also be combined. The cotton fabrics obtained with this process are all the more attractive for their irregularities and chance patterns, while the varying shades of indigo create an impression of mystery.

The resist technique consists of drawing the desired motifs on the cloth with an impermeable material. After being dipped in the dye, the drawn motifs will appear in the original colour of the cloth. Various forms of this technique are used by the Yoruba in the entire region of Ibadan to create the so-called *adire* fabrics (fig. 58). The resist is more often than not drawn with starch, cassava, or candle wax.

In other cases, the decorative designs are drawn in resist on the cloth by embroidering it with raffia threads which are later removed. The Yoruba, again, are masters of this technique, which is also practised by the Bamum of Cameroon and produces highly attractive designs (fig. 59).

In our day, to save time, these designs are often made with stencils cut out of fine sheets of metal. Empty English tea tins are perfectly suited for this purpose.

The Bambara of Mali, on the other hand, were not concerned with saving time in producing their *bokolanfini* fabrics. Their dyeing methods were so complicated and required so many steps that some have even described them as 'aberrant'. The designs, made with yellow pigments and mud baths, called for repeated soakings and rinsings (fig. 60). The resulting patterns were white or yellow on a dark ground. These fabrics were then used to make men's clothing for the hunt (fig. 61).

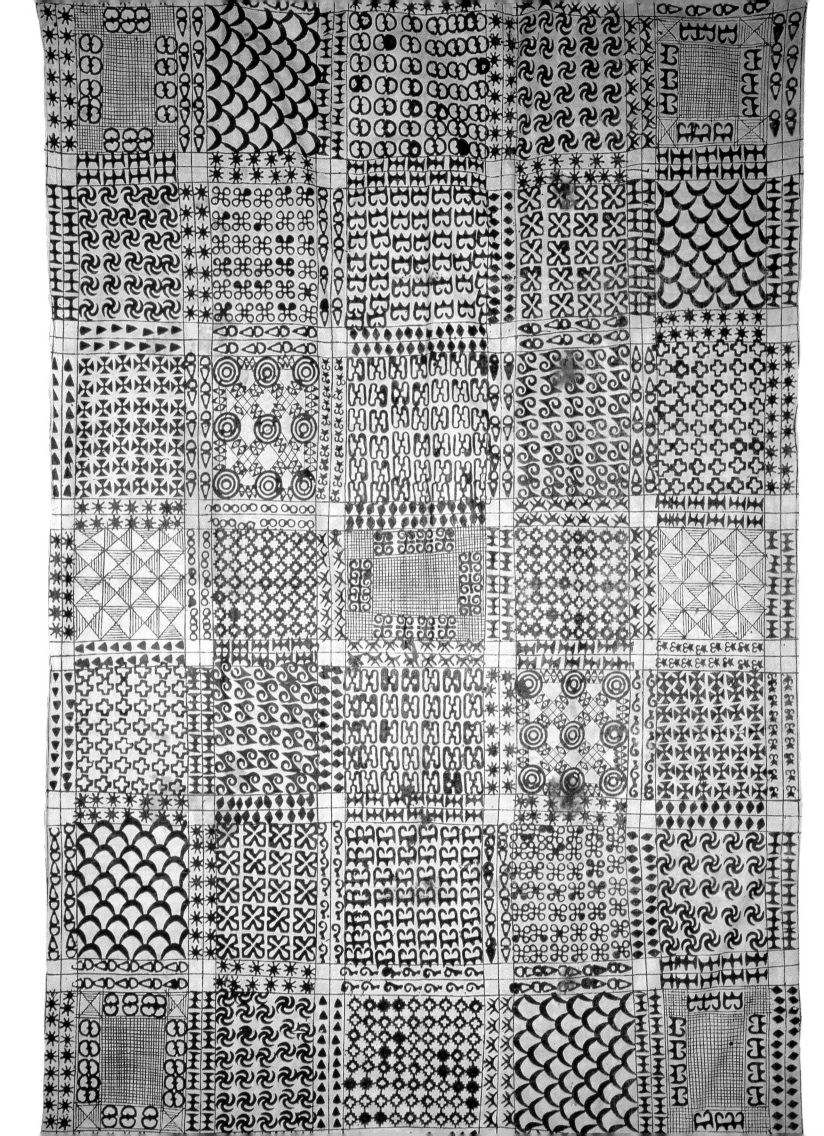

A fairly similar technique was used by the Senufo in the vicinity of Korhogo (Ivory Coast), but the motifs were figurative: animals like antelopes and fish, along with human figures.

In the nineteenth century, a great number of pieces of dyed cotton or raffia were used as currency in the regions adjacent to the Senegal. These were even called 'guineas', and they consisted of narrow strips of material dyed with indigo that were sewn together to be worn as loincloths (fig. 62).

Painted or printed decorations

In the various examples mentioned previously, the entire piece of cloth was soaked in the dye solution. In the techniques to be described next, the artisan drew the designs with pigment in a liquid medium.

True figurative drawings are relatively rare, but, to the south of the Sahara, the Hausa tribesmen paint magic designs and verses from the Koran on their clothes for protection. The technique most commonly used involves stamping the motifs directly on the fabric. The famous *adinkra* fabrics of the Ashanti are also made with this method (figs. 63 and 64). The black pigment is made from tree bark and looks like tar. The stamps are made out of pieces of calabash cut into the desired shapes. The cloth is spread on the ground and divided into squares, each of which will be stamped with a different motif.

Appliqué

In the appliqué technique, decorative designs are cut out of brightly coloured cloth with a stencil and sewn, or 'applied', onto material of a different colour. This is a very popular technique because it permits stunning colour combinations to be obtained. The traditional African colours are brown, red and black; European fabrics with less common colours, like green, are also used nowadays.

The appliqué technique, very widespread in Africa, is used for clothing, wall-hangings or objects intended to highlight the

64. Key to Adinkra motifs and symbols
Source: National Museum of African Art, Wash. D.C.

Head seen from the back. Meaning: valour, bravery, courage. Refers also to a precious traditional fabric made in the north of Ghana.

'If the hen steps on her chicks, they will not die.' Meaning: fitness, wish to protect, patience.

'God, everything which is above, permit my hand to touch it.'

Eagle claws. Alludes to the hairstyle of the Queen-Mother's servants. Meaning: ability to serve.

Moon. Female symbol. Means: fidelity, patience, determination.

Talisman against negative influences. Meaning: good luck.

The highest Adinkra symbol. Meaning: authority, grandeur, firmness, magnanimity.

Five tufts of hair. Evokes the traditional hairstyle of the priestesses.

Chain. Meaning: 'We are bound in life as in death.'

Variant of the preceding.

Windmill. Meaning: ability to face difficulty in life.

Ram's horns. Meaning: humility, excellence, wisdom, knowledge.

Four-storey house, castle. Meaning: government, authority, seat of power.

Opposite

63. Adinkra fabric
Ashanti. Ghana. Cotton printed with vegetable dyes. National Museum of African Art, Washington D.C.

Worn by the Ashanti king Prempeh I in 1897, when he was deposed by the British, this fabric has great sentimental value for the Africans.

prestige of the chiefs and notables. The most famous pieces were made in the former Dahomey by the Fon tribe. The craftsmen belonged to a special guild and worked for the nobles and chiefs, making clothing, wall-hangings and flags for the royal palace (fig. 65). The motifs suitable for the king were lions, white-breasted cows, sharks, or harps, which were all emblems of royalty. These motifs were also used in the decoration of the palace walls. In Benin, the ceremonial costumes of the oba still feature appliqué motifs representing kings, or yellow and black lions against a red background.

The cut-out appliqué motifs mentioned above were generally figurative, even if stylized in a naive register. Among the Kuba of Zaïre, however, the appliqué designs are abstract shapes (fig. 66). Using a piece of woven raffia as a base, they sew on long T- or comma-shaped bands (supposed to represent stylized dog-tails). The space between are filled with circles – a rarity in the art of the Kuba, which generally favours rectilinear designs.

These rectangular pieces of cloth, which can reach a length of as much as 8–10 metres and a width of from 75 cm to one metre, are worn by the women for certain dances, wrapped around their hips. Bright colour effects are not the point here; the monochrome harmonies of beige raffia alone are attractive enough. The works of Paul Klee strongly recall these designs, which have also been imitated by Western textile designers.

In the appliqué technique, the various pieces of cloth necessarily have sharply-defined contours, and so there is no tonal progression or play of shading between the figures and background. This feature is in keeping with the traditions of African art, in which forms tend to have a symbolic value and are not meant to provide equivalents of visual reality.

For more complex drawing effects, using many different colours in a restricted space, the Africans resorted to embroidery.

The refinement of embroidery

Embroidery is the most sophisticated way of decorating a fabric and, theoretically, the one which offers the greatest variety of effects.

60. Working with earth dyes
Orondona Village. Mali.
Photo Library of the
Barbier-Mueller Museum,
Geneva.

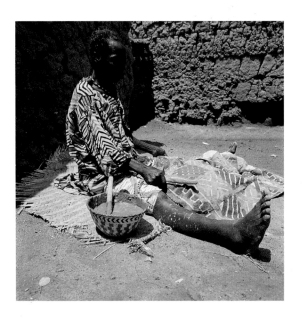

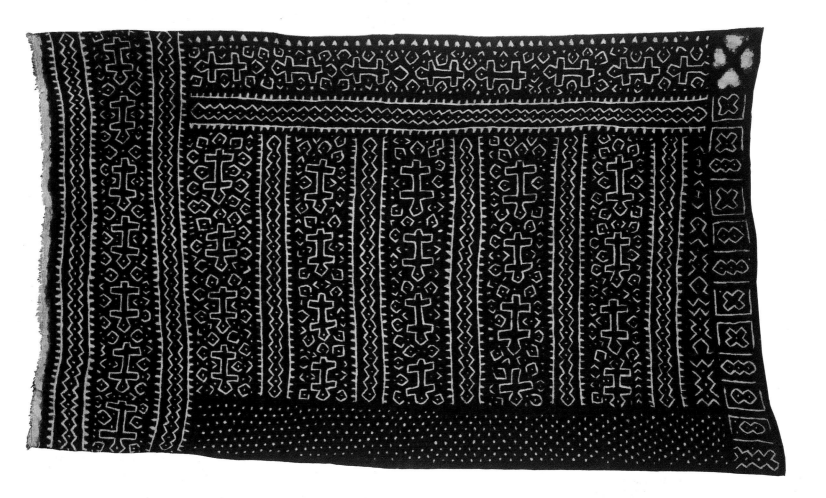

61. Earth-dyed fabric
Bambara. Mali.
W.: 157 cm.
Ethnographic Museum,
Basel.

In West Africa today, fine embroidered clothing may be found among the Islamic tribes, in particular the Hausa (fig. 67), the Peul and the Nupe of northern Nigeria. This craft, among others, is highly developed in the city of Kano, where the men create sumptuously embroidered boubous.

In his autobiography, *Amkoullel, enfant Peul,* [14] the Malian writer Amadou Hampâté Bâ makes frequent references to his father, Tidjani, a respected chief:

'In his youth, he had learned not only how to use the tools of the farmer – shovel, hoe, axe and plough – he was not only an expert marksman and rider, but he also knew how to sew and embroider in the manner of the Arab half-castes of Timbuktu .... the Peul and Tukulor nobles were not allowed to exercise the manual skills of the artisan castes (ironwork, weaving, shoemaking, woodwork), but they were allowed to embroider and sell their work .... Later,

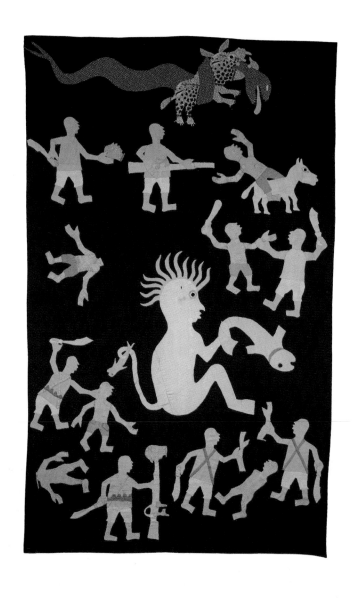

65. Wall-hanging from the palace of Abomey with appliqué motifs
(Copied from an original). Fon. Formerly Dahomey. Republic of Benin. Abomey. 200 x 130 cm. Museum of African and Oceanian Arts, Paris.

I was taught this art too, and I would embroider magnificent boubous which would be priceless if sold today.'

Yet the most remarkable embroidery work is the famous Kasaï velvets* made in Zaïre by a tribe related to the Kuba, the Shoowa (fig. 68). Tradition has it that the civilizing king Shamba Bolongongo (who also transmitted the arts of the smithy to the Kuba) learned how to work velvet abroad and introduced it to his own people in the seventeenth century.

This velvet is always made from a raffia base. The velvet effect is produced by very fine raffia threads which run under the cloth and come out on the other side, where they are cut with a small knife. The velvet designs are generally outlined by embroidery using thread of a lighter or darker colour to bring out the forms.

This type of work was always done by women, who were highly skilled embroiderers (fig. 69), and a tradition used to require it to be done by pregnant women. They created the velvet effects slowly, freehand, starting at one corner to follow the geometric development of the lines. These marvels were, however, not meant to be worn as clothing. Given their great value, they were used at the court of the king, to cover the throne or serve as blankets. They could also be used as currency, do service as dowries, or even be buried to honour a deceased dignitary.

67. Embroidered boubou
Hausa. Nigeria.
Private collection.

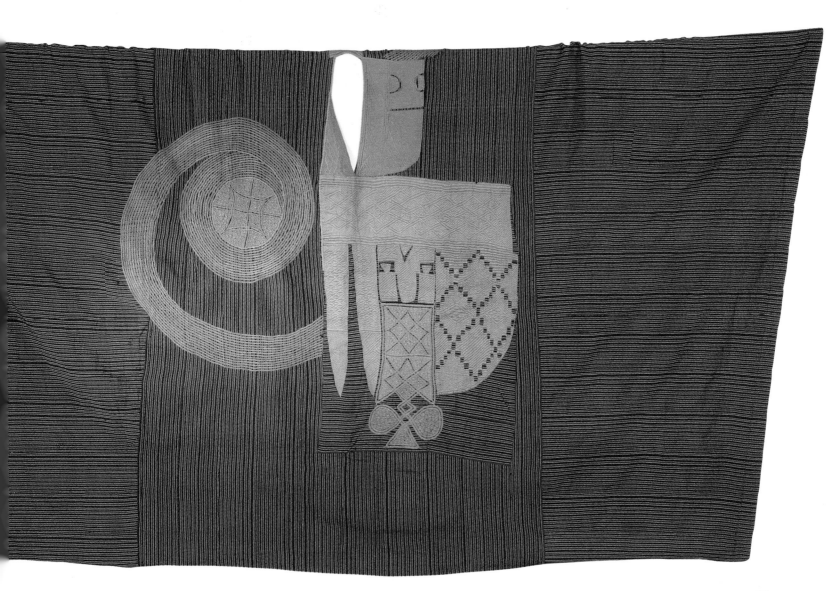

The designs reproduced the ritual scars of the Kuba and the sculptures which decorated many wooden objects (and were often copied in basketwork). The warm harmonies of orange, brown, red, yellow, black and purple tones turn these fabrics into abstract pictures, surfaces articulated with complex undulating, knotted and interwoven designs. The forms are regular enough for the eye to be able to follow the contours, but the sudden changes of direction in these subtly gentle yet obsessive mazes are disconcerting to behold.

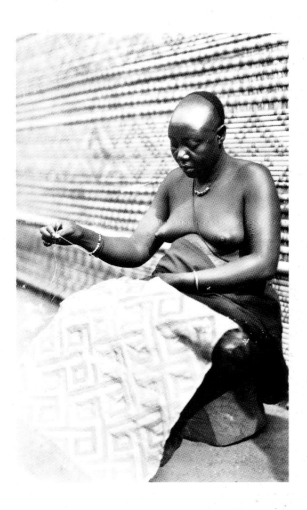

69. Kuba woman embroidering
Postcard. Photo Library of the Barbier-Mueller Museum, Geneva.

Opposite

68. Kasaï velvet
Kuba. Zaïre. Raffia. Barbier-Mueller Museum, Geneva.

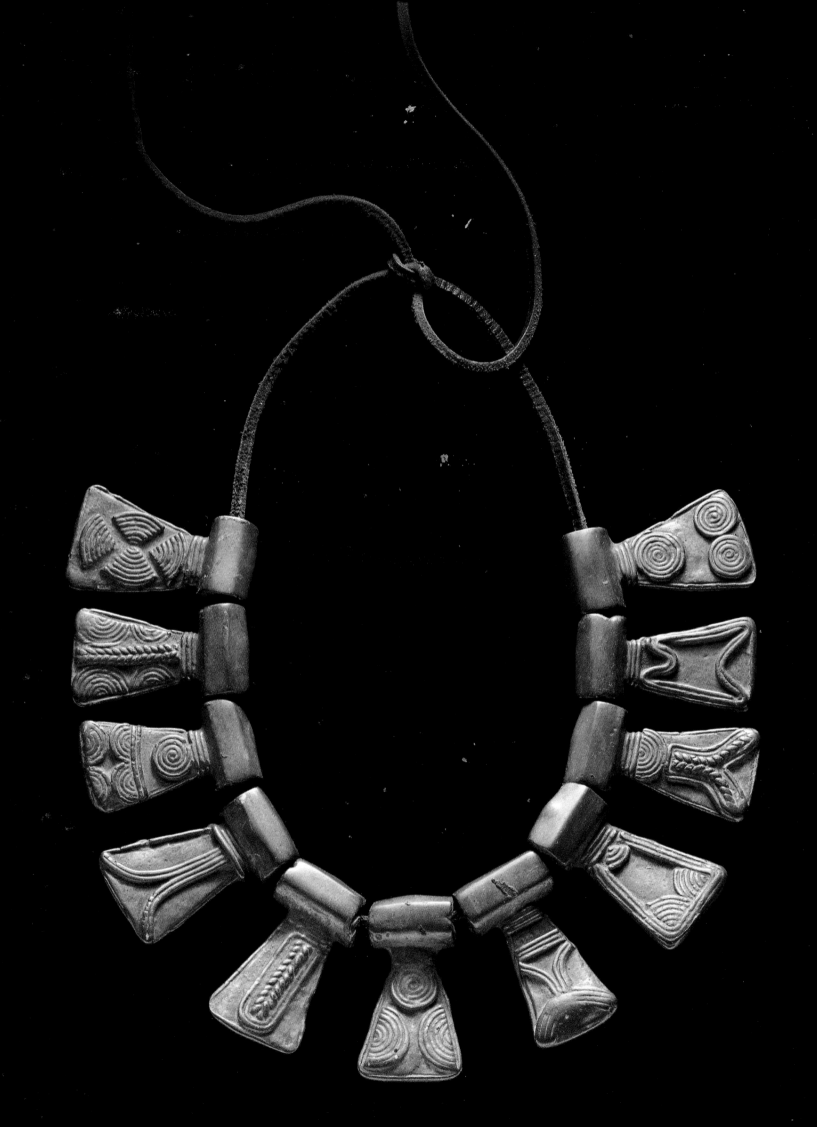

The splendour
of jewellery
and adornments

In Africa, almost everyone wears jewellery, both men and women. Jewels there have always been, and still are, essential accessories of dress, much more so than clothing. They are the culmination of a large series of bodily adornments developed over the course of time. In the past, at the bottom of the scale were tatooes or scars which sometimes covered large portions of the body with symbolic geometric designs, tribal marks, or signs indicating social position or levels of initiation.

Painted designs were combined with scarification, and applied on the body when feasts were celebrated. These designs were precisely determined by tradition and composed of red, black, yellow or white stripes and dots. The most outstanding examples of this body painting could be seen at the *Geerewol* feast among the Fulani (the other name given to the Peul in central Niger, Nigeria and part of Cameroon). The Fulani are nomads who roam over vast territories to graze their herds. The Geerewol is held once a year and assembles about three thousand people. For the young men, it is the opportunity to display their charms, to participate in erotic dances and to wed their beloves. Prior to the festivities, the young Fulani males, convinced of belonging to the most beautiful race in the world, will spend hours before their small mirrors decorating their faces with

Opposite

71. Brass necklace
Dan. Upper-Cavally region. Ivory Coast and Liberia. L.: 29 cm. Barbier-Mueller Museum, Geneva.

78. Ankle bracelet
Baule. Ivory Coast. Brass. Diam.: 10.7 cm. Barbier-Mueller Museum, Geneva. (Probably acquired before 1942.)

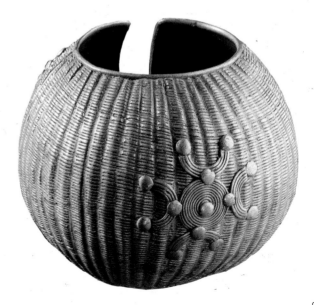

85

the dots, lines and circles that will set off the brightness of their eyes, the whiteness of their teeth, and the line of their fine noses. The results of their efforts at transfiguration, enhanced by embroidered costumes and jewellery, will be judged by the young women in the course of dances.

Body painting among other African populations did not play the same role as among the Fulani, but jewellery is everywhere present. It is an indication of the wearer's age, social status and family situation. Most jewels also have a more or less pronounced talismanic significance; they are supposed to protect their owner and ward off evil influences.

All sorts of materials go into the making of African jewels: gold, brass and other metals, ivory, beads and, in a more modest register, straw, wood and feathers.

Brass necklaces

Brass is widely used in West Africa as far as Zaïre, to make jewels of very sophisticated design. If gold was extensively used among the Akan of Ghana and in Senegal, brass and copper served the same purpose everywhere else. Copper was even more highly valued than gold because of its reddish colour, which was associated with royalty and great prestige.

In Gabon and Zaïre, where the lost-wax process was unknown, the objects were cast in open moulds before being hammered into shape and finished with a burin. In West Africa, on the other hand, the lost-wax process was practised for centuries to make jewels, although it was not the only one used.

A fine example of the lost-wax technique may be seen in a Dan necklace from the Ivory Coast or Liberia (fig. 71). It is composed of trapezoidal plates variously adorned with linear designs and strung on a leather thong. This precious and rare object was above all a magic amulet, even if it evidently advertised the bearer's advanced social status.

In Cameroon, the use of the lost-wax process permitted the production of many rich and complex necklaces intended for the Bamum chieftains. Using a light-coloured brass similar to gold, skilled bronzesmiths cast series of

Opposite

72. Brass necklace with bovine heads
Bamum. Cameroon. Barbier-Mueller Museum, Geneva. Formerly in the Charles Ratton Collection.

73. Royal necklace
Bamum. Western Province. Cameroon. Brass. Decorated with ten heads cast in lost-wax, each with a different openwork hairstyle. Diam.: 32.5 cm. Barbier-Mueller Museum, Geneva. Formerly in the Joseph Mueller Collection (acquired before 1942). Detail on overleaf.

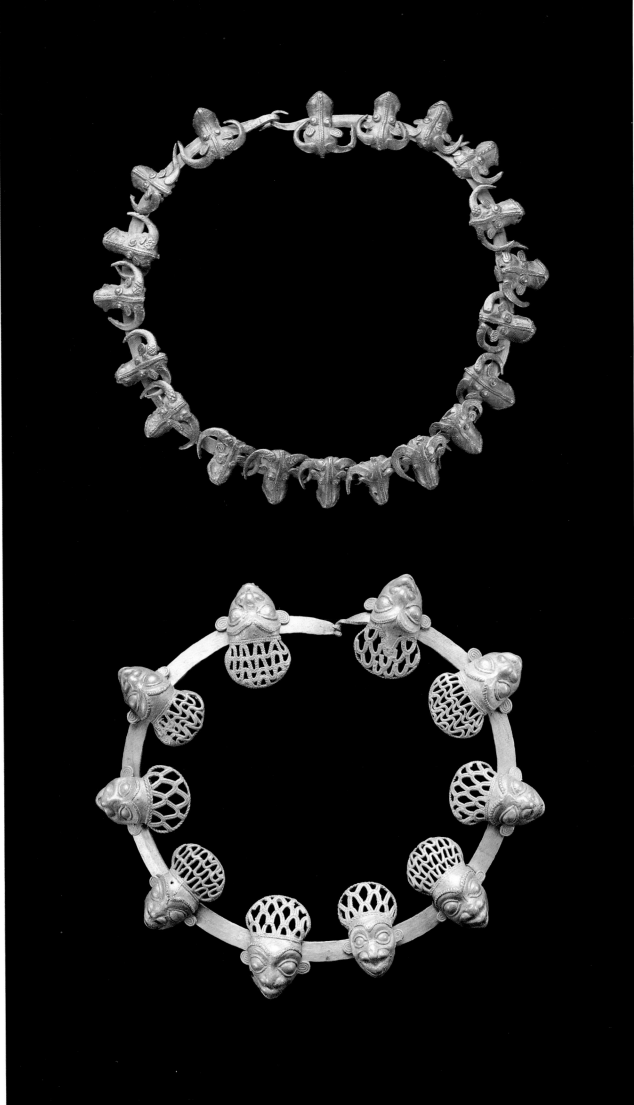

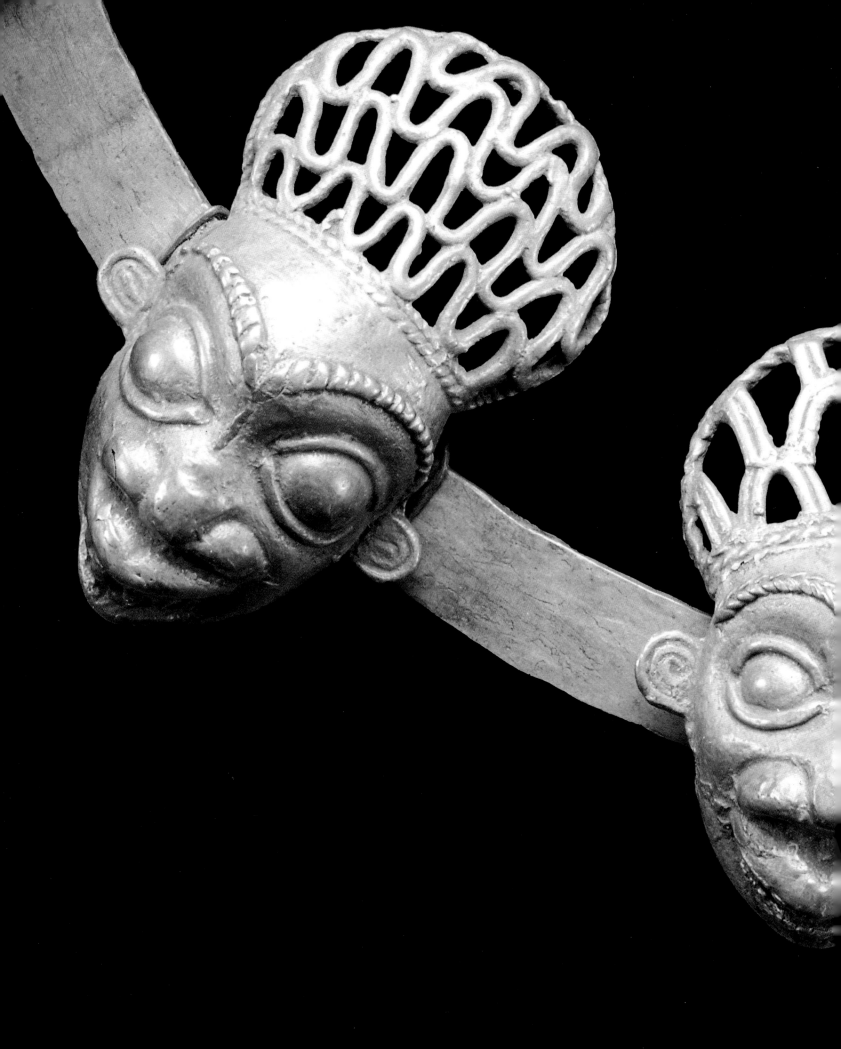

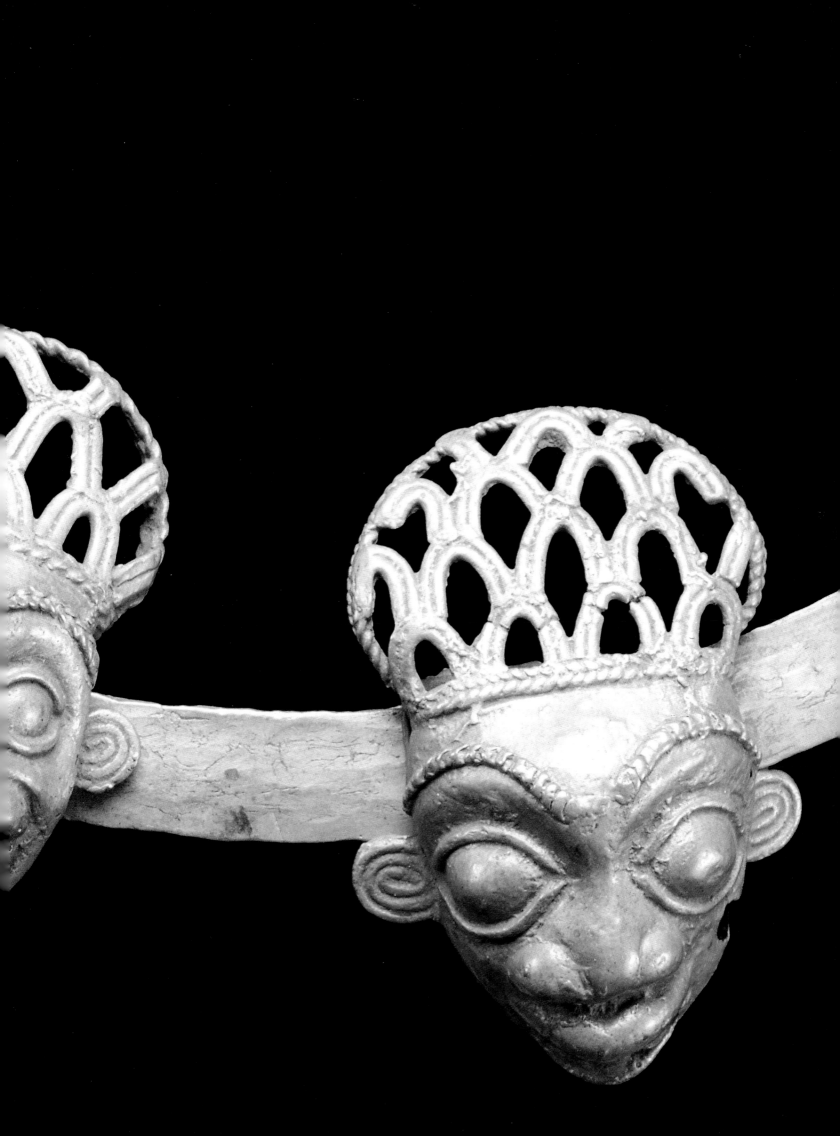

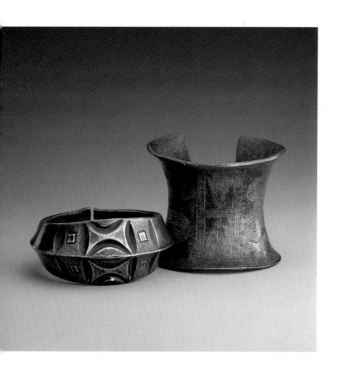

**74. Brass bracelet
and necklace**
Fang. Gabon. Necklace
(left) diam.: 14 cm.
Bracelet (right)
H.:10.5 cm.
Barbier-Mueller Museum,
Geneva. (Both acquired
before 1942.)

heads – from heads of water buffaloes (fig. 72) to heads of kings (fig. 73) – which they welded to rings of the same metal.

The Fang necklaces of Gabon were also made of brass, but were of a much more massive quality. Since they were not articulated, putting them on was a major operation: the fortunate owner had to rest his head on a block while the blacksmith fitted the necklace to his neck with blows of his hammer. According to Louis Perrois, [15] once in place, the necklaces stayed in place for the rest of the wearer's life. They were undecorated for men, and decorated with geometric patterns for women; but this distinction was not absolutely rigid.

In the People's Republic of Congo and in Zaïre, the necklaces were also massive, heavy and cumbersome to wear, but such was the price of prestige. They were cast as one single piece in an open mould and adorned with engraved geometric designs. Among the Teke (Zaïre), certain necklaces were flat and had crenellated edges. Others, of round section, could weigh several kilos; the one reproduced here (fig. 75) belonged to a land chief. The middle part has a steel blade (not visible) which was supposed to increase both its protective power and its value.

Iron was very rarely used in jewellery, even though it was also considered a precious metal. The wrought-iron torque from North Zaïre (fig. 76) is decorated with delicate ornamental designs on its flat ends and is a superb demonstration of the blacksmith's art. Iron could not be cast because of the extremely high temperatures required for its fusion; it was heated until red-hot, then hammered into shape on an anvil.

Heavy arm and leg bands

Brass bracelets or bands for the wrists and ankles were very popular because of their prestige value and to ward off evil spirits. However, they often weighed several kilos and were therefore far from appropriate for the activities of everyday life, and different solutions had to be found to remedy this drawback.

Some of the heaviest and most beautiful models, like the Kota ankle bracelets of Gabon (fig. 77), were supposed to be worn permanently but, in fact, only the lighter ones were so worn. The others were valued in financial terms and could even be used to pay dowries. Their powerful and characteristic sculptural forms make them easy to appreciate by Westerners accustomed to abstract art.

Weight does not seem to have been a consideration for the Fang of Cameroon and Guinea, whose wrists were always graced with heavy bracelets that had been hammered into shape, then chased with a burin (fig. 74). Other armbands worn around the biceps were lighter.

The solution developed by the Baule (Ivory Coast) was more elaborate, and in keeping with their refined artistic tradition. They were masters of the lost-wax process and had learned other precious-metalwork techniques from their Akan neighbours. The larger Baule armbands, or coils, were hollow and made of very fine brass wire, and so much lighter to wear. The technique consisted of laying equally fine lengths of wax 'wire' on a charcoal core which was later removed. This process produced very intricate designs that sometimes imitated basketweaving (fig. 78). These bracelets could be worn without overly hindering the wearer in walking. Originally, they could be removed only by an artisan, but other types of ankle bracelets were developed with hinges that permitted their removal at will.

The Senufo of the Ivory Coast produced large quantities of ankle-bracelets in the shape of boats. These could be worn by men, women and even infants. They were, however, not much appreciated by the men who, being farmers, did not like being hampered in their movements.

The Mossi, Nuna and Bobo tribes of Burkina Faso had ankle-bracelets of similar shape, but the bands were topped with zoomorphic figurines (fig. 79), and in some cases with the representations of ancestors to obtain their favour for the wearer.

Combining jewellery with the sounds and rhythm of dancing, the Dan and the We of the Ivory Coast and Liberia wore bracelets with small spherical bells on their ankles. The bracelet had between three and ten bells, each of which was decorated with symbolic motifs referring to the

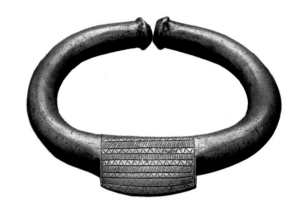

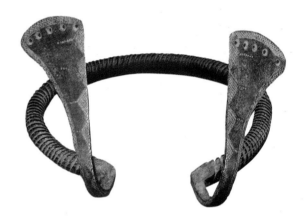

75. Torque from a land chief
Teke. Popular Republic of Congo. Brass and iron cast in a mould. Diam.: 26 cm. Private collection.

76. Torque
Northern Zaïre. Wrought iron. Diam.: 16 cm. Private collection.

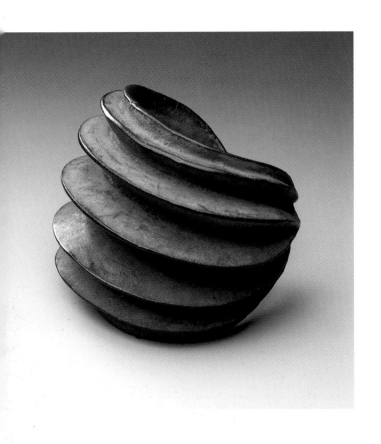

77. Ankle bracelet
Kota. Gabon. Copper
alloy. Diam.: 10.5 cm.
Barbier-Mueller Museum,
Geneva. (Acquired
before 1942).

creation of the world. There were also much richer bracelets with up to five rows of five bells (fig. 80).

Bracelets indicating the bearer's social rank had to be worn permanently. So as to minimize discomfort during work, many tribes wore arm or legbands composed of coils wound tightly around the limbs, as we can see in the photograph of the Banziri woman (fig. 81, Republic of Congo). Günter Tessmann also noted among the Fang of Gabon in 1913: [16]

'The legs and arms are profusely adorned, especially among the women. The arm, forearm, or both, display coils of imported brass wire, or bracelets of hollow brass, which are also imported. The coils adorning the arm are shorter, while those on the forearm cover it completely .... Ornaments on the legs are, on the whole, similar to those on the arms .... the most common model being long spirals that wind from the middle of the shin down to the ankle.'

These same long metal coils may also be found among the pastoral tribes of Kenya and Uganda (Masaï, Toposa, Turkana, Rendille, Pokot). They were worn in accordance with very strict rules, which changed depending on the tribe. Among the Turkana and Pokot, for instance, the bracelets worn by the men indicated not only their age, but also the part they played in conducting raids for cattle. Among the Toposa, when a woman married she was given a metal necklace composed of similar spirals. For the Rendille, the dignity of a married woman was indicated by a bracelet worn on the forearm, to which was added a second bracelet when her first male child was circumcised.

Brass rings

The few remaining bronze or brass rings still worn in Africa belong to old men and mainly have a prestige value. Mounted on many of these rings is a figurine (made with the lost-wax process) which gave it a magical significance: to curry favour from ancestors or the spirits of the brush. The rings could be decorated with representations of masks used in dances, with animal motifs – water-buffalo, bird, or

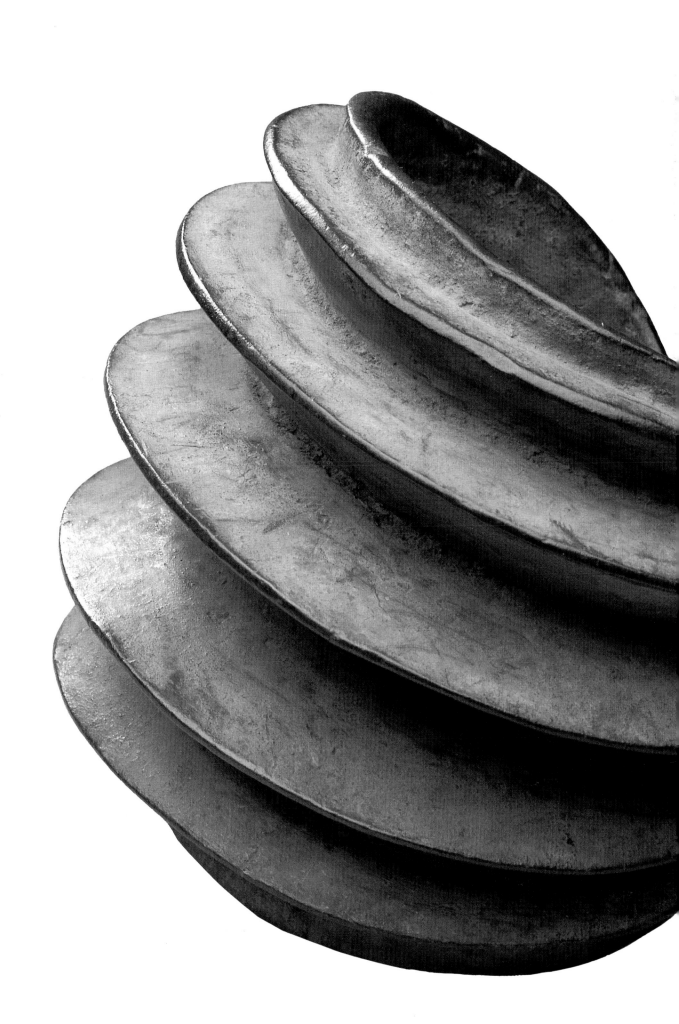

79. Ankle bracelet with zoomorphic decoration
Nuna. Burkina Faso. Brass.
Diam.: 15.5 cm.
Private collection.

82. Ring with mounted warrior
Dogon. Mali. Brass.
H.: 6.5 cm.
Private collection.

83. Bracelet with figurines
Former Dahomey.
Republic of Benin.
Silver. Diam.: 12 cm.
Private collection.

This jewel was made out of old silver coins from Europe.
The figures include a cannon, a bird of prey, a gourd, a fetish horn, and a lion devouring a monkey.

Opposite

80. Ankle bracelet with five rows of five bells
Dan. Ivory Coast or Liberia. Brass. H.: 11 cm.
Inner diam.: 11 cm.
Barbier-Mueller Museum, Geneva.

81. Banziri woman from the Sango tribe
Former French Congo.
Postcard.

Among the many jewels worn by this woman may be noticed some metal coil armbands and bead necklaces.

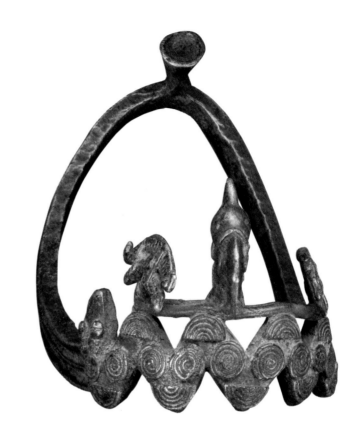

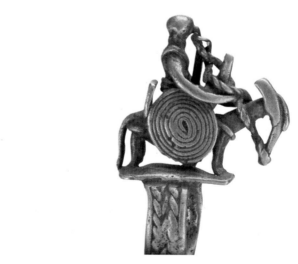

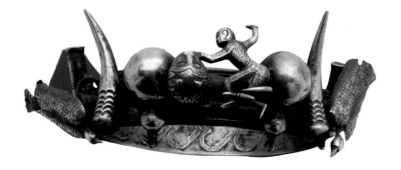

frog – or with human figures, as on this Dogon ring from Mali (fig. 82), which shows a warrior on horseback. Rings of this last type were given by the *hogon*, or high priest of the Dogon, to the military chief to the village, who was supposed to wear it during prayer.

The Dogon are not the only tribe to have produced such rings. A similar type was also made by the Senufo (Ivory Coast) and by the Bobo (Burkina Faso). The figurines are fine miniature sculptures represented with a greater or lesser degree of stylization.

Rings worn by the dignitaries among the Bamum of Cameroon often bore the well-known motif of the six-legged spider. The spider, believed to possess magic powers, was a symbol for intelligence.

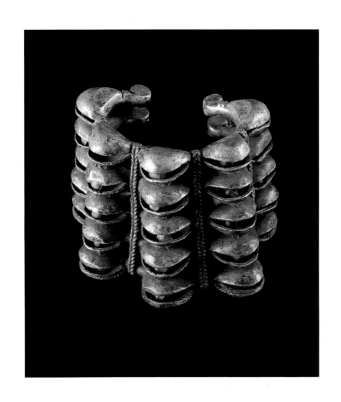

Other metal ornaments

Iron, often considered a precious metal in Africa, was sometimes used to make jewels. Today, this metal has largely been replaced with aluminium.

In Northern Zaïre, among the Mangbetu and their neighbours, the Zande, many ornaments were worn on the head. Hairpins made of steel cut out into elegant shapes were permanently stuck in the hair of the men, giving them a very impressive bearing.

Silver was used more rarely than brass or gold. Among Islamic tribes it replaced gold, because, as the ethnologist Angela Fisher points out, [17] it is considered to be 'the pure metal blessed by the Prophet, while gold, the metal of the Devil, is feared and believed to attract misfortune'. In the Sahara, silver is worn by everyone who can afford it.

Throughout the savannah, from Senegal to Lake Chad, silver rings were very popular and worn by both men and women, though those of the men were of larger size. They reproduced the design of traditional non-figurative rings, but, like those from the region around Djenne, could imitate the tall architectural forms of this city's famous mosque.

In the nineteenth century, a great many prestigious and decorative objects were made in the former Dahomey

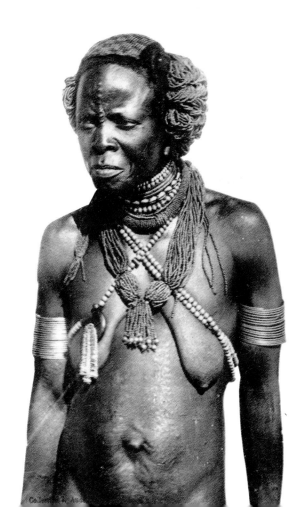

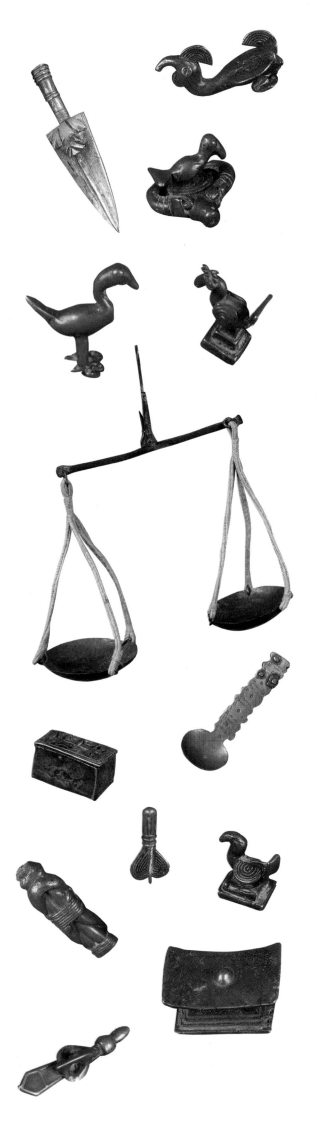

(today's Republic of Benin). The bracelet with several figurines reproduced here (fig. 83) probably stems from this tradition. Most of the figures are zoomorphic.

The fascination of gold

Gold jewellery is to be found only in certain areas of West Africa. It can be found in the Sahel regions, from Senegal to Mali, in Niger, in Ghana (formerly the Gold Coast, home of the Akan), in the Ivory Coast, and in certain areas exposed to Akan influence.

The most productive mines are located in Senegal (Bambuk) and Guinea (Bure), but there are many others of lesser importance in Liberia, Ghana, and Togo. Panning for gold in rivers or collecting it on the ground after rain are both widely practised. The women do the work of sifting through the gold-bearing sand with calabashes.

Europeans usually associate gold with South Africa and its famous mines. This precious metal, however, was rarely used to make jewels, for people generally preferred coloured glass beads as ornaments.

The use of gold on the African continent was limited by several factors: apart from the restrictions of Islam, there was the fact that those populations who had remained loyal to animistic beliefs were reluctant to use this yellow metal because they believed it held evil influences. Up until recent times, ritual ceremonies and sacrifices were performed to neutralize its occult powers and prevent cave-ins in the mines.

In gold trading, the Akan merchants use brass figurines as weights (fig. 84). These are of figurative or abstract design and were made with the lost-wax process. Certain representations of social types are remarkably full of life and movement. The gold trader's equipment also included scales, tiny caskets, and brass spoons for the gold dust (fig. 85). The caskets and spoons were often decorated with correspondingly fine motifs. These objects were always handed down from father to son.

Although gold is a durable metal, very few ancient jewels have come down to us. There is the famous pectoral of Rao (Senegal), excavated from a seventeenth- or eighteenth-

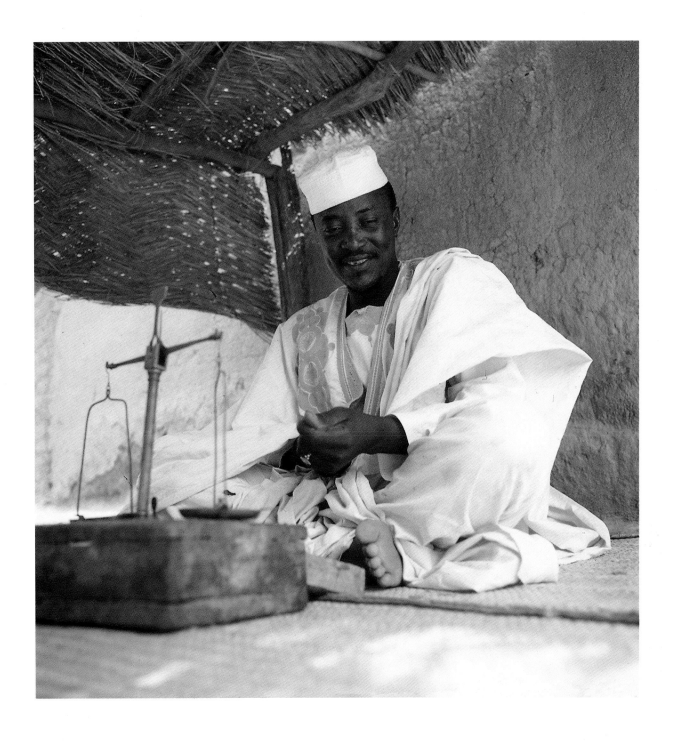

Opposite

85. Utensils of a gold trader
Akan. Ghana.
Musée de la Monnaie (Mint), Paris.

Scales, weights
and a tiny round spoon
made especially for gold
dust which was kept
in a small brass

rectangular box
decorated with fine
motifs. The weights
shown above and below
the scales could be
of figurative or geometric
shape. One represents
the sacred stool
of the Ashanti. These
weights were calibrated
and corresponded
to a certain quantity
of gold dust and metal.

84. Gold trader in the city of Djenne, Mali
Photo Library of the
Barbier-Mueller Museum,
Geneva.

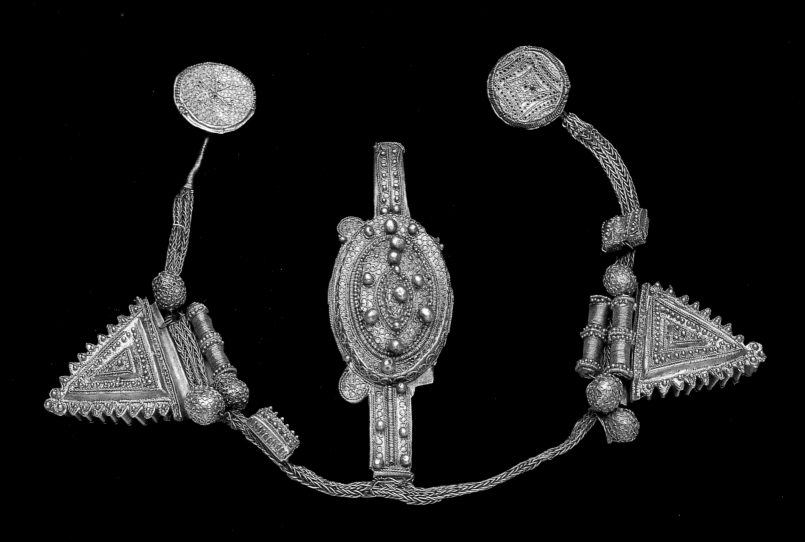

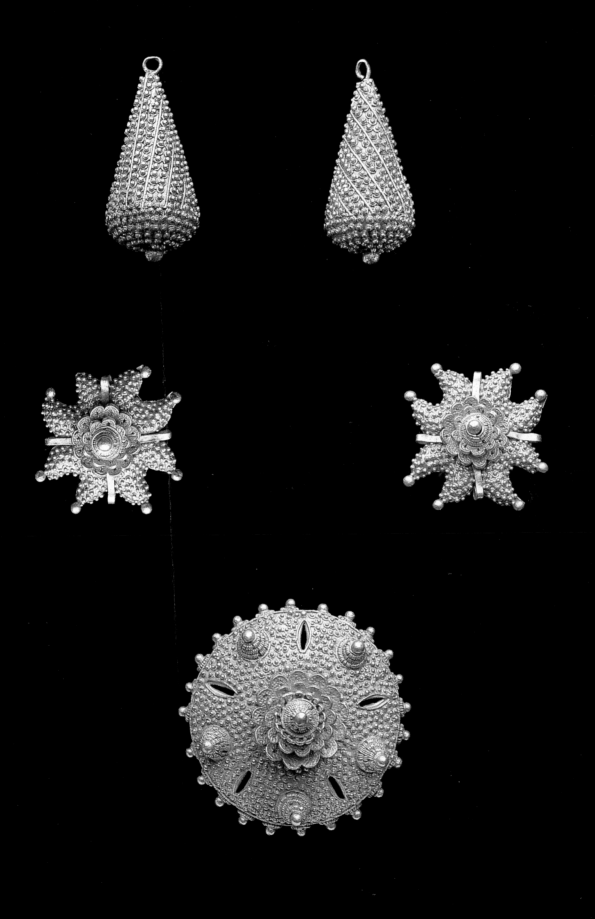

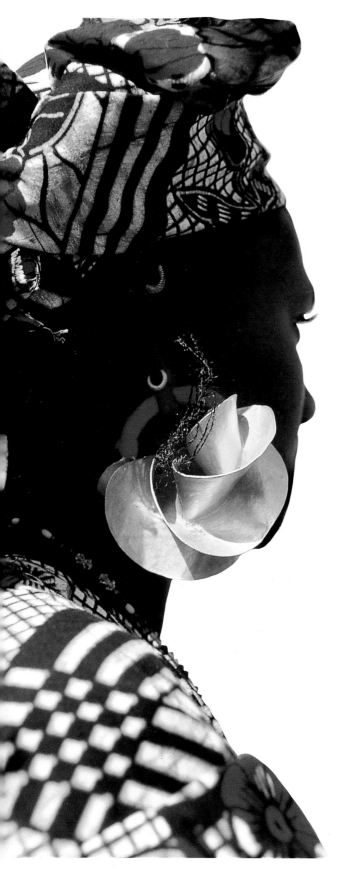

century royal tomb, and the so-called 'Amadou Treasure' (fig. 86), which included objects made by complex techniques used for centuries by the goldsmiths of Mauretania and Senegal. Countless pieces of jewellery have been lost, having either been melted down for economic reasons or transformed into designs more in keeping with the latest styles. The oldest jewels made of gold date back to the nineteenth century, but most are from the first half of the twentieth century. Of these, the most sumptuous are undoubtedly the earrings worn by married Fulani women (fig. 87) and made by Malian goldsmiths, which are works of art in their own right. The large curved, crescent-shaped 'wings' are made by beating a single stick of gold into shape. These women are often quite wealthy and also sport large amber beads in their hairpieces, as well as gold filigree jewels around their neck or in their hair.

The goldsmiths of Senegal, a region very permeable to outside influences, produced a great deal of jewellery for Europe. They made scores of pendants in the shape of flower-baskets, using filigree and granulation to save on the precious material. To find designs more in keeping with the African spirit, one must look for jewellery made specifically for the Africans (fig. 88).

The Akan goldsmiths of Ghana are rightly famous for the richness of their jewels. They often reproduced traditional designs, as we can see thanks to the illustrated diary of the French merchant, Jean Barbot, who travelled to the Ivory Coast in 1678–79. Small jewels of similar design were found in the wreck of a ship that sank in the eighteenth century.

Today, the jewels have become bigger and even more luxurious. The splendour of the Akan ceremonies is without equal anywhere. The king of the Ashanti, the *Ashantihene*, and the rulers of the other kingdoms, sport jewellery all the time, and their subjects are, so to speak, not far behind. Every feast, and the feast of the yam in particular, becomes the occasion for a fabulous display of wealth. When a king dies, young women bedecked with gold perform ritual dances at the funeral festivities.

Rings worn by wealthy Akan men and women display an amazing variety. Some have abstract, torsade designs, but most represent animals of all kinds – fish, birds, porcupines –

or plants, and even coveted objects, like cannon, and barrels of gunpowder.

The beads used for necklaces often reproduced traditional models which Jean Barbot also recorded in his drawings. Over the course of time, other representational forms – often amusing – were added to the ornamental repertory. There was no end to the variety of motifs: teeth, padlocks, keys, ears of corn, snails, and even figurative pendants, but the whole was always harmonized by the soft, warm colour of the gold.

Larger pendants were also made without being part of a necklace. These were worn for ceremonial occasions on their bare chests by notables of high rank in the king's suite. The basic form was the circle, which was decorated with filigree rosettes. In addition to these chest pendants, there are also pendants for swords – often representing reptiles and lions (fig. 89) – which are noteworthy for their large size (from 20 cm to 30 cm long), and for their textured surfaces.

The Akan bracelets are reserved for kings and queen mothers, and since they are huge, they are often hollow or made of gold leaf around a wood core, which considerably lightens the load. These are only a small part of the regalia which will be discussed later.

The influence of the Akan in the Ivory Coast extended to the Baule and to the lagoons area tribes, but the designs have changed. The realism of the Akan gave way to a stylization that verged on abstraction. The goldsmiths are masters of the lost-wax process. As with the bracelets in brass, they create surfaces made of extremely fine gold wire to produce a sort of precious matrix which elevates these jewels beyond mere realistic representation to the rank of true works of art. Discovering these outstanding works in the seventeenth century, Jean Barbot wrote: 'Even European artists would be hard put to imitate them.' The jewels made in this way were intended for personal use by men and women alike. There were few rings, but a great number of beads of all kinds – flat, round, or rectangular – which were superbly crafted and hung from the doorways of notables on special occasions to publish their wealth (fig. 90).

Pendants are also made in great quantities, to be worn attached to a necklace or in the hair. In the form of small heads (fig. 91), they are associated with ancestor worship

Page 98

86. 'Treasure of Amadou'
West Africa. 19th cent.
Gold, silver and leather.
Museum of African and Oceanian Arts, Paris.

Overleaf

88. Various forms of hair ornaments
Tukulor. Wolof. Senegal.
Gold.
Barbier-Mueller Museum, Geneva.

Opposite

87. Women with gold earrings
This form indicates that she is married. Her lips are made up with kohl. Fulani/Peul. Near Mopti, Mali.
Photo Library of the Barbier-Mueller Museum, Geneva.

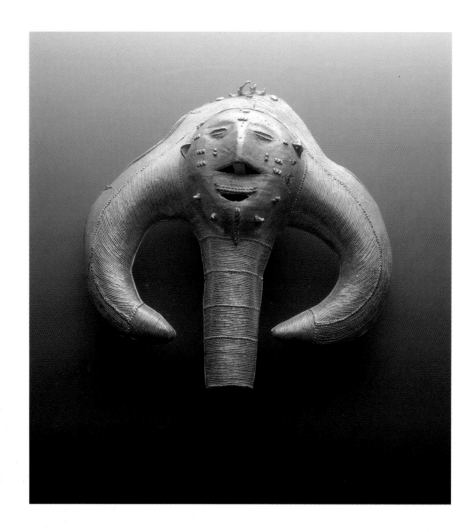

**92. Ornament
decorated with human
face and ram's horns**
Lagoons area tribes. Ivory
Coast. Late 19th cent.
or early 20th cent.
H.: 12.5 cm. Barbier-
Mueller Museum, Geneva.

Opposite

**91. Pendant
in the shape
of a stylized head**
Southeastern region,
Ivory Coast. Gold.
Barbier-Mueller Museum,
Geneva.

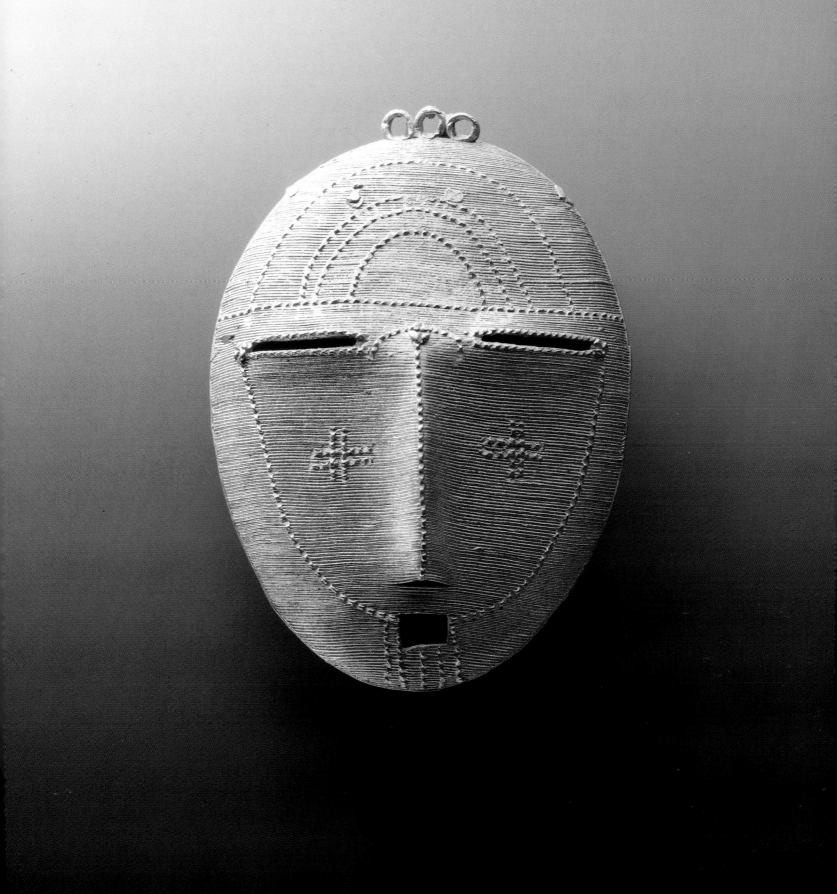

and are so stylized as to exclude portraiture. Unusual juxtapositions can be seen among the lagoons area tribes, such as this human face with ram's horns (fig. 92). Today, these jewels belong to the family heritage and are occasionally exhibited to proclaim a nobleman's prestige.

Only in the areas populated by the Akan has gold played – and still does play – such an essential role in determining high social rank. Elsewhere, copper, brass, and ivory had the same purpose. In the court of ancient Benin, ivory was valued almost as highly as brass.

Princely ivory

In former Benin, as in many other African kingdoms, ivory was above all the prerogative of the king. Each time an elephant was killed at the hunt, one of the tusks was reserved just for him. The second tusk could be bought by the nobles, but only if they had permission to have jewels made by the ivory-carvers of the court. Great quantities of ivory ornaments were produced for the *oba* or his officials in Benin or in the neighbouring city of Owo, a major ivory-carving centre. The bracelet from the Lagos museum reproduced here (fig. 93) gives a good idea of the skill of the carvers. Created out of a single piece of ivory, it is made according to a standard design: one cylinder fitted into another so that they could rotate independently. The inner cylinder, entirely pierced with small holes, serves as a background for the carved designs on the outer cylinder.

In more recent times, many other tribes began to use ivory to make their jewellery, but the style is no longer the same. The refinement of the sculptures has given way to broader forms with simple contours, handsomely brought out by the warm tones of the ivory, which was tinted either by contact with the body or through the use of pigments mixed in an oil medium. The latter was the case with anthropomorphic pendants, which are fine sculptures in their own right. These were worn as talismans, for they represented ancestral spirits who were supposed to protect the living. Ivory was often chosen because of its pale white colour, making for a striking contrast with the dark masses of hair; which is certainly why so many hairpins were made. These

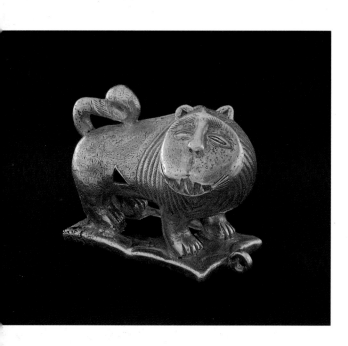

89. Sword ornament in the shape of a lion
Akan. Ghana. Cast gold. Weight: 743 gr. Barbier-Mueller Museum, Geneva.

This pendant hung from the sword grip by a ring attached to one end of the gold plate.

Opposite

90. Flat beads
Baule. Ivory Coast. Gold. Barbier-Mueller Museum, Geneva.

These flat beads, strung in series of thirty, were hung outside of the houses of rich dignitaries on the occasion of certain feasts.

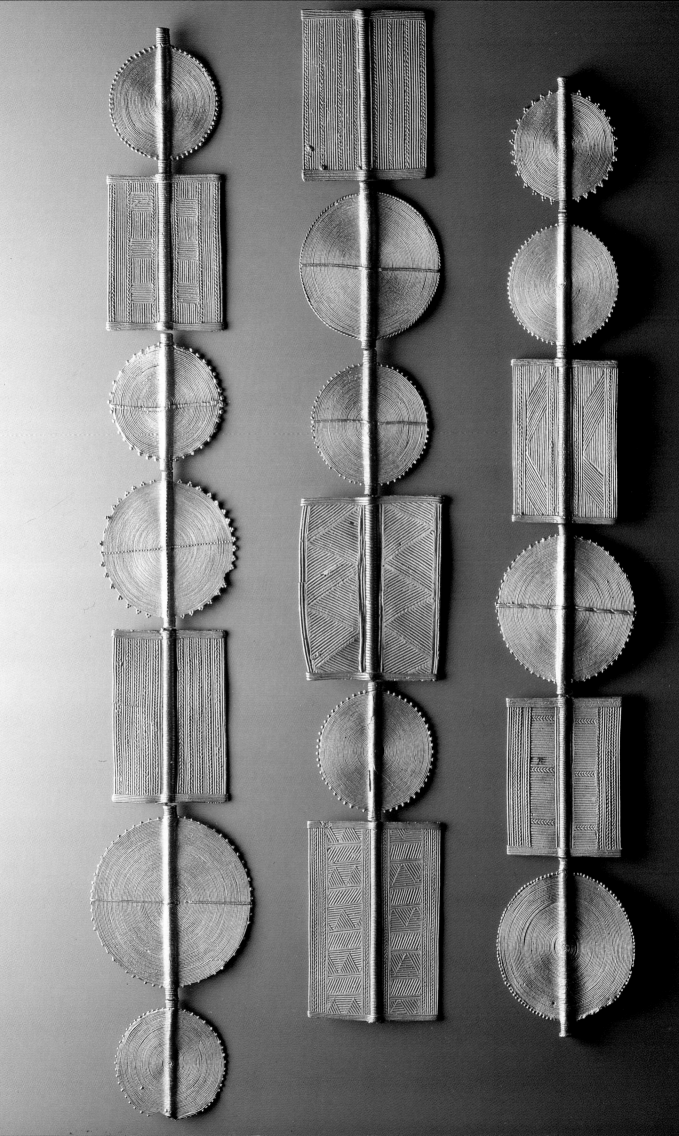

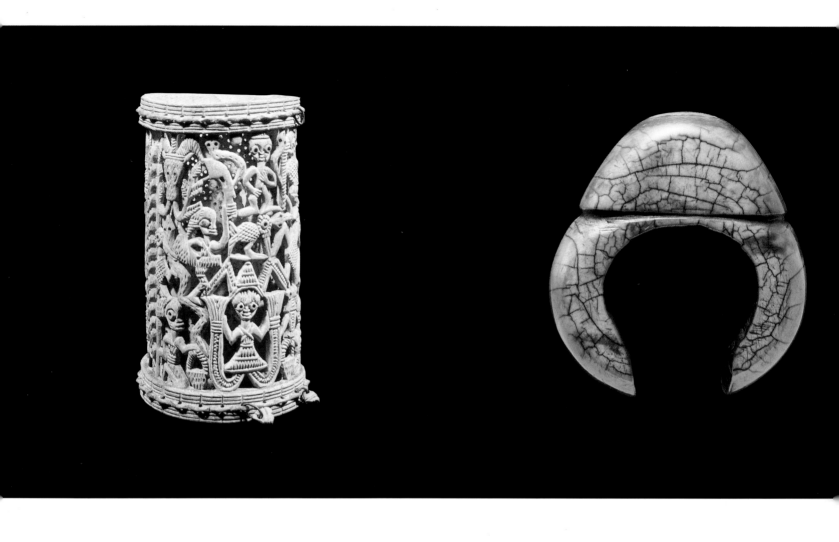

Left to right

93. Cuff bracelet
Benin. Nigeria. 16th cent.
Ivory. H.: 15.7 cm.
National Museum, Lagos.

94. Bracelet of a chief
Bamum. Cameroon.
Western Province.
Ivory of reddish colour.
W.: 9 cm. Barbier-Mueller
Museum, Geneva.
(acquired before 1942).
Formerly in the Joseph
Mueller Collection.

were decorated either with figurative motifs or geometric shapes.

Because of its density, ivory was often used to make bracelets of very simple and abstract design. The Yohure of the Ivory Coast, as well as the Lega and Songye of Zaïre, were very fond of arm-rings with a round section and full forms. In Cameroon, on the other hand, bracelets made for the chiefs (fig. 94) demanded more original designs. In other regions, bracelets were made out of plates of ivory that had been given a more or less curved shape. Among the Nuer and Shilluk of Sudan, for example, we can see some remarkable models (fig. 95) whose warm and light tones stand out beautifully against the dark skin.

This play of forms was one option for the ivory-carvers, but if they wanted to add graphic designs, they could use silver or lead studs arranged in geometric patterns. Bracelets decorated in this fashion may be found among the Hausa of Northern Nigeria and the Songye of Zaïre.

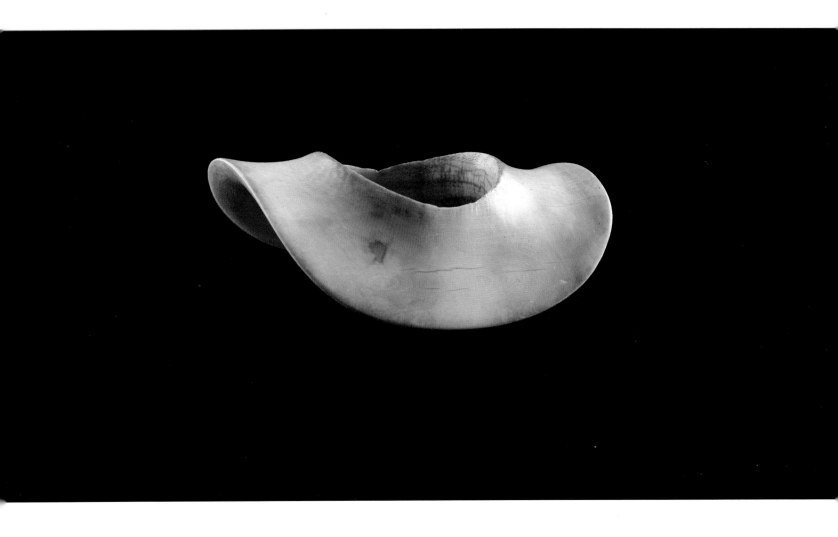

The Dinka of Kenya probably appreciated ivory more than any other tribe. The size of the bracelets worn by the men was supposed to be proportional to their wealth or prowess in warfare. If an ivory bracelet broke, the pieces were re-carved to make pendants, earrings or rings. The pale tones of ivory were often contrasted with brightly coloured beadwork.

95. Bracelet
Shilluk. Sudan.
Ivory. Diam.: 17 cm.
Barbier-Mueller Museum,
Geneva.

Coloured beadwork

The fondness of Africans for beads goes as far back in time as one cares to go. Even before glass beads were invented, one could see this taste in the Nok region (Nigeria), where, as early as the first century BC, certain terracotta statues* were adorned with rows upon rows of necklaces. Quartz beads have been found by the thousands in excavations at Igbo-Ukwu (ninth century) and

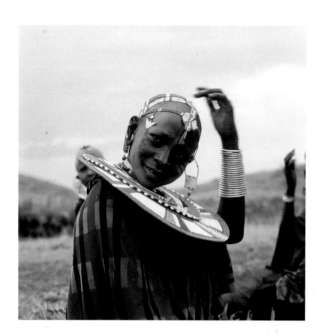

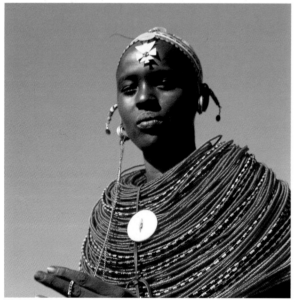

**96. Masaï girl
wearing
a beadwork collar**
Masaï. Tanzania.
Photo Library of the
Barbier-Mueller Museum,
Geneva.

97. Married woman
Rendille. Tanzania. Photo
Library of the Barbier-
Mueller Museum, Geneva.

Her social status is
indicated by the cross
on her forehead and by
the kinds of earrings she
is wearing.

Ife (twelfth century). Quartz is still used in many areas of Africa to make beads by polishing them on a hard, wet stone.

Beads made of coral were widely used in Benin for prestigious ornaments. Already in the fifteenth century, portrait heads of kings were cast in bronze and decorated with necklaces containing coral. These heads were also decorated with headdresses featuring both coral and agates. The use of such jewels has continued down to the present day; on feast days, the oba appears garbed in a tunic made of coral beads, and wears other ritual jewels made of coral and ivory. Ancient bronze plaques that decorated the galleries of the palace (fig. 108, p. 118) show that the courtiers also wore coral necklaces.

Many other stones besides agate were used in Africa: bauxite, steatite, calcite, cornaline and jasper. Agate and cornaline beads imported from India were replaced in the mid-nineteenth century with German copies made in the Rhineland. In addition to these semi-precious stones, cowries and pieces of seashells were often used to make jewels, with or without beads.

Glass is, however, by far the preferred material for making beads. The explorers of previous centuries always brought along all sorts of beads to barter for more precious materials. Venice, once a major centre for the manufacture of glass beads, has been replaced by Bohemia today. Often, too, the glass used in industrial packaging is recycled in Africa, either by breaking up and polishing the glass, or by re-melting it and casting in clay moulds.

The uses of these beads vary according to the region. In Nigeria, very fine objects decorated with beadwork are produced. Strictly speaking, these are not jewels but finery worn on the occasion of certain ceremonies, like the brightly coloured beadwork tunic made for the *oba* of Benin, which can be seen at the National Museum in Lagos (fig. p. 5).

The chief of the Yoruba, in southern Nigeria, wore a beadwork crown which covered his face with a beaded veil (figs. 171 and 172, p, 184). Animal figures on the crown – usually birds – were also covered with beads.

The use of glass to make jewels and finery for non-courtiers is characteristic of the regions of Eastern and Southern Africa.

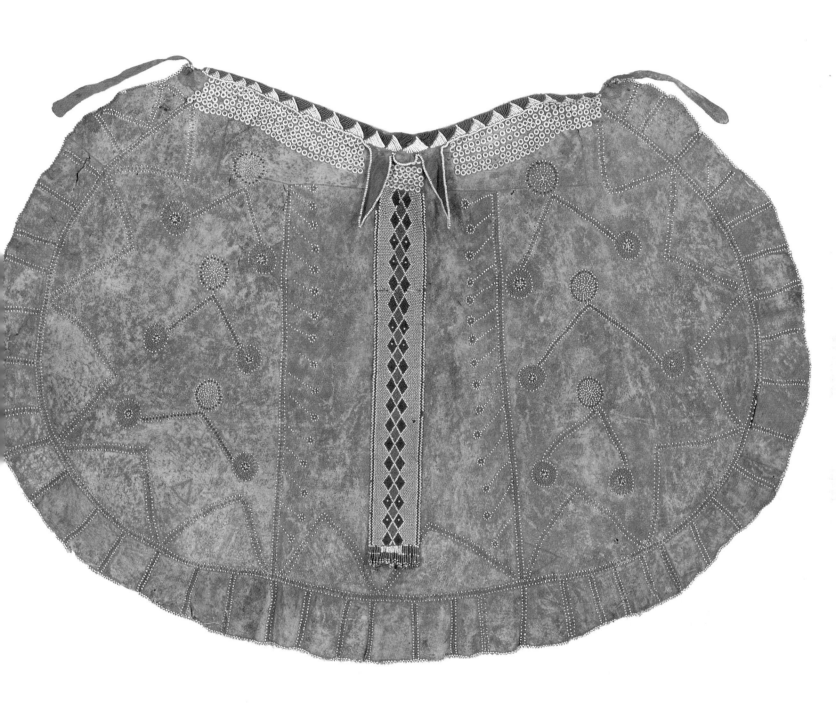

100. Beadwork cape
Nguni. South Africa.
Sheepskin, thread, beads.
W.: 161 cm.
Private collection.

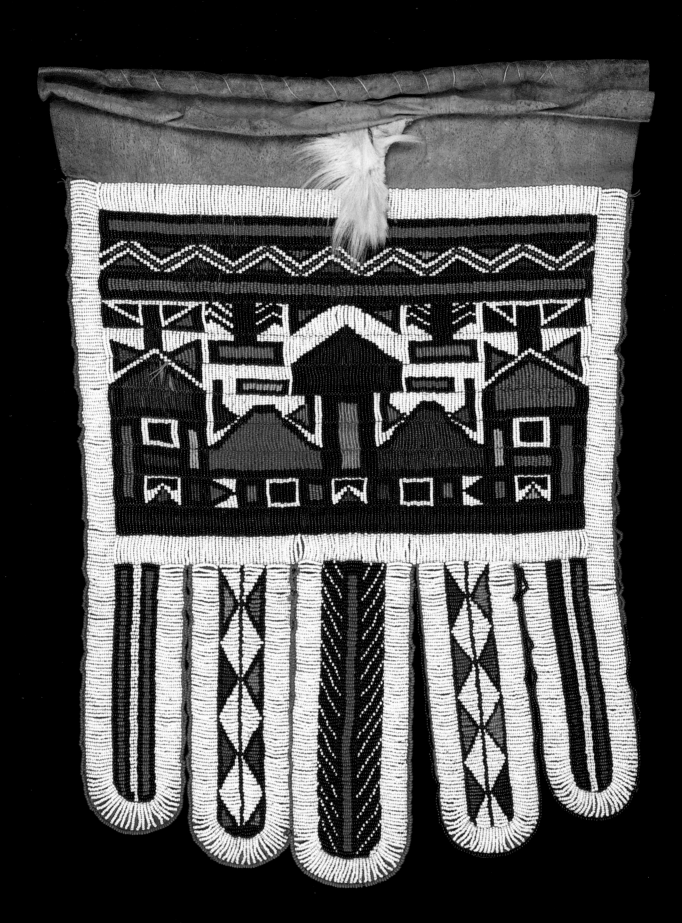

The semi-nomad pastoral tribes of Kenya lack the equipment to melt metal. Yet both the men and women of these tribes are fond of adorning their bodies with colourful and shimmering ornaments. Glass is perfectly suited to meet this demand. Rows of necklaces complete the body painting practised everywhere and acts as a code to identify the wearer's social position.

Among the Masaï of Kenya and Uganda, the women and warriors wear the most beadwork. The women learn how to produce over forty designs worn on broad flat collars (fig. 96), with the blue beads being reserved for married women.

Even more than the Masaï, the Dinka (Kenya) are consummate masters in making decorative beadwork. Warriors wore tight-fitting corselets around their chests with the appropriate colours for their age. The daughters of wealthy Dinka families also wore this type of corselet, but they were necessarily looser fitting and transparent, shawl-like garments that let the forms of the breasts show through rows of beads. Each row of beads was worth an ox. Such a corselet was an eye-catching and seductive device that meant many heads of cattle for the future husband, who often had to take on heavy debts to meet the price. By way of compensation, the cowrie-shells attached to the finery vouched for fertility.

In southern Africa, among the Bantu-speaking tribes, in particular the Ndebele, the Xhosa and the Zulu, the use of beads is as widespread as among the tribes of Kenya, but in different applications. Beads are worked into the weaving of fabrics sewn onto goatskins to make certain types of clothing worn for everyday use, mostly by women. They are signs of social rank, as well as magical protection against the spirits. In the Transvaal region, newly married Ndebele women were given objects made of white beads painted with coloured designs to be worn on her breasts, back and head. Beneath a leather cape embroidered with white beads, she also wore a beadwork apron, called a *jocolo*, from which hung five finger-like flaps (fig. 99). This apron was subsequently worn on feast days. In her everyday activities, she wore a simpler apron (*mapoto*), which was also decorated with beadwork. The Ndebele women also

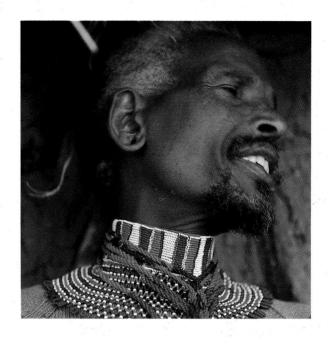

98. Beadwork necklace worn by an elder near the village of Dogobesh
Iraqui. Tanzania.
Photo Library of the Barbier-Mueller Museum, Geneva.

Opposite

99. Married woman's apron (jocolo)
Ndebele. South Africa.
British Museum, London.

Overleaf

101. Chief's headdress
Mangbetu. Zaïre. Feathers on a basketwork cap.
Private collection.

111

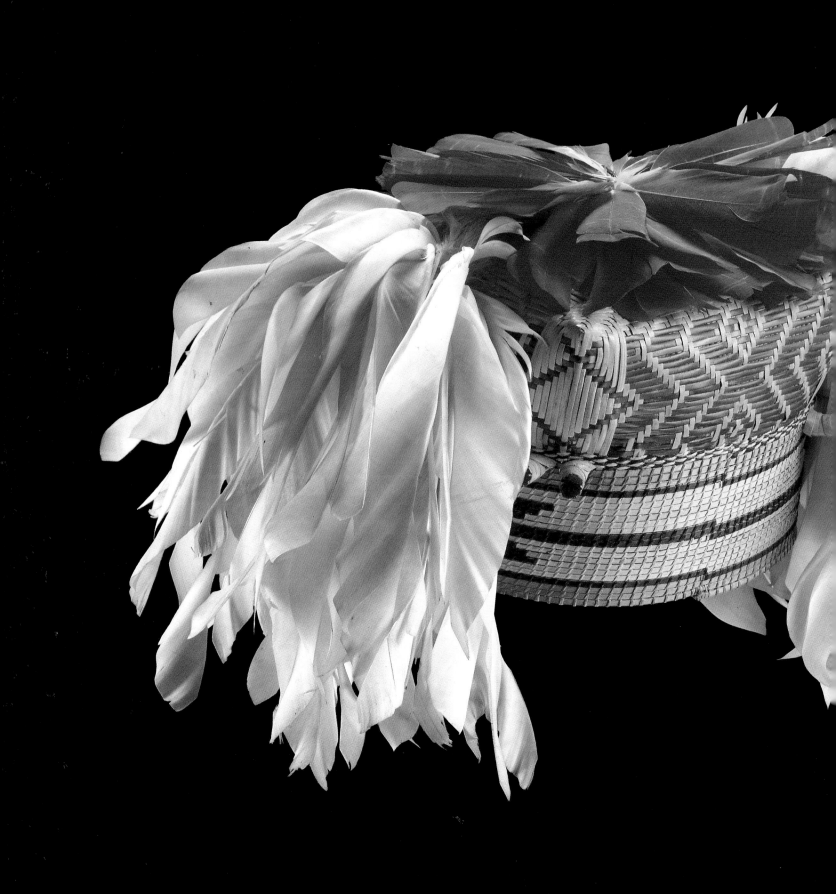

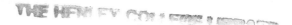

made and commonly wore hoop-like necklaces composed of bundled grass and covered with beads which they took off only on the death of their husband.

Like the Ndebele of Transvaal, the Nguni of South Africa created beautiful beadwork capes (fig. 100). The finesse of their decorative elements and the artistry that went into their creation suggest that these luxury objects were intended to underscore a chief's prestige.

The Zulu wear rectangular garments with beadwork designs on their chests to ward off evil spirits, as well as bead necklaces as love tokens. Each necklace consists of from five to ten squares of beadwork 3–4 cm to the side strung on a thong. The colours and designs used by the young girl who makes them will tell her beloved what he needs to know and how to act on it.

Not everyone in the tribe could afford beads for their adornments. In such cases there were always natural materials close at hand.

Feathers and plant matter

Thanks to any number of inexpensive natural materials, the Africans have always been able to give full vent to their need for self-expression and their taste for bright colours.

The hats of the Mangbetu, well known for their plumes, were generally made out of a basketwork cap topped with feathers. Red feathers from certain species of parrots were the exclusive privilege of chiefs (fig. 101). These hats were in any case intended only for the men. Hunters would make a special type of hat if they had killed an okapi and needed protection against its vindictive spirit.

When hats or headdresses were not worn, then a comb did the trick as ornament for the hair and was usually worn all the time. Certain combs among the Baule of the Ivory Coast were topped by fine figurative or non-representational motifs covered with gold leaf. The combs of the Ivory Coast lagoons area tribes were made of plain wood and with characteristically harmonious curves (p. 205).

After the head, the sex organs were endowed with special significance by many African populations. [18] As the source of life and seat of fertility, the sex organs were

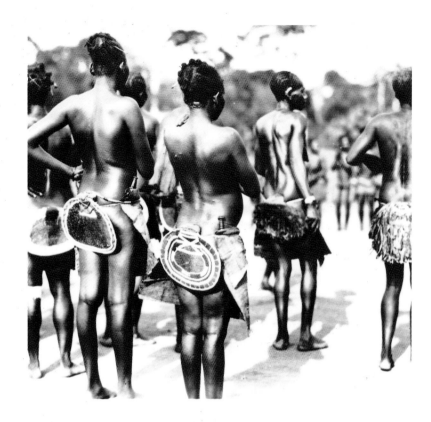

103. Mangbetu women wearing buttock-screens woven out of plant fibres
Mangbetu. Zaïre.
Detail from a postcard.
Photo Library of the Barbier-Mueller Museum, Geneva.

Opposite

102. Penile sheaths
Somba. Republic of Benin. Gourd with pyrographic designs.
L.: 24.5 cm. (left) and 23 cm. (right).
Private collection.

celebrated with ornaments of all kinds, usually made of natural materials. The Somba men of the former Dahomey wore penile sheaths (fig. 102) made of tube-shaped gourds decorated with finely-traced pyrographed motifs. On the female side, the Mangbetu women rivalled with each other in creating new motifs for the buttock-screens which they wove out of banana leaves (fig. 103).

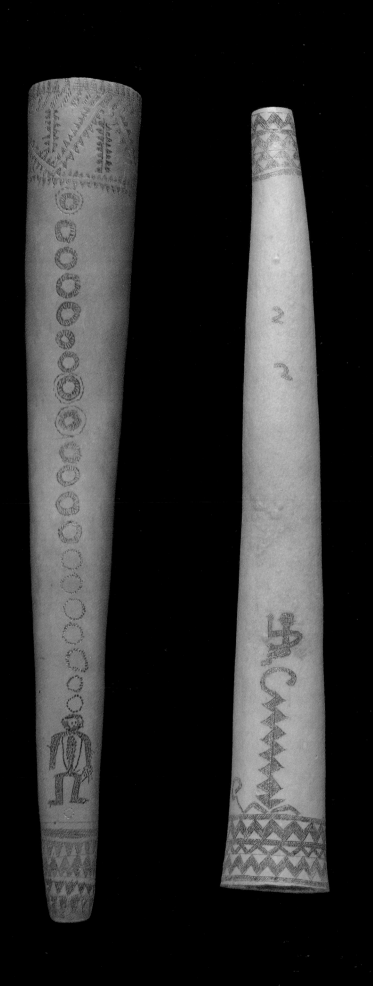

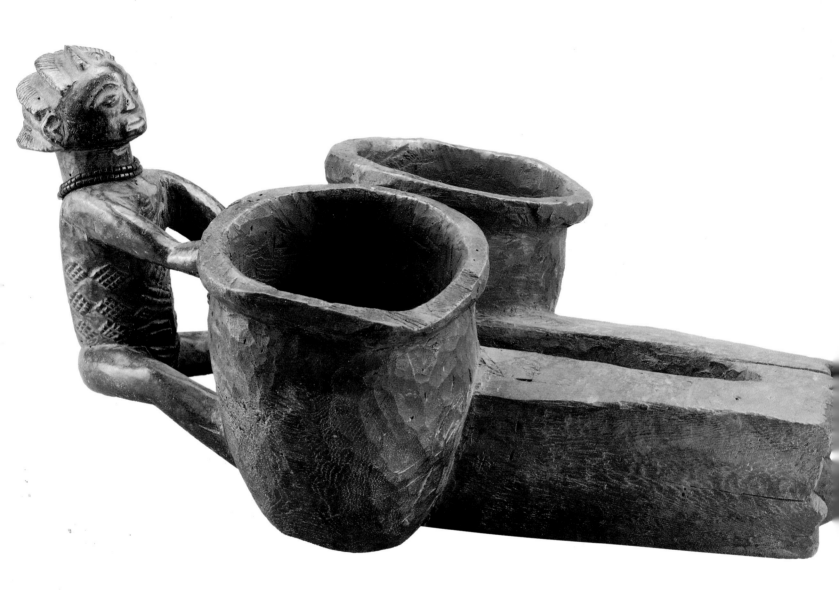

Weapons for combat and prestige

For the African man living in the grasslands and jungle, weapons are a vital necessity. Weapons for hunting, arms for offensive and defensives purposes, have existed since the earliest times and have evolved considerably since the days of the flint knife. Arms of remarkable quality were created with a significance that went far beyond their original function. Like jewels, they became insignia of rank and attributes of royal power. Their effectiveness and their beauty were the product of the mastery of metalwork achieved by the African craftsmen.

Opposite

105. Bellows
Luba-Shankadi. Zaïre.
Before 1930. Wood,
beads. L.: 69 cm.
Private collection.

**106. Blacksmiths
in Zambeze**
Postcard reproducing
an old engraving.
Photo Library of the
Barbier-Mueller Museum,
Geneva.

The art of metalwork

The making of weapons requires knowledge of techniques for working brass, copper, and most of all iron. The production of brass, copper and bronze is documented in Africa since the beginning of the first millennium AD. The so-called bronze (actually brass) plates which covered the gallery walls of the palace in Benin* in the seventeenth century (fig. 108) were a striking demonstration of the skill of local bronzesmiths working with the lost-wax process, which is one of the most difficult casting techniques of all. In most cases, the brass and copper were worked with hammer and

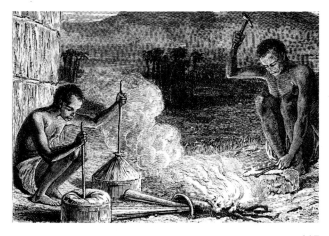

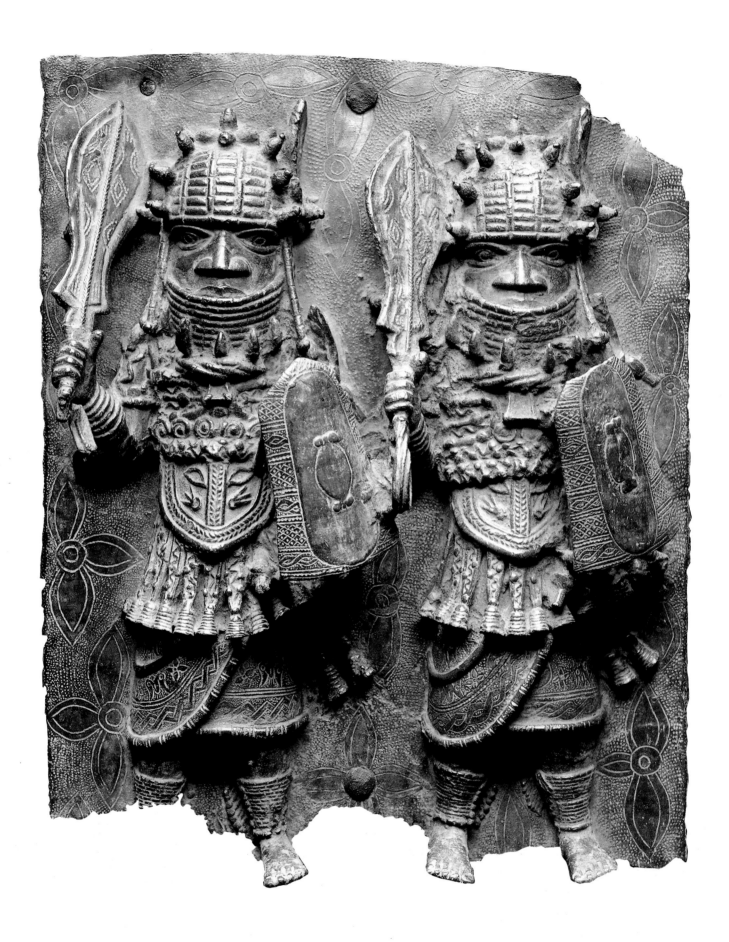

anvil. However, this technique could not offset the major drawback of these metals: their lack of solidity.

Steel and iron, being more resistant, were better suited to warfare. The Iron Age in Africa began in the eighth century BC in Niger and Nigeria, then spread to West Africa at the beginning of the Christian era. Traces of iron production from as early as the third century have been recorded in Rwanda, and from the sixth century in areas around the Upper Zaïre River. Arab documents from the twelfth century even mention exportation of iron to India.

The techniques used by blacksmiths have not varied much over the centuries. Iron ore could be found in abundant quantities in surface deposits at numerous sites. This ore was melted down at low temperatures in furnaces consisting of a hole in the ground covered by round constructions in which layers of metal were alternated with layers of coal. Bellows (fig. 105) provided air for the fires which were kept burning for two days. The resulting mass of iron mixed with slag then had to be purified, divided into ingots, and worked again in the fire, before finally being hammered into shape on an anvil. An old engraving (fig. 106) shows the blacksmiths at work in a scene that could be witnessed by ethnologists at the turn of the century. One man hammers a piece into shape on the anvil with a hammer, while his assistant works the double bellows to feed the fire.

The blacksmith's tools were few and rudimentary: hammer, anvil, chisels, burins and a wire-drawing bench to make metal wire of different gauges. Nevertheless, this scant equipment did not prevent him from working wonders.

The remote past

Many figures sculpted prior to the nineteenth century represent all kinds of soldiers in arms. Some fourteenth- and fifteenth-century terracottas from the lower Niger delta* represent cavalrymen with helmets strapped on, sheathed daggers on the forearm, and quivers on the back. These were professional soldiers organized into veritable armies and very conscious of their importance.

A bronze figure in the Metropolitan Museum of Art depicts a more humble, but energetic warrior with

Opposite

108. Wall-plaque from the palace of the oba of Benin
Represented are two warrior nobles in full armour, with shields and swords. Kingdom of Benin. Nigeria. 17th cent. Brass. H.: 40 cm. Barbier-Mueller Museum, Geneva.

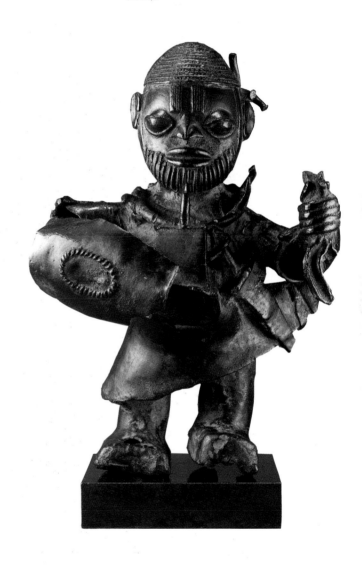

107. Warrior figure
Ijebu or Owo. Nigeria. 1450–1640. Bronze. H.: 32.4 cm. The Metropolitan Museum of Art, New York.

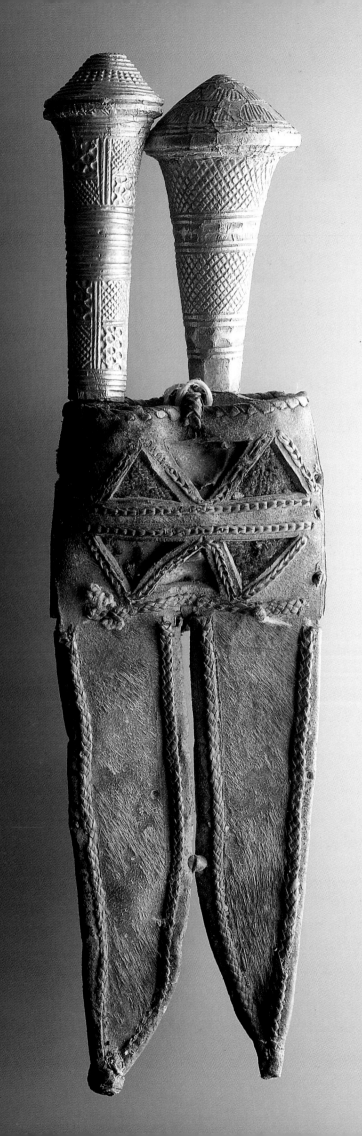

convincing realism. This foot soldier from the Lower Niger (fourteenth–fifteenth century) is armed with a shield and two swords; one hanging from his belt and the other brandished (but broken) in his left hand. The ornaments he wears – a square bell around the neck and a glass-bead and leopard-tooth necklace – have more of a magical than a martial or aesthetic function. The important thing was to have protection against magic spells and evil spirits, and then to ensure victory.

Produced one or two centuries later, the plaques from the royal palace in Benin (fig. 108) record the image of the noble warriors who fought in the service of the *oba*, as the king of Benin was known. Each one wields a broad ceremonial sword, called *eben* and a shield. All of these accessories were decorated. The fine pattern of linear motifs on the wooden shields covered with leather are very similar to those which appeared on the costumes (cloth or leather) worn by these same courtiers. These were ceremonial costumes and weapons. Another plaque from the same source, today preserved in the ethnological museum in Leipzig, shows the warriors preparing for combat. Their swords there have long, smooth and pointed blades. The ornamentation is sparse, but they wear a variety of pendants with magical charms and amulets.

In his *Description of Africa*, written in the seventeenth century, Olfert Dapper provides information which completes the representations on the plaques. In fact, the Dutchman had never been in Africa himself, but compiled the testimony of the travellers of his day: [19]

'This tribe is armed with pikes, shields, javelins, and bows with poisoned arrows. The nobles who go to war and want to make an impression wear handsome scarlet costumes, a necklace with elephant and leopard teeth, a stuffed red turban with a horsehair tail .... The army is led by a general who commands by the rod and who reserves all of the spoils for himself. Nevertheless, these soldiers are very courageous and generous; they never abandon their post, even if death should stare them in the face, and after the battle they go to thank the Prince for the honour of having been able to serve him.'

Except for the statues, this kind of text is the only remaining record of the arms used prior to the nineteenth century,

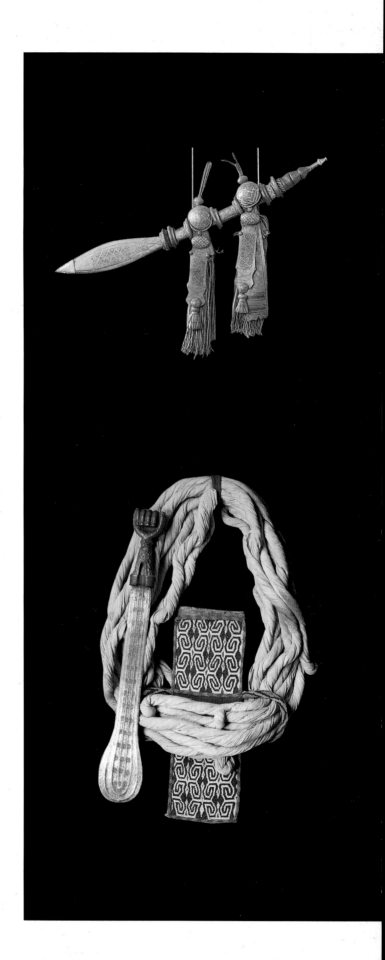

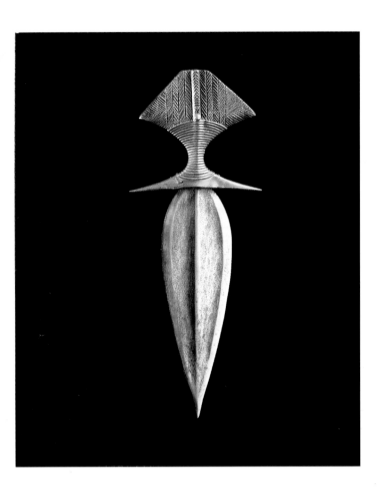

113. Dagger
Nzombo and Ngiri. Zaïre.
Hammered wrought-iron
blade. Wood grip
wrapped in brass wire.
L.: 40 cm. Barbier-Mueller
Museum, Geneva.

for they have all been lost. Metal is costly and hard to come by, so that worn and damaged weapons were invariably melted down to make new ones.

Closer to our time

Most of the weapons in the existing collections date from the end of the nineteenth and beginning of the twentieth century. This was a period which saw the culmination of the metallurgical arts, before firearms imported from Europe replaced the traditional arsenal. As their highly refined ornamentation testify, these weapons were the property of kings and not of common soldiers. Ordinary arms have forever disappeared into the crucibles of the foundries.

The classification of these weapons is not a simple task. We will use the classification which is generally adopted and which makes a first distinction between offensive and defensive armament. Offensive arms are subdivided into four categories: hand weapons (swords, daggers, knives), projectiles (bows and arrows, throwing knives), thrusting weapons (shafts tipped with metal points, like spears, pikes, and axes). The fourth and last category, which includes shock weapons like war clubs and maces, is of less aesthetic interest.

The defensive arms included all kinds of shields and some body armour, which was very rare.

In Africa, where nothing is left to chance and occult forces are at work everywhere, these weapons were sanctified by priests and sacrifices in ritual ceremonies. Accordingly, magic substances were often enclosed in the handles and grips to increase the warriors' chances of victory. The grips could also be carved with the likeness of an ancestor or protective spirit.

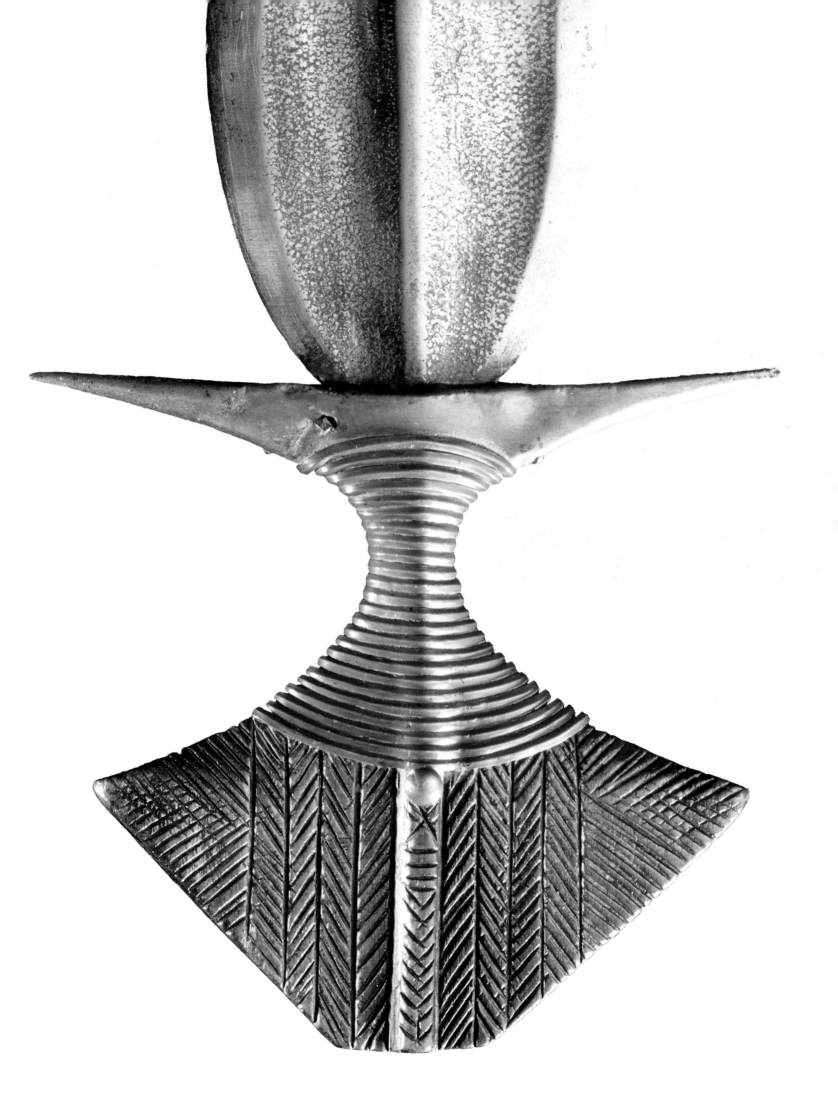

114. Ceremonial dagger
Nkutshu. Zaïre.
Hammered wrought-iron
blade. Carved wooden
grip. L.: 32.5 cm.
Barbier-Mueller Museum,
Geneva.

115. Ceremonial sword
Ngombe and Doko. Zaïre.
Hammered wrought-iron
blade, engraved.
L.: 76 cm. Barbier-Mueller
Museum, Geneva.

Page 120

**110. Two daggers with
gold-leaf grips in a
double sheath**
Baule. Ivory Coast.
Late 19th–early 20th cent.
L.: 25.3 cm.
Barbier-Mueller Museum,
Geneva.

This two-dagger set
was a prestigious item
that also illustrated
a Baule proverb: 'The
knife blade cannot carve
its own handle', which
means that 'what you
cannot achieve alone,
can be achieved through
cooperation'.

Page 121

Above

**109. Sword with
leather sheath**
Mande. Mali/Guinea.
The top of the grip and
the tip of the sheath are
in brass. L.: 84 cm.
Deutsches Leder-
Museum, Offenbach
(Main).

Below

**111. Commander's
sword with beadwork
sheath**
The broad belt which
accompanies it is made
of cotton. Bamum.
Cameroon. H.: 17.8 cm
(grip). L.: 69 cm. (sword).
Museum für Völkerkunde,
Berlin.

A nearly endless variety of hand-held weapons may be found in every part of Africa, but their possession is regulated by strict codes. Only tribal and military chiefs were allowed to own them and, if the need arose, to supply them to their men. Ordinary mortals disposed of knives for agricultural tasks, and bows and arrows for the hunt or for warfare. The Scotch explorer Mungo Park [20] described what he saw as a captive of the Hausa of Niger in 1796:

'The black people of the town of Benowm came, according to their annual custom, to show their arms, and bring their stipulated tribute of corn and cloth. They were but badly armed – twenty-two with muskets, forty or fifty with bows and arrows, and nearly the same number of men and boys with spears only. They arranged themselves before the tent, where they waited until their arms were examined.'

Certain combat weapons intended for chieftains evolved towards a more refined aesthetic treatment and have become objects of great prestige. They were kept in more or less decorated sheaths made of wood, leather or basket-work which protected the object no less than the bearer.

The forms given to hand weapons were manifold, for they reflected the traditions and lifestyles of the different tribes. The Mande sword (Mali or Guinea), with a sheath decorated with colourful leather tassels (fig. 109), is easy to imagine at the side of a dashing horseman, ready to be drawn and brandished, its blade flashing in the sun. The style of this weapon speaks for the influence of the Tuareg and Berbers of North Africa, with whom the Mande were once in contact.

The Baule of the Ivory Coast are geographically quite close to the Mande, yet their weapons seem to express a completely different vision of the world. Working with the usual refinements of their arts, they produced arms of great luxury, often decorated with gold, a commodity of which they disposed in abundance (fig. 110). For royal ceremonies in the palace, they created ritual swords imitating the superb ritual sabres of the Akan* (Ghana).

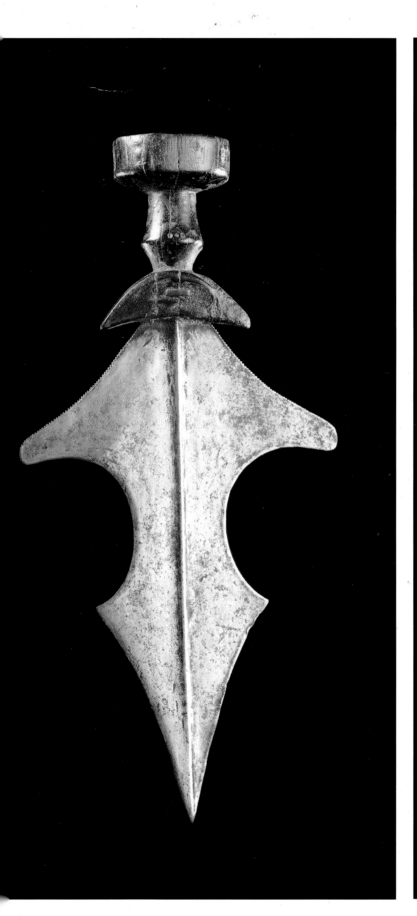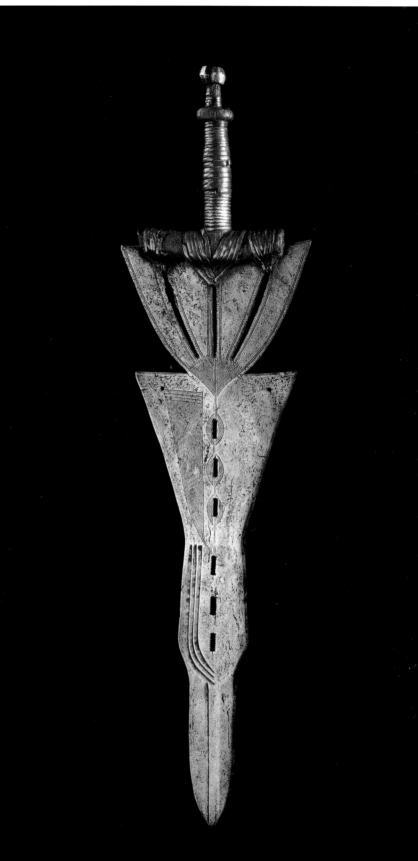

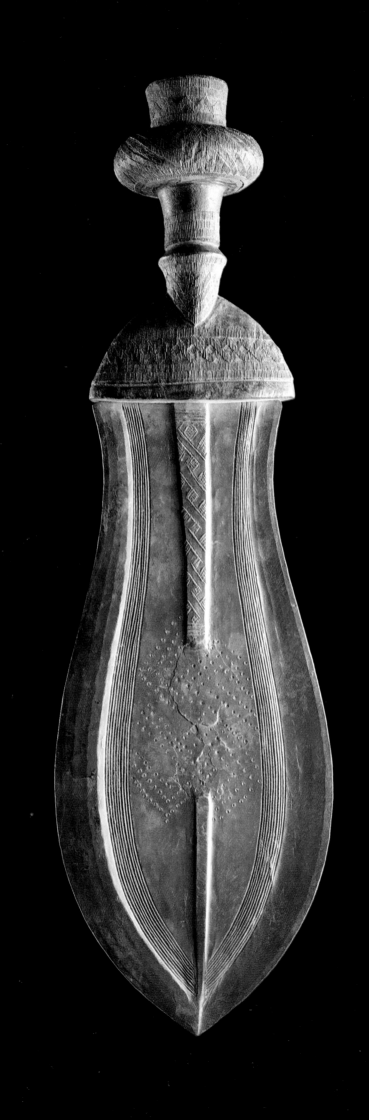

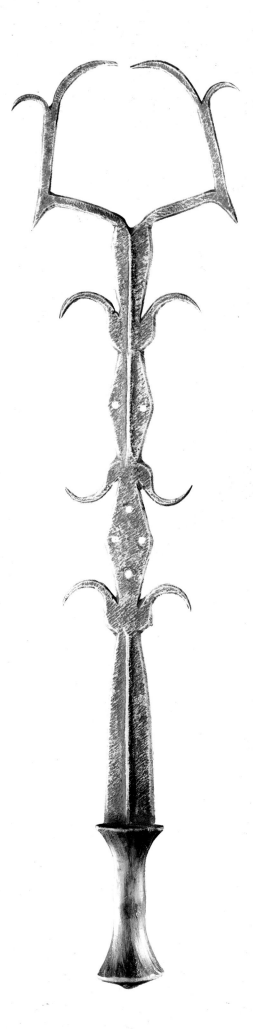

Opposite

117. Ceremonial sword (ikul)
Kuba. Zaïre. Brass blade, wooden grip with pewter incrustations. Dotted lozenge motif in the middle. Barbier-Mueller Museum, Geneva.

This weapon was only an accessory of the Kuba nobleman's costume, and not meant to be used in warfare.

116. Parade sword
Konda. Zaïre. Hammered and engraved steel blade. Carved wood handle. L.: 60 cm. Barbier-Mueller Museum, Geneva.

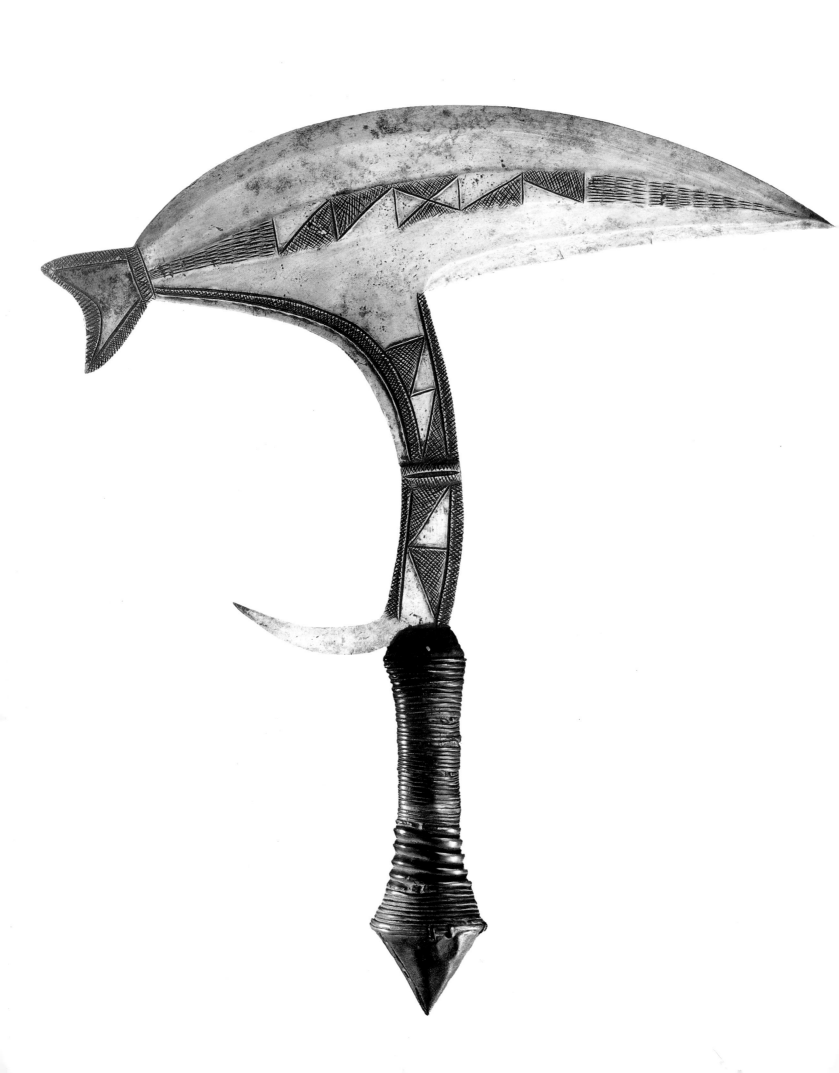

Moving from the Baule tribe to the Bamum of Cameroon, we see refinement giving way to power. Reserved for the rulers of the grassland kingdoms, these swords (fig. 111) were generally equipped with a beadwork sheath and a broad cotton sash of the kind still worn by dignitaries. The specimen at the ethnological museum in Berlin has an unusually rounded tip and a carved grip. These remarkable weapons show the degree of skill achieved by the Tikar blacksmiths settled in the northern grasslands.

Another picture emerges from Zaïre, which saw the production of a great variety of forms, each more beautiful than the next. The Mangbetu and Zande prided themselves on their daggers with handles topped by anthropomorphic figures carved out of wood or ivory (fig. 112).

In other regions of Zaïre, among the Nzombo and Ngiri, for example, the artisans played on the contrast between the unadorned silvery blade and the warm tones of a grip wrapped in brass wire (fig. 113). Among the Nkutshu, the blades were given elegant contours (fig. 114). The Ngombe, finally, were enamoured above all by sophisticated forms (fig. 115). The colours of the copper wire set off the design and refined ornamentation of the blade. The sword reproduced here was of course the property of a chief and was used purely for show; whether it could have withstood the rigours of actual combat is open to question.

To the Konda of Central Zaïre, however, would go the prize for the most ornate and extravagant sword-blade design of all (fig. 116): it is awesome and ostentatious, but totally unsuited for warfare. In any event, weapons in Zaïre were not necessarily intended to be functional; they just had to indicate the owner's social rank. If need be, the weapons were made only of wood.

Why wooden swords?

Wooden swords may be found in Central Zaïre among the Kuba who regulated their lives according to the phases of the moon. They normally had swords with metal blades, but during periods of the new moon, only wooden blades were allowed. The reason why is revealed by the ethnologist Joseph Cornet: [21]

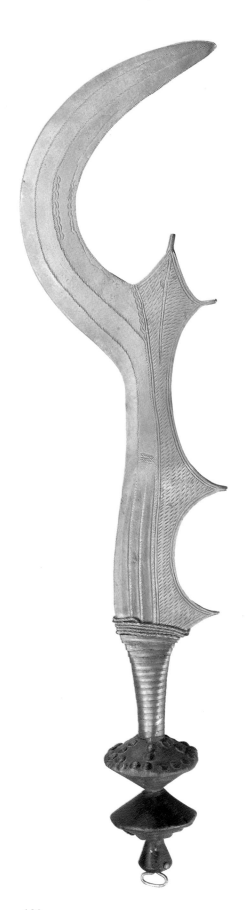

'This custom is supposed to have begun with Kot a-Pey, a king who ruled between 1902 and 1916. Filled with remorse at having participated in the assassination of King Miko mi-Kyeen, his predecessor, Kot a-Pey feared reprisals from the spirit of the defunct king. To appease him, he ordered that only wooden knives could be borne at the beginning of the new lunar cycle.'

Secluded in his palace, the king surrounded himself with his wives, whose chants were supposed to summon the vanished orb to return. When this came to pass, the king would emerge and proclaim the new month which for the Kuba followed the phases of the moon.

The wooden swords of the Kuba were copies of existing models of short-swords made of copper or iron (fig. 117). The gracefully formed blade was topped by a carved wooden grip. These short and broad swords were not reserved for the king, but the royal sword – a long, slender, and pointed affair – and the royal bow and spear, were his exclusive privilege.

All of the weapons discussed so far had a symmetrical shape and a central axis. There were also many asymmetrical models, the most noteworthy of which were the sickle-shaped knives.

Sickle-shaped knives

The famous Fang* knives, with blades in the form of a bird's (or toucan's) beak, were long thought to be throwing knives. The latest ethnological research, however, tends to consider them to be like a 'bird-headed axe'. Certain variants of this type of knife even take on very clearly the form of a fish, tail-fins included (fig. 118). These ancient weapons were originally intended for hand-to-hand combat and not for ritual use. Their production was stopped at the turn of the century.

A weapon very similar to the toucan-beak design may be seen on a mid-nineteenth-century engraving representing King Mbunza of the Mangbetu tribe (Zaïre), except that the handle is longer and straight. These sickle-shaped Mangbetu knives (fig. 119) were worn essentially for prestige effect, hence the elaborately carved wooden or ivory handles. Copper versions of this sickle-knife were also made, but only for the monarch.

These knives had no ritual function. Other arms of similar design were made for capital executions.

Arms for executions

Asymmetrical knives of the sickle type may be found among the Ngombe and Doko of Zaïre (fig. 120). Two European travellers, Camille Coquilhat and Lieutenant Vangele (quoted by G. Gosseau), witnessed their use in 1883. [22] Coquilhat described the din of drums and the crowd's excitement at the sight of the condemned slave, whose head was wrapped in a woven-reed net and attached to a curved pole:

'The executioner strode to the place of execution wielding his huge knife, whose curved blade seemed to have been designed to accommodate a human neck .... Taking off his cloak, he knelt on the left side of the slave, facing him, his right hand resting on the ground. Rubbing his cheek with some earth, he arose, made a trial run, then, with a sudden blow, struck the hapless victim .... The head was projected through the air. Immediately after, the crowd rushed to the decapitated body, their knives at the ready.'

The Ngombe knives were used not only for executions, but also for war, and in times of peace, as insignia of rank and worth. In the latter case, they were held with the blade turned upward, like sceptres.

Other sickle-shaped knives made by the Ngombe and Doko were given a symmetrical form (fig. 121). These were used for executions, but also as insignia of rank. More recently, less robust models were to be seen on the occasion of parades and dances.

The blades of these weapons were remarkably tooled with fine ridges and grooves, and the wooden grips decorated with brass studs. They all display the 'awesome beauty of instruments of death', as the ethnologist Marc Félix once described it. [23]

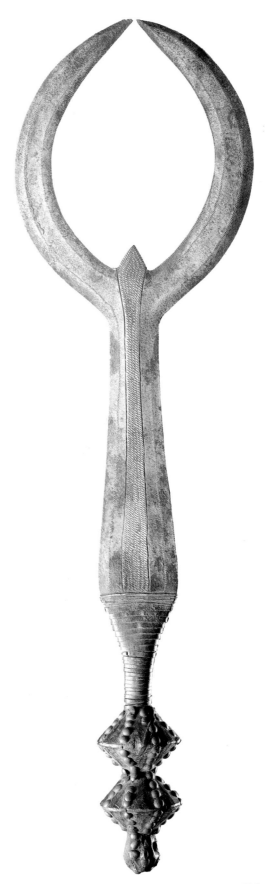

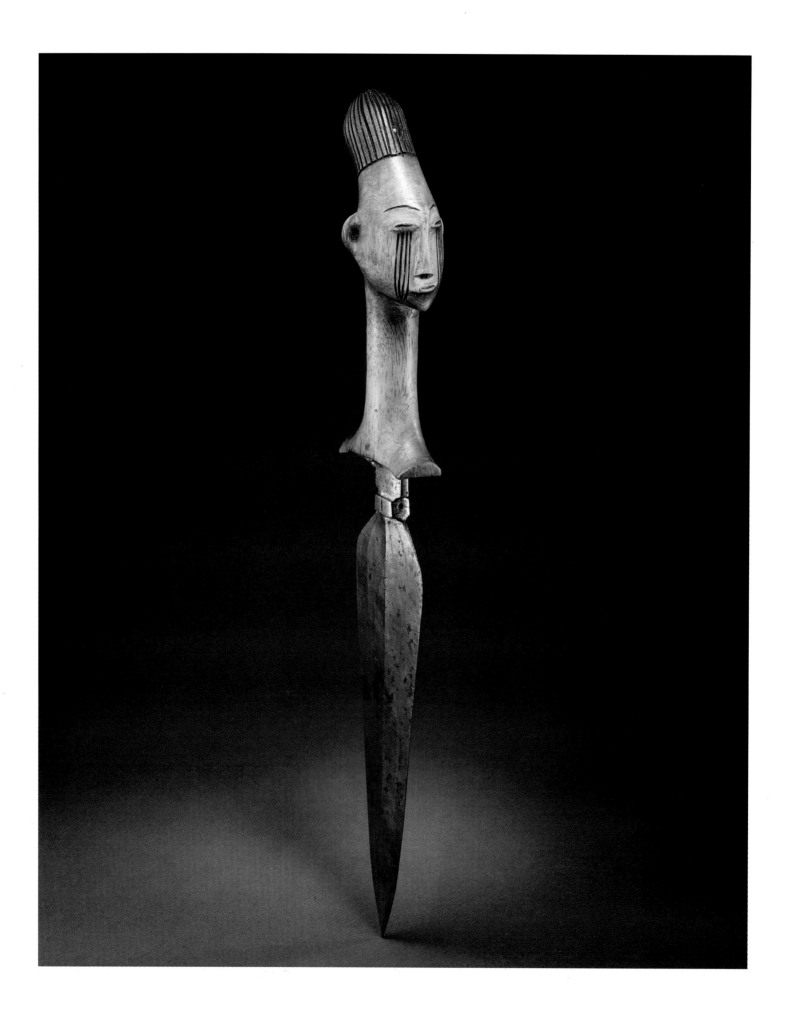

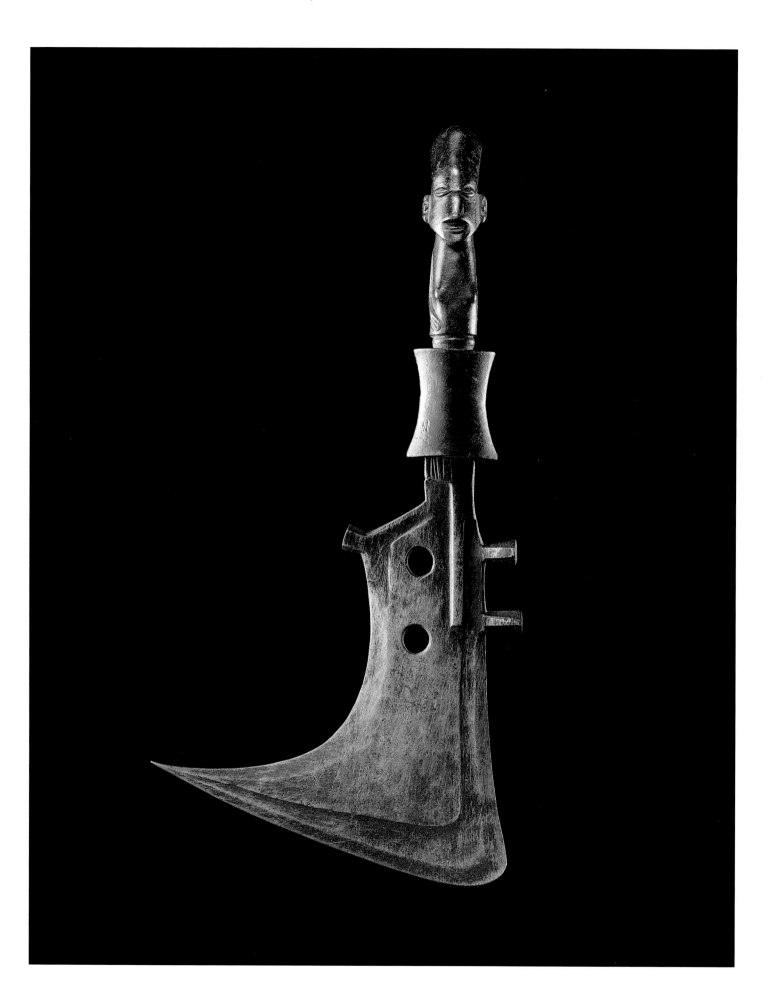

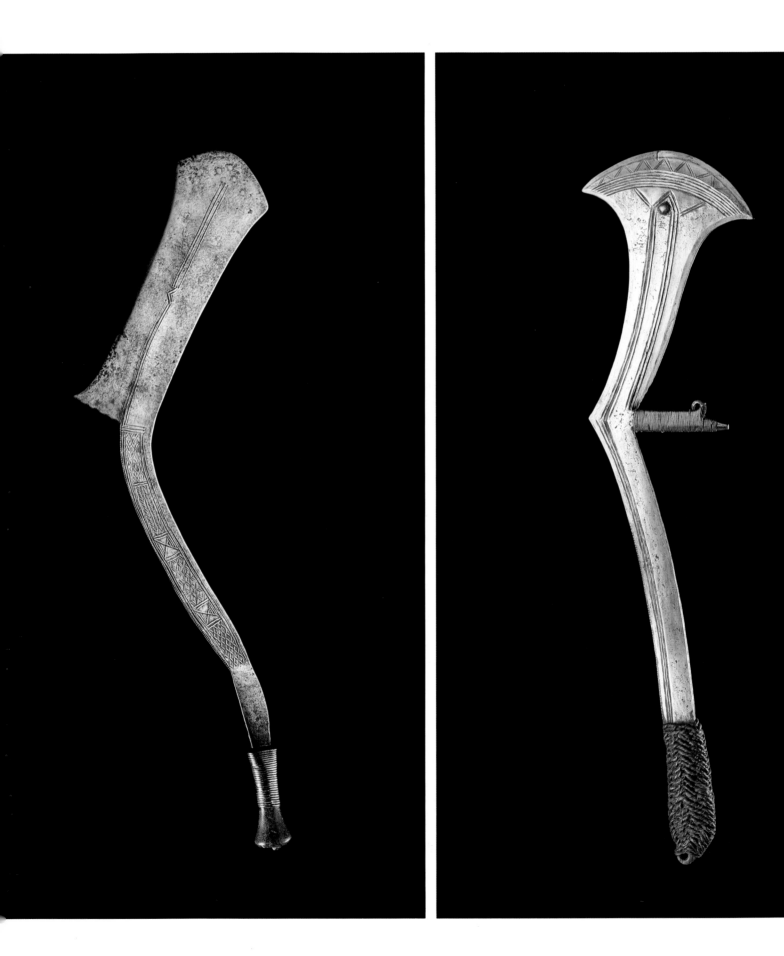

Among the many forms of sickle-blade knives, certain models show a development in the direction of the throwing knife.

From sickle-knives to throwing knives

Throughout northern Zaïre and in some of the adjacent areas (Congo, Gabon, the Central African Republic and the south of Sudan), many populations made weapons (sometimes called sabres) which combined a long, flowing blade and a short grip. There are fine models from the Nzakara and the Binja (fig. 122). The blade, engraved with fine designs, also presents inlaid copper disks that create a striking effect.

Other weapons of a similar shape present an added spur or hook. This is the case for the weapons of the Biyanda and the Gbaya (Republic of Central Africa and Cameroon, fig. 123). Here again, aesthetics were always a consideration. Accentuating the curves and grooves, a brass stud gives a colourful finishing touch. This weapon was intended mainly for show.

Along with these knives, which only had one sharp edge, there were models with many blades. One may be seen on an old postcard showing an Ubangi fetish-maker (fig. 124).

Throwing knives and playful curves

In warfare, the throwing knife was a weapon of deadly effect, and so greatly feared by the enemy. With its many points and cutting edges, it was well-balanced for throwing, and almost invisible and silent in flight.

This type of weapon is specific to Africa and existed in many different forms. The blacksmiths skilfully combined its curved shapes into a harmonious whole, without ever sacrificing any of its efficacy. The Matakam knife (fig. 125) from north Cameroon is still used as a weapon and worn on the shoulder as an insignia of social rank. It was mostly undecorated and owed its elegance to an artful play of curves of which an abstract sculptor would be proud.

The Zande knife (fig. 126), more complex in design, had

Page 132

112. Dagger
Mangbetu. Zaïre. Wood, steel. L.: 32 cm. American Museum of Natural History, N.Y.

The top of the grip is decorated with the deliberately stylized head of a Mangbetu woman.

Page 133

119. Sickle-shaped knife
Mangbetu. Zaïre. Wood handle, steel blade. L.: 42 cm. Barbier-Mueller Museum, Geneva.

Opposite

122. Sickle-shaped sword
Nzakara and Binja. Zaïre. Hammered wrought-iron blade with copper incrustations. Carved wood grip partially enrolled in steel wire. L.: 62 cm. Barbier-Mueller Museum, Geneva.

123. Throwing knife
Biyanda, Gbaya and other tribes. Central African Republic and Cameroon. L.: 59 cm. Barbier-Mueller Museum, Geneva.

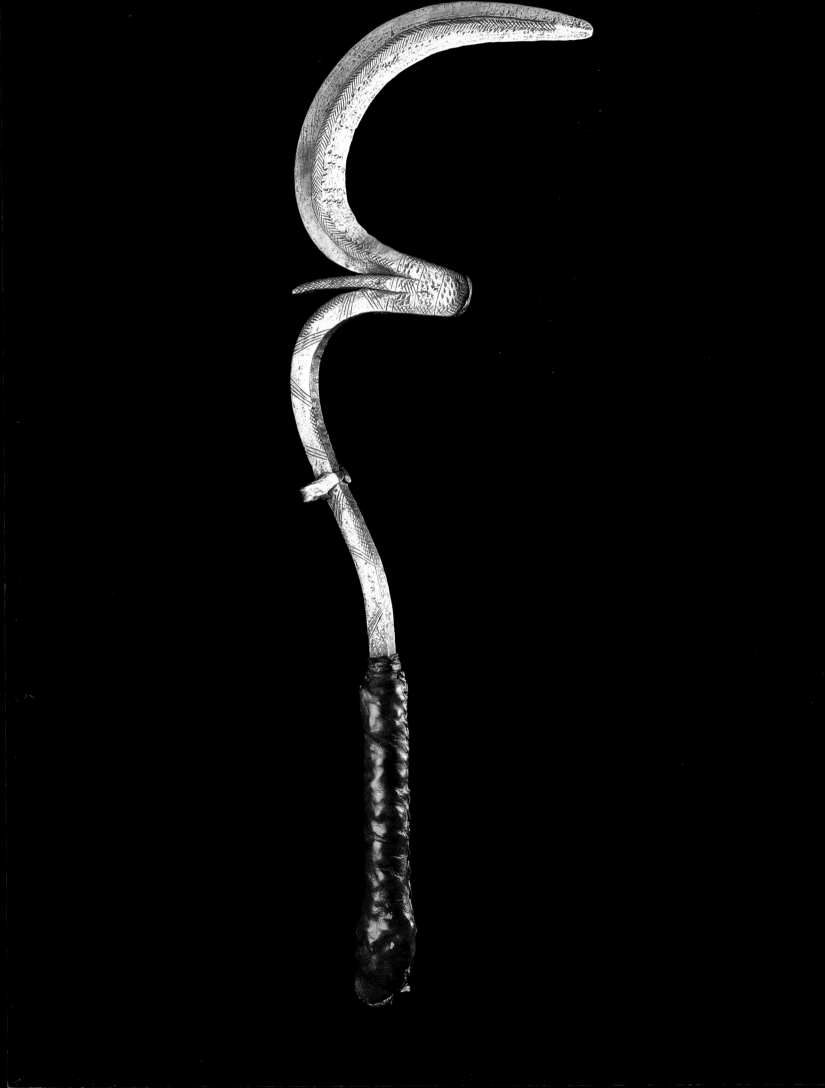

blades that were decorated with slits and engravings. The Zande soldier normally carried four knives, which he used only if necessary, after he had used up his provision of sharpened stakes. Zande knives were always used as weapons until the end of the nineteenth century; since then, they have served more as ritual objects for ancestor worship.

There are many different types of throwing knives. Among the Yakpa of the Central African Republic, the blade was given very rounded forms which almost evoke a flower (fig. 127). This model represents the last stage of a long development. Other categories of weapons also display designs of great beauty.

Thrusting and shock weapons

Thrusting weapons consist of sticks or poles fitted with blades at the top. Weapons for hurling and jabbing, like spears and stakes, were widely used and could be decorated with metal incrustations. Most noteworthy among this class of weapons are the war-axes. Once again, Zaïre offers the finest designs, especially the Songye axes, which are marvels of the metaworker's art.

The Songye were tough warriors who conquered vast territories. Their weapons had to be both resistant and beautiful, for they proclaimed the dignity of their chiefs. The ceremonial axes of the Songye are easy to recognize by the characteristic design of their blade; it is attached to the handle by five separate stays, giving the whole an elegant openwork decoration which in no way weakens its effectiveness. The different parts of the axe were made separately. The blacksmith decorated each of the stays with heads, the details of the eyes, nose and mouth being carefully carved out with a burin. There was the same number of heads on each side of the stays. Some of these elements could also be given a twisted shape. These stays were themselves reinforced by curved, obliquely placed stays. Only when this work was done was the blade itself welded to the stays, and the whole attached to the handle, which was normally covered with a thin sheet of metal.

Opposite

125. Throwing knife
Matakam, Mafa or Kapiki.
Northern Cameroon,
Northern Nigeria.
Barbier-Mueller Museum,
Geneva.

**124. Fetish-maker
with throwing knife**
Ubangi region.
Photo Library
of the Barbier-Mueller
Museum, Geneva.

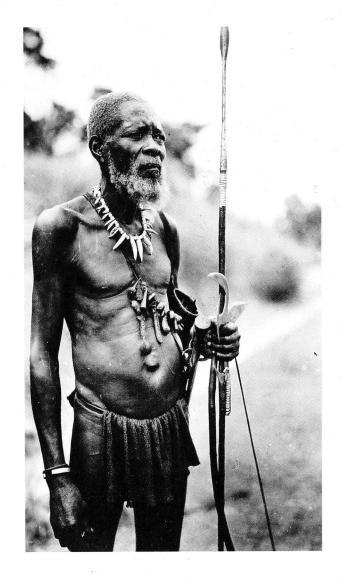

137

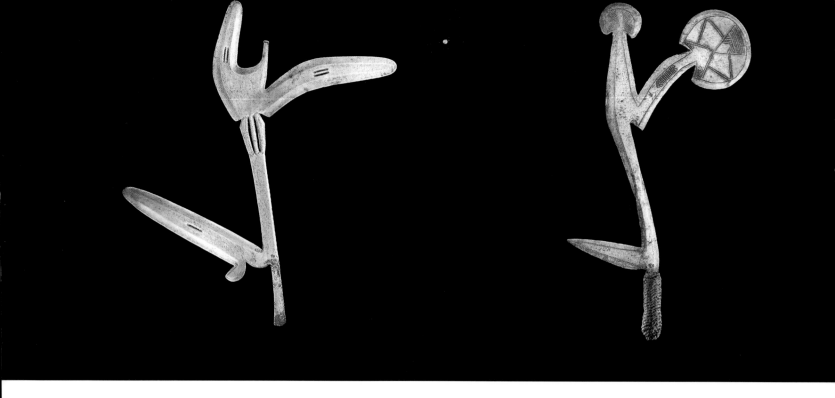

Left to right

126. Throwing knife
Zande, Adio, Nzakara.
Zaïre. Steel. The handle
may originally have been
covered with leather,
or perhaps even ivory.
L.: 48.5 cm.
Barbier-Mueller Museum,
Geneva.

127. Throwing knife
Yakpa and Wada. Central
African Republic. Forged
steel. L.: 42.7 cm.
Barbier-Mueller Museum,
Geneva.

Generally similar in shape to the axe is the adze, which differs in having the blade being fixed in a plane perpendicular to the handle. These have become purely objects of prestige intended for chieftains, and will be discussed separately.

The fourth and last category of arms to be considered are the shock weapons – more often than not maces and war clubs with rounded tops. These could be decorated with carved figures or metal studs, like this Nuer mace from Sudan, on which the studs were arranged in the shape of a human figure (fig. 129).

Defence and protection

African warriors used a variety of shields for protection in battle. The simplest kind were made of tightly woven basketwork or of wicker decorated with painted designs. Others, like those of the Mangbetu (Zaïre) were made of wood with a rectangular shape and devoid of ornament. In Kenya, the oval-shaped shields of the Masaï were decorated with painted geometric designs which had a heraldic meaning; in this way, the enemy could tell to which clan or age group the warrior behind it belonged.

Some of the shields made by the Songye were true works of abstract art. The specimen at the Barbier-Mueller Museum (fig. 130) stands out by the elegant design of its

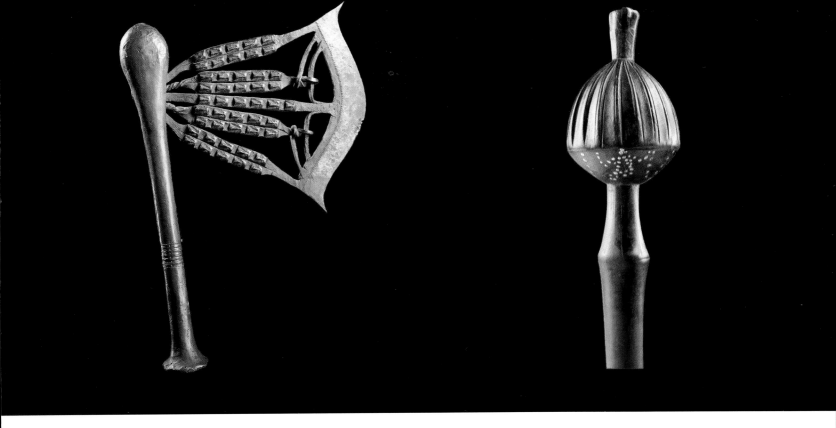

contours, which is enhanced by the bold opposition between the characteristically striated patterns and the miniature *kifwebe* mask set in the middle. Only craftsmen with a very highly developed sense of form could produce such a harmonious whole out of such disparate, if simple, elements.

While defensive arms were made of plant or animal materials, the offensive weapons were made of metal, principally iron and steel. These indispensable items were often used as a form of currency in commmercial trans-actions.

From weapons to money

Prior to the colonial period, commercial and trading transactions in Africa were never conducted with coins or the like. They were effected by means of barter with products deemed valuable because they were either rare, useful or desirable. All sorts of goods could serve this purpose: cattle, cotton fabrics (fig. 62, p. 70), beads, cowrie shells, salt, kola nuts, and, most of all, metals.

These were traded in various forms. In the case of gold, it was in the form of gold dust or small jewels, as in West Africa, among the Akan of the Ivory Coast, in Mali, and on the Trans-Saharan trade routes.

But the metal that was in the highest demand, because it was the most useful, was iron. In his *Travels in the Interior*

Left to right

128. Parade axe
Nsapo of the Songye group. Steel blade, wooden grip. H.: 57 cm.
Barbier-Mueller Museum, Geneva.

129. Mace
Nuer. Sudan.
Wood and metal nails.
Private Collection.

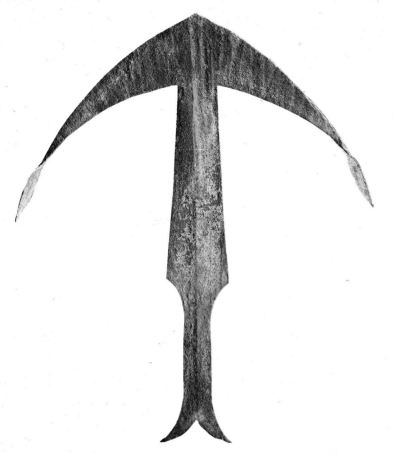

131. Metal blade used as money
Kwele. Gabon.
Hammered steel.
L.: 50 cm.
Barbier-Mueller Museum, Geneva.

Opposite

130. Shield
Songye. Zaïre.
Middleweight wood.
Black and white pigments. H.: 76.5 cm.
Barbier-Mueller Museum, Geneva. (acquired before 1942).

These shields decorated the lodge in which the masks of the *Kifwebe* society were preserved.

Overleaf

132. Metal blade used as money
Ndengese, Songo-Meno, Nkutshu. Zaïre. Steel.
Barbier-Mueller Museum, Geneva.

This object was originally a sign of social status. It gradually became used as currency in trade and commerce. Only rare specimens still exist.

of Africa (1796), Mungo Park wrote concerning the inhabitants of Gambia: [24]

'The article that attracted most notice was iron. Its utility, in forming the instruments of war and husbandry, make it preferable to all others, and iron soon became the measure by which the value of all other commodities was ascertained. Thus, a certain quantity of goods, of whatever denomination, appearing to be equal in value to a bar of iron, constituted, in the traders' phraseology, a bar of that particular merchandise. Twenty leaves of tobacco, for instance, were considered as a bar of tobacco ; and a gallon of spirits (or rather half spirits and half water) as a bar of rum.'

At the end of the eighteenth century a slave was worth 150 bars. In Sierra Leone, these iron bars were called *barriferri*.

In other regions, iron was traded in different forms: as hoes in northern Zaïre and as bells along the Ubangi River. Among the Guro of the Ivory Coast, payments were made with *sompe*, long bars with wing-like shapes at the ends, and among the Fang of southern Cameroon and Gabon with *bitchies*, small iron bars strung along plant-fibre rope which served as small change.

There were even more surprising variations. The object lost its original function as a tool (e.g. the hoes) or weapon and took on a more symbolic role as money. Having lost their original meanings, these objects evolved towards simpler forms, until they became a sort of abstract sculpture. In Tanzania, the hoe was completely flattened under the blacksmith's hammer and can now be admired as pure form. Among the Kwele of the Congo, the shapes were more complex: the perfectly shaped curves end in spear tips to create a striking formal design (fig. 131). In Zaïre, the Dengese, Nkutshu, Songo-Meno and Kela tribes have adopted the forms of the Zande throwing knife and created a type of money which is a remarkable formal achievement in its own right (fig. 132).

Copper alloys were also widely used as money in the form of small St Andrew's crosses (*croisettes*) or large bracelets called *manilles*.

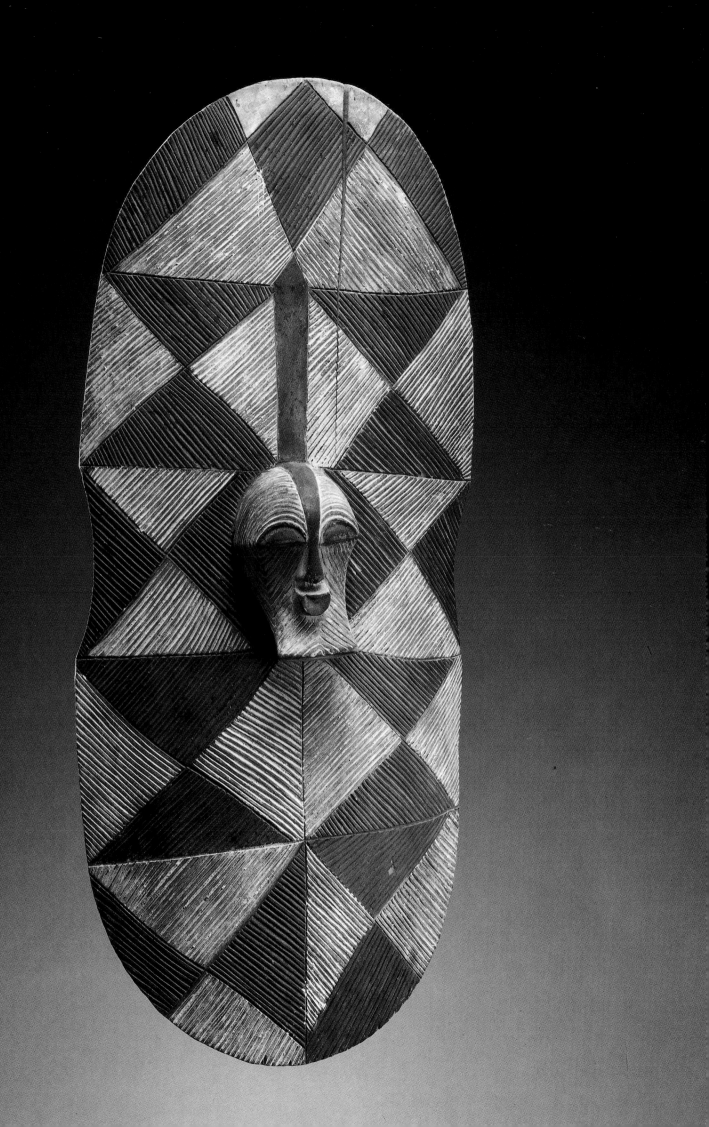

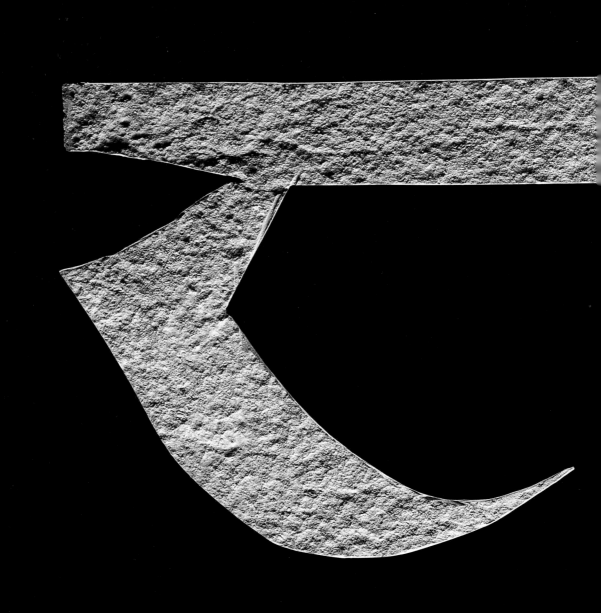

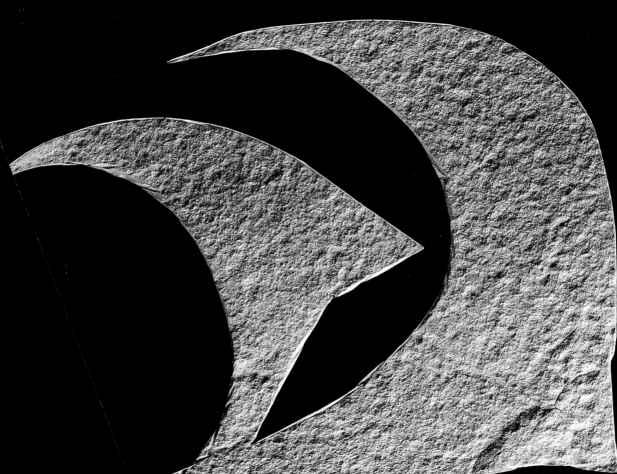

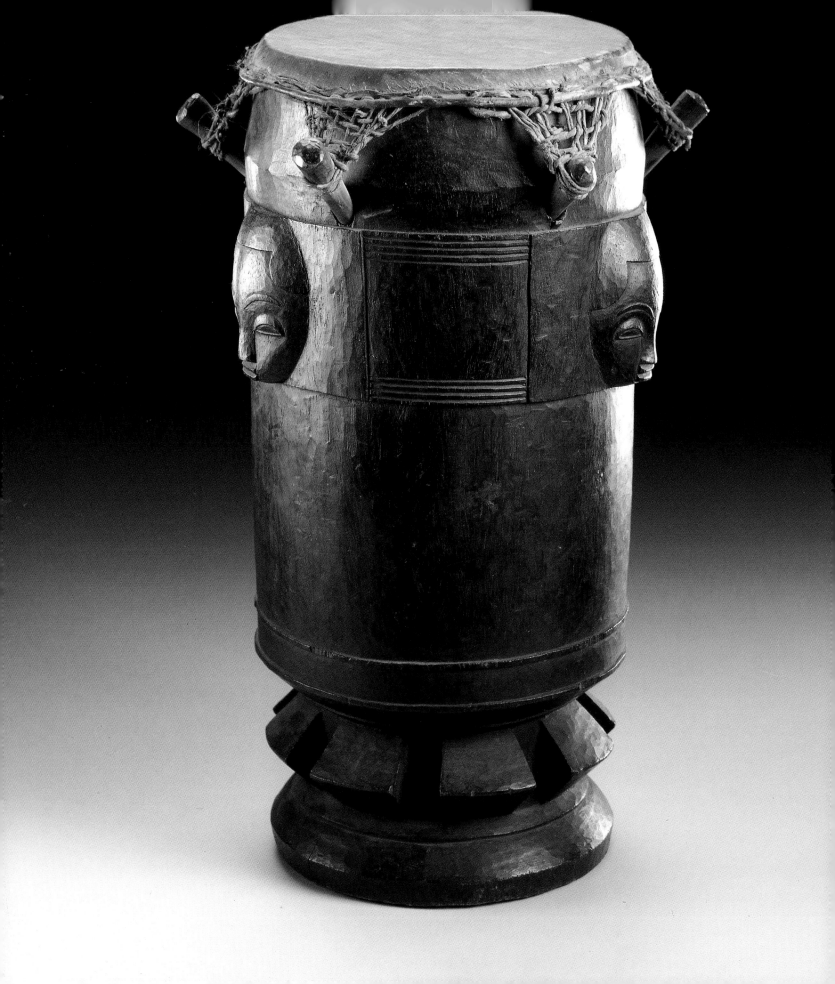

The pleasures of social life: music, games and tobacco

Entertainment in African life – feasts, dances, banquets and singing – are often organized when there is a need to reduce tension or deal with anxiety. Participation is open to all. One such occasion is described by the Malian writer Amadou Hampâté Bâ in his previously-cited autobiography: [25]

'Over a dozen children in the neighbourhood were to be circumcised at the same time. As custom dictated, the ceremony would be preceded by all-night festivities, from sunset to sunrise. All the relatives and friends of the families were informed. The preparations for the feast lasted a good month .... Finally, the big night arrived.'

The writer then tells of the arrival of the *griots* and of the itinerant musicians who go to feasts to praise the families in song. He was especially struck by the woman-griot, Lenngui: 'She sang the whole night through, going from shepherd songs to wedding songs, from war songs to love songs, from the epic to the nostalgic mode. The tambourines gave the beat, while the crowd, clapping hands in alternating rhythms, kept up the cadence.' Other griots also participated, including a master of genealogies: 'Lightly swaying his body and his head back and forth, he went through the audience in turn. Using the usual onomatopeias,

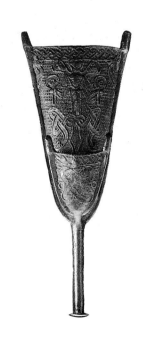

133. Double gong
Kingdom of Benin.
Nigeria. 15th–19th cent.
Copper alloy.
H.: 34.5 cm. W.: 14 cm.
National Museum, Lagos.

A number of decorative motifs advertise the king's prestige: the figure in the middle with knotted legs represented the *oba* ever since one of them had paralysed legs. The silurid fish has its origins in the same tradition. The python head was represented throughout the Palace of Benin as a symbol of power.

Opposite

134. Skin drum
Yohure. Ivory Coast.
Wood, animal hide.
H.: 46 cm.
Barbier-Mueller Museum, Geneva.

135. Slit drum
Lobala. Zaïre. Ubangi
region. Wood. Barbier-
Mueller Museum, Geneva.

Opposite

**136. Lobala drum in
its original context**
Black and white
photograph. Photo
Library of the Barbier-
Mueller Museum, Geneva.

he would present the melody he had chosen, slow or fast, cheerful or sad, and the crowd took it up in a chorus.'

This description gives us an idea of the importance of music and dance in African life. Apart from these major feasts, other, more accessible, pleasures could always be organized to promote conviviality. These could be games, puppet shows, or rituals involving the use of tobacco or Kola nuts.

In all of these situations, the participants used objects that were made to fulfil aesthetic requirements as much as their explicit functions.

The omnipresence of music

In Africa, music is everywhere. The natural gifts of the Africans in this domain is well known. Even when there are no musical instruments around, the activities of everyday life are enlivened by songs. Rhythm, even if only by the clapping of hands, is king.

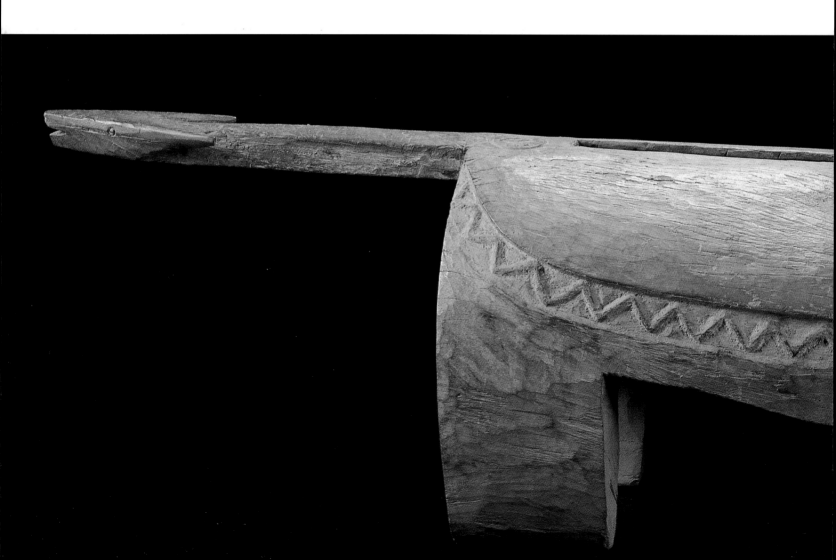

These talents are not related to the actual evolution of the tribes in the cultural sphere. Even today, the pygmies of northern Zaïre, who still live mainly from hunting and fruit gathering, are known for the beauty of their polyphonic chants, which accompany their everyday activities, rituals or leisure.

The subject of this section, however, is not African music, but the appearance and design of their musical instruments. It is one of the areas in which the African aesthetic sense is at its most immediately apparent, nourished, as always, by a vivid imagination.

Nevertheless, the decoration of the instruments is not the product of pure fancy on the sculptor's part. It is ruled by tradition and the symbolic meanings associated with the instruments and the occasions on which they are used, as well as by the nature of the instrument. It is inconceivable that the ornamentation of a harp could ever be the same as that of a drum. At the same time, the craftsmen enjoy a certain latitude in interpreting the chosen theme or design, and in responding to the musicians' wishes.

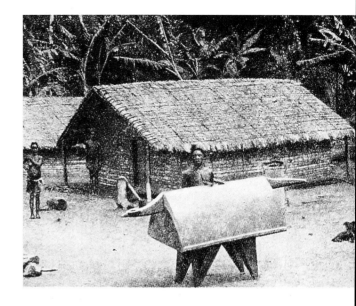

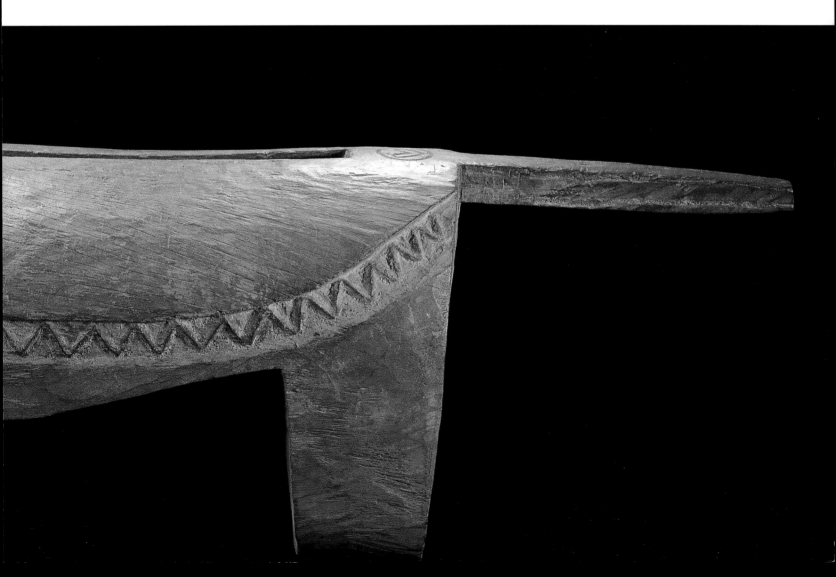

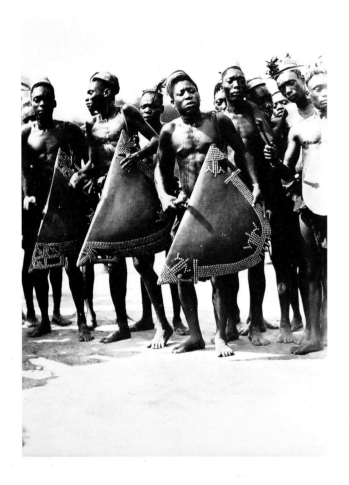

**138. Men
playing slit-drums**
Mangbetu. Postcard.
Photo Library of the
Barbier-Mueller Museum,
Geneva.

Opposite

137. Slit drum
Momvu/Mangbetu.
Northeastern Zaïre.
Hardwood with dark
polish and brass nails.
36 x 81 x 15 cm.
Barbier-Mueller Museum,
Geneva.

The most frequent motifs are stylized or idealized anthropomorphic figures. This is probably an expression of the communion and identification between the musician and his instrument. Indeed, the instrument transmits the vibrations from the musician's body and soul. This fusion is all the more easily achieved as the notion of soul or spirit is paramount in the African mind. Moreover, the Africans describe sounds in terms of the human voice.

Instruments with zoomorphic carvings also exist, although in lesser numbers; the forms are often of bovines or of birds (an obvious choice). Often there is a combination of anthropomorphic and zoomorphic elements, as in the case of masks.

These carvings do not exclude other forms of ornamentation – mobiles, coloured cloth or raffia, leather tassels – which give the music a visual impact that creates a transition with the world of the dance.

Leaving the village compounds for the royal courts, we can see that music has also contributed over the centuries to reinforcing the prestige of the rulers. Thus, on the carved plaques that decorated the palace of the *oba* of Benin in the eighteenth century, which were a sort of visual chronicle of the period, we see the king very often preceded or accompanied by musicians playing a variety of instruments. These have been identified, and they include ivory horns, gongs (fig. 133), bells, drums, castanets and flutes.

Drums for all occasions

The drum is the African instrument par excellence, and it played a very important role both in the life of the village and in the life of the court. The rhythms of drums accompanied special occasions of all kinds that would have been unthinkable without them. They came in a great variety of shapes and sizes, and can be divided into two major groups: skin drums and slit drums. In the first group, the hides and tightening strings do not play an ornamental role, but the wooden body lends itself to carvings and any number of three-dimensional treatments. The sound-box can take the form of a cup, while the feet can be carved in the shape of a human figure or a horse, as in the case of the Baga caryatid

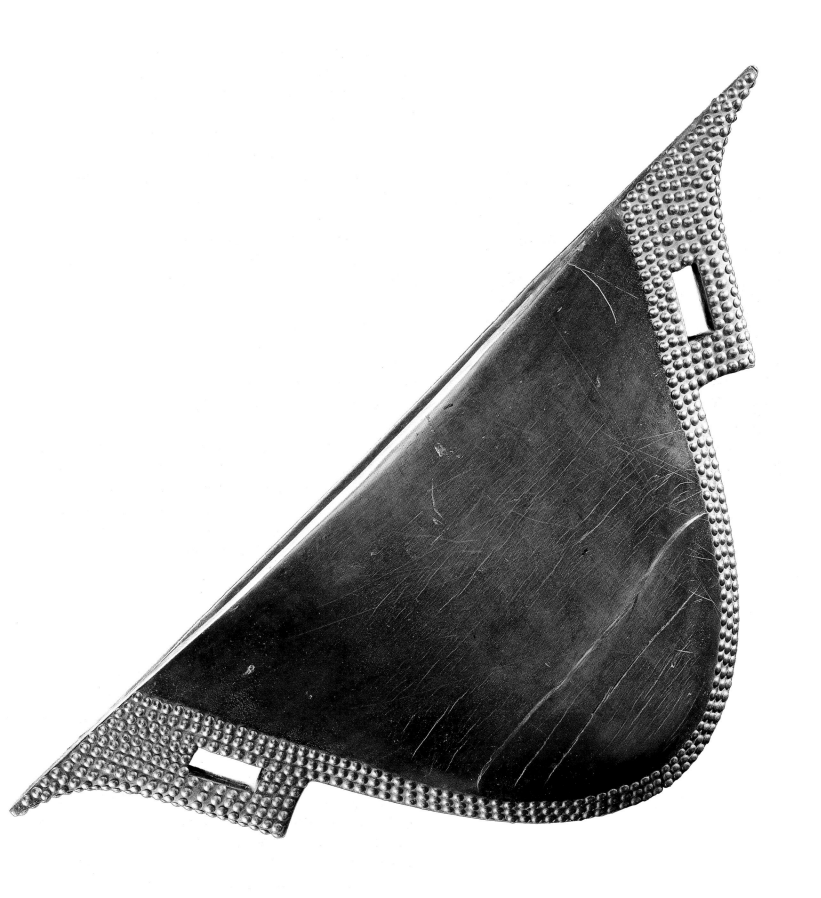

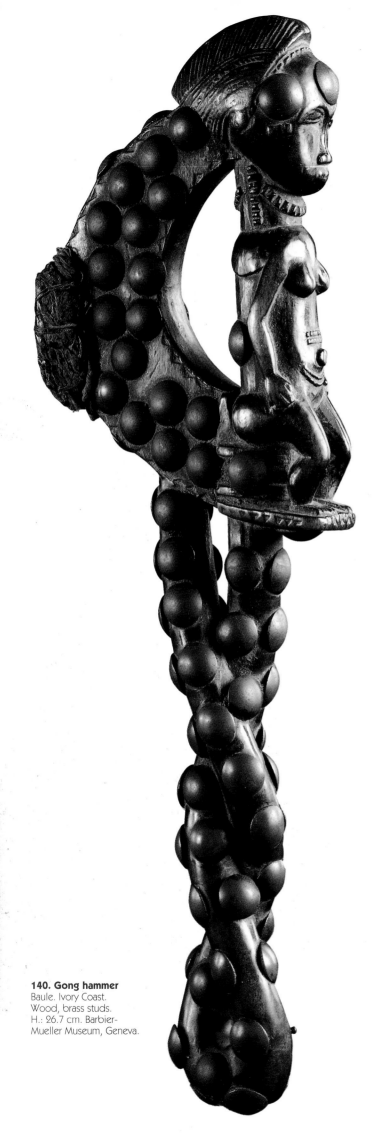

140. Gong hammer
Baule. Ivory Coast.
Wood, brass studs.
H.: 26.7 cm. Barbier-
Mueller Museum, Geneva.

drum from Guinea.* Its height enabled it to be played standing up for funerals or other ceremonious occasions. The delicacy of the carvings, the complexity of the forms, and the gravity of the faces represented, attest to the importance given to these drums.

In other cases, anthropomorphic figures, entire bodies or just heads, were carved in relief on the sides of the drum. Here, too, there were countless variations. The beautiful Yohure drum in the Barbier-Mueller Museum (fig. 134) is worth mentioning because of the extreme refinement of the sculptures produced by this tribe. The faces have delicate features and appear totally serene beneath high and smooth foreheads. The foot of this instrument is balanced and lightened by geometric volumes similar to those of certain Yohure chairs. Drums such as these were used to announce important events or deaths in the village.

The variety is just as great in the category of slit drums. Thus, in certain regions of equatorial and central Africa, the sound-boxes (made of a single piece of wood) could be imagined as an animal body, and by adding a head and a tail, one obtained the likeness of a bovine. A stylized lobala drum (figs. 135 and 136) seems to hover somewhere between strict geometry and an evocation of the animal's powerful flanks. These instruments were of major importance because they were made for the chiefs. The ethnologist Gabriel Seligmann wrote about a similar drum [26] in the form of an ox, life size, and with great horns, which was captured during a military campaign in 1905: 'It belonged to the Zande sultan Yambio of Avungura, whose power fell with the loss of this venerated instrument.'

Leaving the Ubangi territories in which these buffalo-drums were made, and heading east towards the Uele Valley where the Mangbetu live, one can see that zoo-morphic slit drums were used alongside other drums with abstract forms (fig. 137), which were decorated with the brass studs that are greatly valued in this region. The zoomorphic drums, which stem from a rural context, were used to transmit messages from village to village, while the triangular drums were played in the royal orchestra and underscored certain special occasions in the king's life, as when he drank palm wine or hosted the visit of another chieftain. The elegant shapes of these drums were well suited to a regal decor. They are shown in action on an old postcard (fig. 138), and we know that in some cases they were accompanied by xylophones or rattles.

The body of the instrument, whether a skin drum or slit drum, was always made of wood. Other instruments had sound-boxes made of gourds. This was the case with the *balafon*, a typically African instrument which is composed of a sort of xylophone placed over a series of gourds that amplify the sound. They are still widely used today.

For Europeans, drums and bells do not have that much in common. In Africa, however, some bells can be very close in design to a drum.

Very unusual bells

Bells in Africa can be made of very different types of material: wood, iron, bronze or even ivory. Often they have no clapper, because they were played like drums, with a stick.

The wooden Kongo bells of Zaïre were often crowned by human figurines. Their dull tones were used in ceremonies conducted by a healer. In more prosaic cases, they were attached to the necks of hunting dogs. Among the Zande of Zaïre, a wooden bell was sounded when the chief drank wine. The handle of one such bell (fig. 139) is topped by a beautifully carved head worthy of a master sculptor.

The mallets which were used to strike metal bells or gongs during certain ceremonies could be remarkable works of art in their own right. The Baule mallet in the Barbier-Mueller Museum (fig. 140) combines an almost free-standing statuette with a double-torsaded handle entirely decorated with brass studs. A cushion made of plant fibres was added to dampen the sound of the gong, which was meant to gently awaken the gods and ensure their presence. The most distinguishing aesthetic feature of this object is the fusion of otherwise very different three-dimensional forms into a harmonious whole, further graced, in the words of A.M. Boyer, by 'skilful oppositions of form and light'. [27]

139. Bell
Zande. Zaïre. Wood, fibre rope. H.: 33 cm. Acquired by Herbert Lang at Poko in 1913. American Museum of Natural History, N.Y.

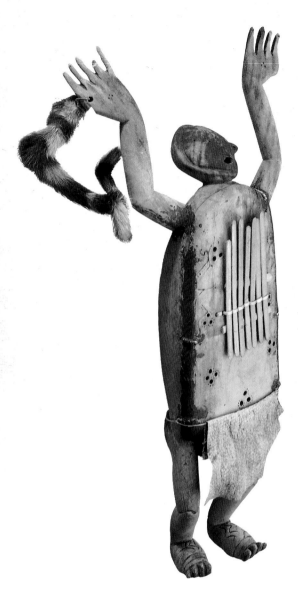

The search for harmony

Harps, especially those from Zaïre, are among the most beautiful of all African instruments. The sculptor of this Mangbetu harp (fig. 141) has given the entire neck a human shape. Very often the sound-box takes on the form of a woman's body which is prolonged by a graceful head of dignified countenance. There could also be legs, but they do not add to the instrument's basic charm. Its beauty resides in the matchless elegance of the forms, which, in the musician's mind, were surely wedded to the harmonious sounds that it permitted him to produce.

The exceptionally beautiful Zande and Mangbetu harps were not the only ones of their kind. Anthropomorphic harps could also be found among the Kwele of Gabon. Among the Fang, the harps used in ancestor-worship ceremonies expressed the link between the living by its body, and the dead by its sounds.

The *kora* is still played today in West Africa (Guinea, Senegal, Gambia, Mali). This is a sort of harp-lute with twenty strings and is often equipped with a sound-box made out of a gourd. In Mali, the *dan*, a smaller version of the kora, was also a very popular instrument. Amadou Hampâté-Bâ has left us an especially evocative description of a dan-player: [28]

'He was called Danfo Siné, which means Siné the dan-player, because he never parted from his dan, a sort of five-stringed lute made with one half of a large gourd. He played this instrument with amazing virtuosity .... His hands did what they wanted, and so did his voice. He could make his audience tremble with fear by imitating the roar of a furious lion, or lull it by imitating a chorus of trumpet-birds .... And when he danced, he would have inspired envy in Mister Ostrich himself, that king of the bush dancers, when he courts his sweetheart.'

When the strings of the harp or lute were replaced by rods of bamboo or steel lined up on a sound-box, the result was called a *sanza*, or thumb-piano, another widespread and typically African instrument. Like the harp, the sanza was often given a human form, which permitted the musician to identify closely with his instrument and to

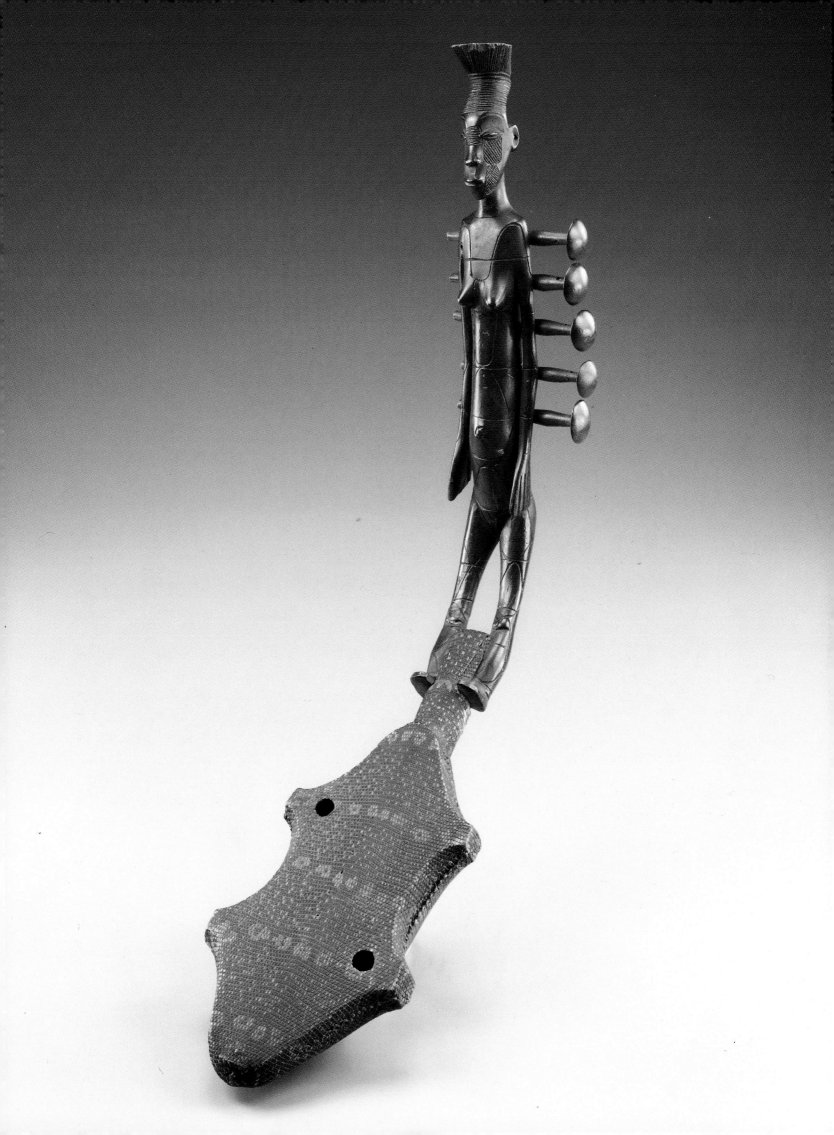

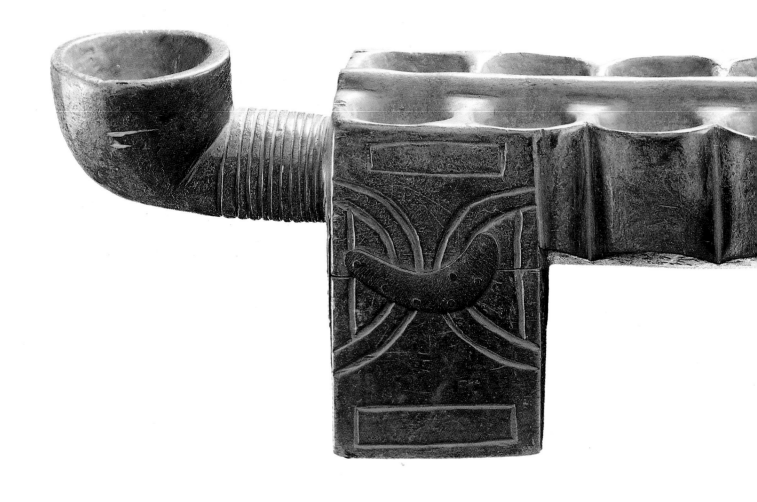

144. Ma kpon game
Dan. Liberia and Ivory
Coast. Wood with dark
patina, metal, and beads.
L.: 72 cm. Barbier-Mueller
Museum, Geneva.

communicate that much more easily with the supernatural realms through sound. Among the Zande in the Uele region of Zaïre, sanzas in the shape of a woman with joyfully outstretched hands have been found (fig. 142). Other sanzas featured a much less realistic form of decoration that distantly remind one of a woman's face, like a shadow falling across the sound-box. In other cases, one sees only purely abstract designs.

The common feature of all of these string or plucked instruments – harp, lute, kora, sanza – is that they create a certain poetic atmosphere when they are used to accompany songs. The same cannot be said of the trumpets, whistles, and other wind instruments that were designed to be used in a more dynamic context.

Shrill wind instruments

This last category of instruments comprises horns, trumpets, and whistles which have been in use since ancient times. The explorer Pigafetta, writing in his

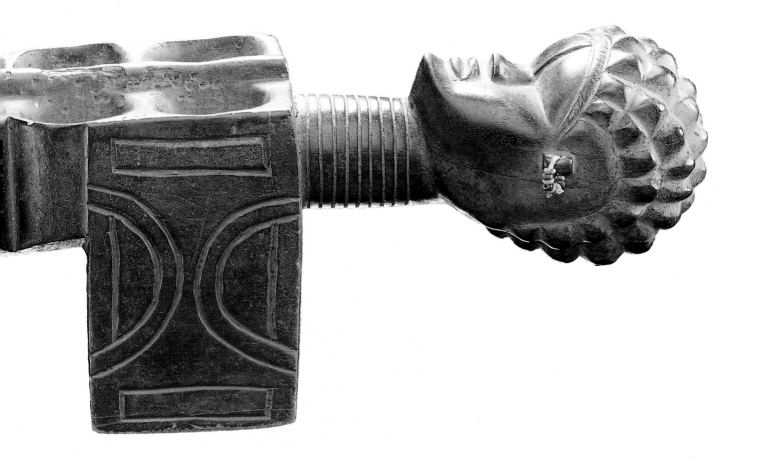

Description of the Kingdom of Kongo (1591), noted that 'at the court of the king, there were also flutes and fifes which were played with art; the dances performed to the sound of these instruments were solemn and dignified'. Later, he mentions transverse trumpets made of elephants' tusks. His descriptions are confirmed by the scenes on the bronze plaques from Benin (seventeenth-century), which show musicians playing horns that might well have been made of ivory.

Very finely crafted transverse ivory trumpets have indeed come down to us. Made at the end of the fifteenth century by carvers in Sierra Leone for exportation by Portuguese merchants, they were carved with delicate relief decorations, but the designs were of European inspiration. Transverse ivory trumpets from the Kingdom of Benin, more authentically African, are preserved in various museums. The pure, harmonious forms of these instruments are decorated with geometric or figurative designs. They were played on the occasion of the king's public appearances and during the ceremonies at which he presided.*

Whistles of all shapes and sizes may be found

143. Megaphone
Vili. Congo. Wood.
L.: 84 cm. Luigi Pigorini
Museum, Rome.

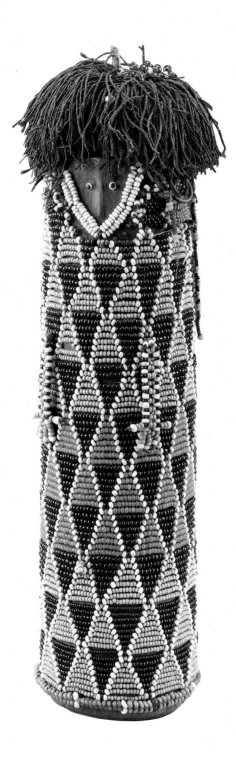

145. Beadwork doll
Zulu. South Africa.
Private collection.

This doll entirely covered
with beadwork is
an especially refined
object, quite different
from the types more
commonly found.

throughout Africa and were associated with a variety of social events, but mostly with the hunt. They were used to celebrate the great deeds of the hunters (among the Bambara of Mali), or as a means of communication between hunters out in the field (among the Tshokwe, p. 204). The latter type was small and often decorated with head carvings, but zoomorphic or abstract designs could also be found in other parts of Zaïre.

For coded messages, whistles sufficed, but in situations where detailed orders had to be given and the human voice was necessary, megaphones were used. The association of the human voice and animal heads, so strange to European eyes, appears on two megaphones attributed to the Vili tribe (Congo) which were collected in 1889 and 1899. The one on display at the Pigorini Museum in Rome (fig. 143) was carved out of a single piece of wood into the shape of a dog's (or crocodile's?) head with glass eyes and an open maw. It is decorated with alternating red and black stripes. The vigorous stylization of the forms and their implicit violence fully express the urgency of the message to be delivered.

The decorations on these megaphones, as well as on the various types of flutes and whistles, present very complex associations of motifs: the craftsmen chose human and animal forms that were related to the messages to be transmitted, which they then artfully transposed onto the instruments, even managing sometimes to portray the listeners' reactions. Use of these instruments was therefore linked with a moment of particularly high social tension and collective emotion.

The games to be discussed in the following section were intended to occupy moments of inactivity and calm, and to integrate them into the life of the group.

Games and toys

In Africa, as on other continents, there are many different types of games, and the Africans have demonstrated no less inventiveness and creativity in their play than in their art. In

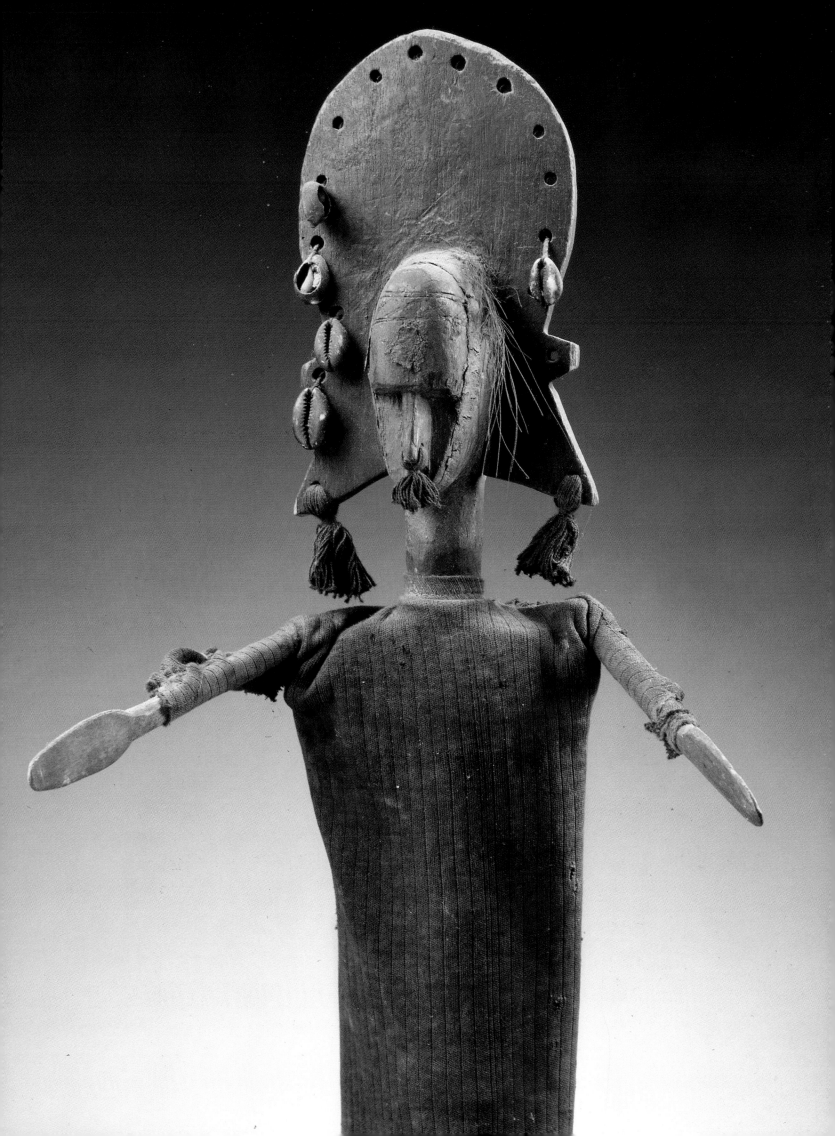

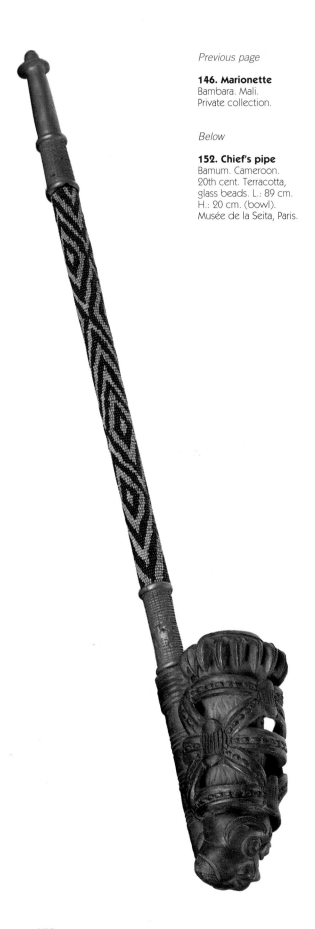

any event, these two aspects of their lives – games and art – were never totally separate, but mutually reinforced each other.

The game of *awele* (also called *mancala* or *ma kpon*) which, though widespread, is played more particularly in West Africa, involves moving pawns according to certain rules on a board with two rows of six holes. The goal is to capture the pawns in the opposite row. The pawns can be made out of seeds, pebbles or pieces of metal. At either end of the board there are two cups to hold the captured pawns. In some cases, one of the cups is given the shape of a human or animal head carved in the style specific to the tribe. A set from the Dan tribe of Liberia (fig. 144) displays the powerful modelling and the smooth and lustrous patina typical of their artwork. The hair is carefully groomed, the ears adorned with beads, and the neck covered with lateral folds which are considered marks of beauty among the Dan. In spite of the stylization of the face into powerful geometric shapes, one can still identify the handsome features as those of a woman. M.N. Verger-Fèvre wrote about this piece: [29] 'Most of the carvers explain the replacement of the cup with a female figure by saying that they want to complete the beauty of the object.'

To play the simpler game of *abia*, all that was needed was a number of fruit stones carved with different kinds of motifs. The Fang of Gabon were such passionate players of this game that the men would play their own wives as stakes. To prevent abuse, it was eventually forbidden by the German authorities.

Dolls immediately come to mind when one talks about toys made for children. Certain kinds of dolls used in magic or religious contexts, however, cannot be considered as toys. This was the case of the *akua-ba** dolls, which young women wore as amulets to ensure fertility.

The real dolls were made by the children themselves. The body could be fashioned out of an ear of corn or a long bone: a goat's shinbone did the trick perfectly. A ball of clay at one end served as a head, and a stick attached crosswise would do for the arms but this was not absolutely necessary. On the other hand, some kind of adornment was invariably added, like bits of cloth and the all-important beads. In the realm of play, where one's imagination alone is the limit, one very often comes across objects that could be considered toys only in the mind of the beholder.

More elaborately carved wooden figurines with recognizable anatomical features – head, breasts, and even navel – were also made. Certain types of dolls, although very rare, were covered with beadwork and could easily be classified as works of art (fig. 145).

Marionettes

The Bambara of Mali, like the Ibo and Ibibio of Nigeria, made a type of marionette that cannot be considered as a toy. They represented effigies of more or less satirized social types which groups of young adults used in public performances. The ones made by the Bambara were rather archaic in appearance (fig. 146). Some were activated simply by a handle, while others had all sorts of strings and wooden levers. The clothes were made of rags or plant fibres, but the crudely carved heads were always very expressive.

In other regions, the marionettes were less crude. Traces of pigments have been found on certain heads, some of which were covered with metal leaf and studs. Among the Ibo, the faces were polished and the arms could be moved forward.

Pipes for pleasure and status

Tobacco played an important part in the social life of the Africans. Originally imported from America, this plant was introduced in Africa in the sixteenth century, after the age of great explorations. The oldest terracotta pipes excavated in West Africa date from around 1600. Very likely, neither tobacco nor hemp were smoked in Africa before then. Cigarettes became common in cities only around the end of the nineteenth century. Even today, in rural areas, the pipe is the preferred way of smoking.

Both men and women smoked pipes, but the design of the pipe itself had to be appropriate to the smoker's social station. Smoking was mostly done individually, whereas taking snuff was a convivial affair. Water pipes, inspired by

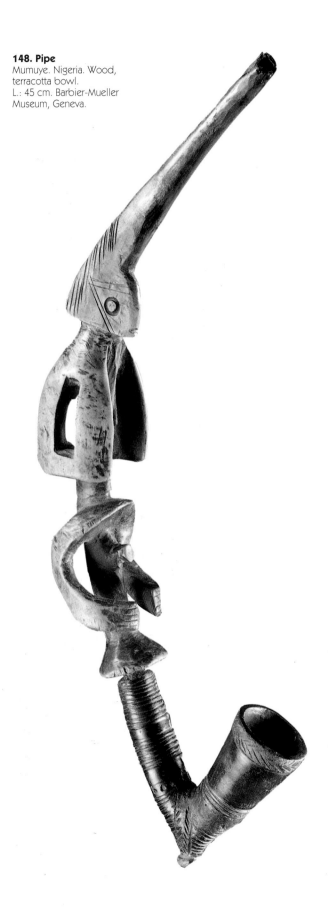

148. Pipe
Mumuye. Nigeria. Wood, terracotta bowl.
L.: 45 cm. Barbier-Mueller Museum, Geneva.

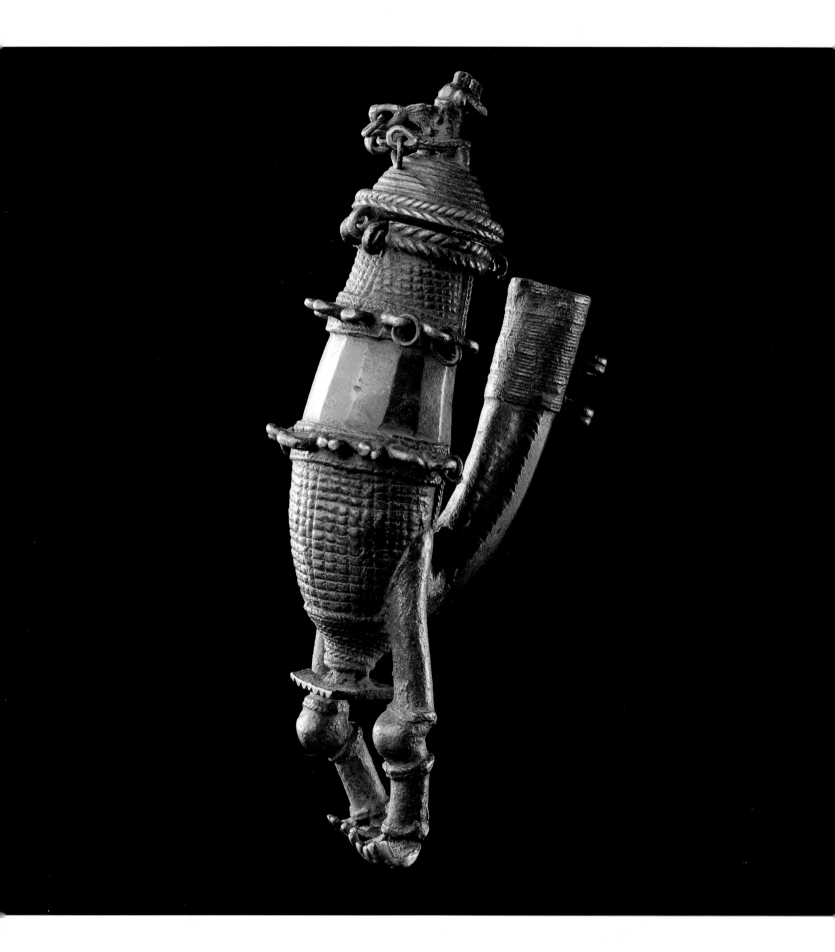

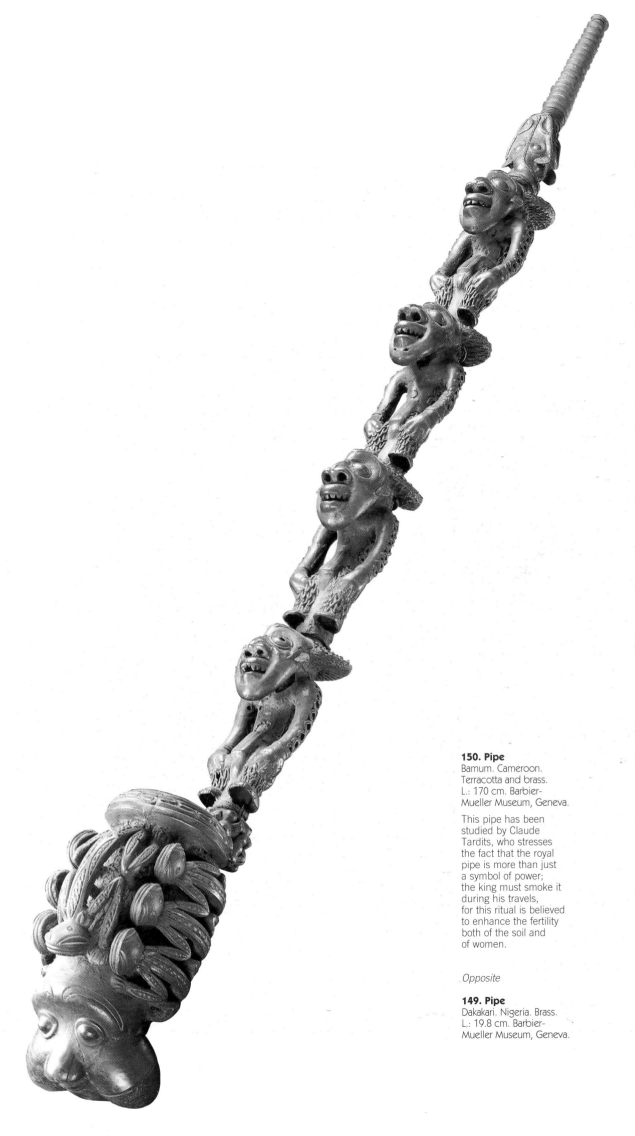

150. Pipe
Bamum. Cameroon.
Terracotta and brass.
L.: 170 cm. Barbier-
Mueller Museum, Geneva.

This pipe has been
studied by Claude
Tardits, who stresses
the fact that the royal
pipe is more than just
a symbol of power;
the king must smoke it
during his travels,
for this ritual is believed
to enhance the fertility
both of the soil and
of women.

Opposite

149. Pipe
Dakakari. Nigeria. Brass.
L.: 19.8 cm. Barbier-
Mueller Museum, Geneva.

151. Three pipes
Bamileke. Western
Provinces. Cameroon.
The bowls are made of
terracotta. L.: 32.5 cm.
(left); 28.5 cm. (right);
32 cm. (middle).
Barbier-Mueller Museum,
Geneva (acquired before
1939). Formerly
in the Joseph Mueller
Collection.

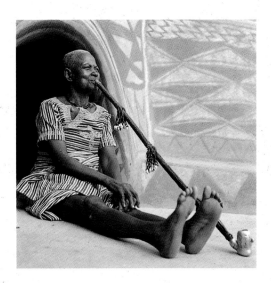

147. Pipe smoker
Photo Library
of the Barbier-Mueller
Museum, Geneva.

The model being
smoked has all
the characteristics
of African pipes:
very long stem and bowl
resting on the ground.

Indian or Arabian traditions, can be found in eastern Africa and Sudan, but the great majority of pipes that have come down to us correspond to the familiar European type.

René Caillié, recounting his travels in northern Guinea in 1827, wrote: [30]

'The men smoke big pipes with stems three feet long and as thick as a little finger; they are made of grey-coloured earth and are well-varnished; the part in which the tobacco is inserted is as large as a coffee cup and decorated with such skilfully carved motifs that I could scarcely believe that it was local work, but this fact was so consistently maintained that I was finally persuaded.'

This description could apply to pipes from many different regions of Africa in existence at the end of the nineteenth and beginning of the twentieth century. Since Caillié rarely mentioned the beauty of the objects that he saw during his travels, his reference to the 'skilfully carved motifs' takes on that much more importance.

African pipes were made of different materials and in an endless variety of designs: terracotta, stone, metal, gourds, horn etc. They could be of very simple design, with bowl and stem (generally long) made up of plain but no less graceful forms (fig. 147). Others were artfully decorated, adding a visual pleasure to the use of a cherished personal object or giving expression to differences in social status which such elaborate ornamentation implies.

The superbly crafted Mumuye pipe from Nigeria in the Barbier-Mueller Museum (fig. 148) could only have belonged to a nobleman. The complex forms reflect the enigmatic structure of Mumuye statuary, which never reproduces the human form realistically. The treatment of the torso as a hollow and of the shoulders as a horizontal bar demonstrates great formal ingenuity.

Many of the pipe bowls had lids, as we can see in this Dakakari model from northern Nigeria (fig. 149), which also stands on legs and is topped with a small bird. These surprising features probably alluded to a now-forgotten legend or traditional myth. This finely decorated pipe was made by the lost-wax process and was intended for a high official.

The number and variety of pipes was perhaps greater in Cameroon than anywhere else. Bamessing, a major centre

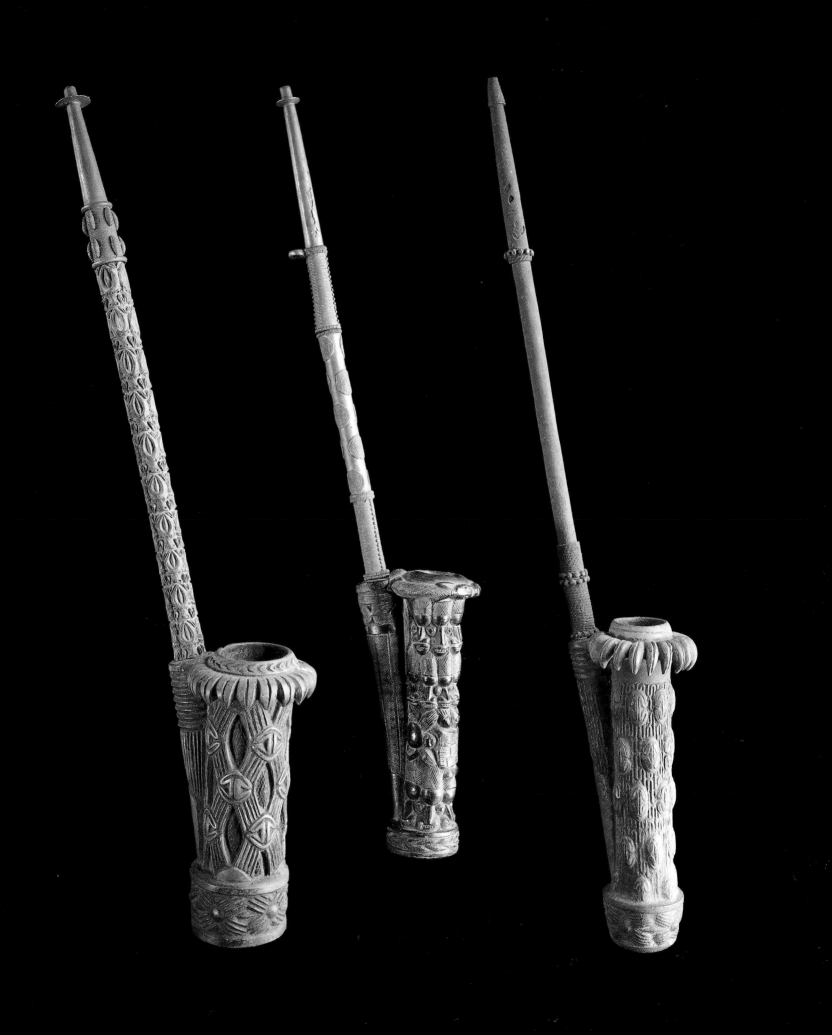

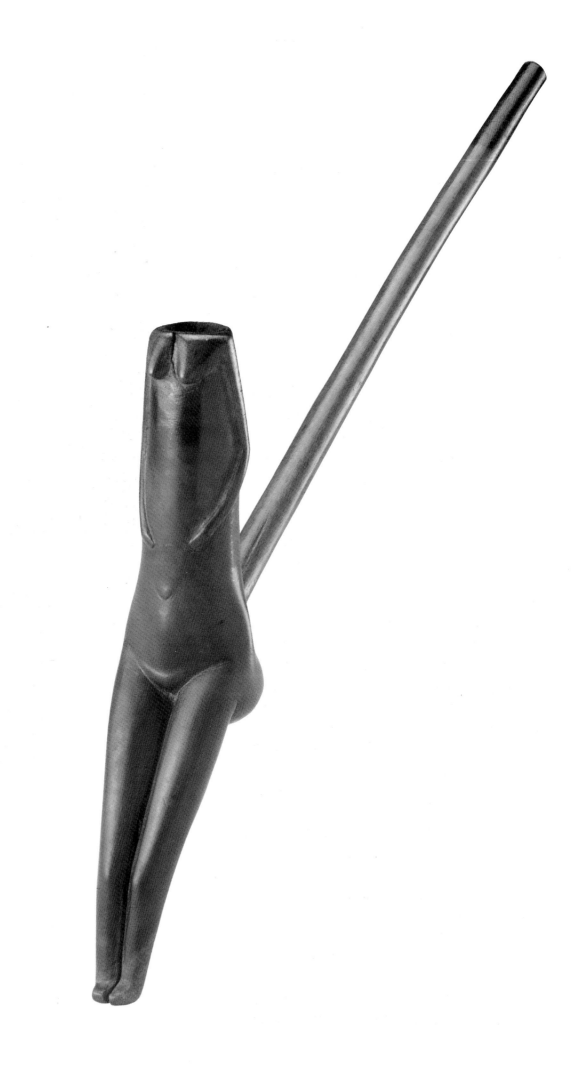

of pottery-making, was famous for its terracotta pipes, which only men were allowed to manufacture and only the smallest models, known as 'travelling pipes', were really smoked. The stem was long because of the poor quality of African tobacco, which is very strong. This is the reason why prestigious pipes, which could have stems of up to two metres long, were not actually used for smoking. Dignitaries would only touch their mouths to the stems during official ceremonies. The king's pipe was carried behind him by a servant.

The decoration of pipes in Cameroon was regulated by a strict code: geometric patterns were good enough for the common man, but high-ranking members of the brotherhoods could indulge in zoomorphic imagery, especially if the animals represented were related to their totems. Only the highest ranking chiefs and members of the royal family were allowed to have pipes with anthropomorphic motifs.

The pipes of the Bamum tribe had bowls made of terracotta or brass. King Njoya was known for the richly decorated pipes that he gave as wedding presents, but none could rival the one he offered as a token of gratitude to Glauning, the German captain who lent him his support during a tribal uprising (fig. 150). This pipe is one of the outstanding masterpieces of Bamum art. The stylized chameleons on the terracotta bowl symbolize fertility, justice and social peace. The pipe can be rested in a balanced position on the ground thanks to the puffy-cheeked face, a popular motif in Bamum art which can be seen on many masks. The stem is formed by a series of four royal servants which were cast by the lost-wax process.

Other profusely decorated pipes (fig. 151) combined several different kinds of motifs: spiders and frogs, toads, or heads of noblemen. Not infrequently, one can find pipes with beadwork stems decorated with lozenge patterns (fig. 152).

At the southern end of the continent, an anonymous Zulu sculptor carved a wooden pipe in the shape of a woman's body, creating an object of rare elegance, even if the head-shaped lid which presumably completed it has been lost (fig. 153).

Ground into a fine powder, tobacco could be taken as snuff or chewed. It was given as an offering to ancestors or

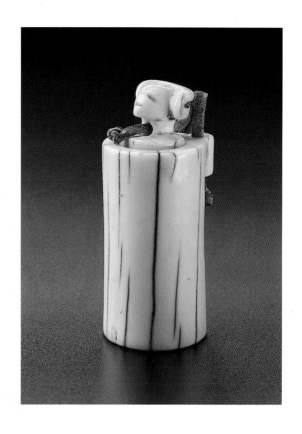

**155. Mortar
for snuff tobacco**
Tshokwe. Angola. Zaïre.
Ivory. Private collection.

Opposite

**153. Pipe
with bowl in the shape
of a woman's body**
Zulu. South Africa.
Wood. L.: 37.5 cm.
National Museum
of African Art,
Washington, D.C.

**154. Mortar
for snuff tobacco**
Tshokwe. Angola.
19th cent. Wood, glass
beads, gourd, leather,
human hair. H.: 31 cm.
Museum für Völkerkunde,
Berlin.

as a gift to friends and visitors. The old blind hunter, Ogotemmêli, Marcel Griaule's Dogon informer in Mali, was familiar with these customs: [31]

'Having sat down on his threshhold, Ogotemmêli scraped in his tobacco pouch and gathered some yellowish dust on the flap: "Tobacco," he said, "clears up the sense of judgment." And he began to reconstruct the system of the world, for one had to begin with the very beginning of things.'

In Zaïre, tobacco was ground in small wooden or ivory mortars which were sometimes decorated with tiny carved figures. Among the Tshokwe of Zaïre and Angola, these mortars were precious luxury items highly cherished by their owners. In the one reproduced here (fig. 154), the tobacco was kept in a small drum-shaped container balanced on the head of a female figure, whose elaborate hairdo suggests that she represents either the king's first wife or his mother. Other types of tobacco mortars were made out of carved ivory (fig. 155). The ground tobacco was kept in containers made from dried fruits – often decorated – or in small gourds that were hollowed out, adorned with colourful metal wires, and eventually polished to a lustrous sheen by passing through countless hands.

The kola nut, like tobacco, played a special role in African social life. Because of their high caffein content, kola nuts worked wonders against hunger and fatigue. They were offered to friends and visitors on special trays as a token of hospitality. These trays were often decorated with symmetrically opposed heads to express the conviviality and reciprocity which they fostered.

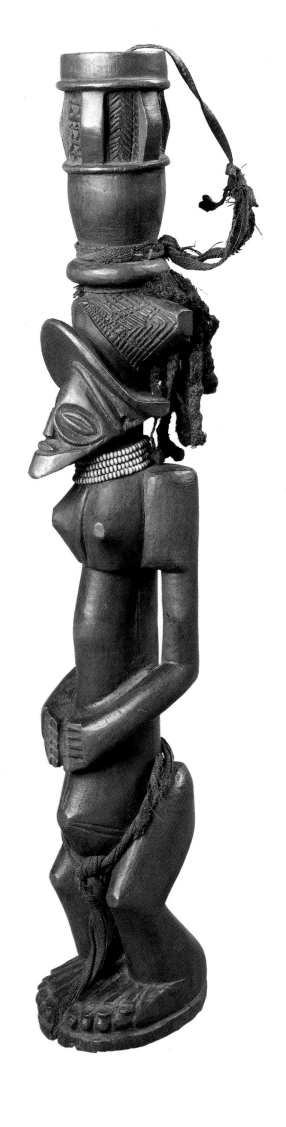

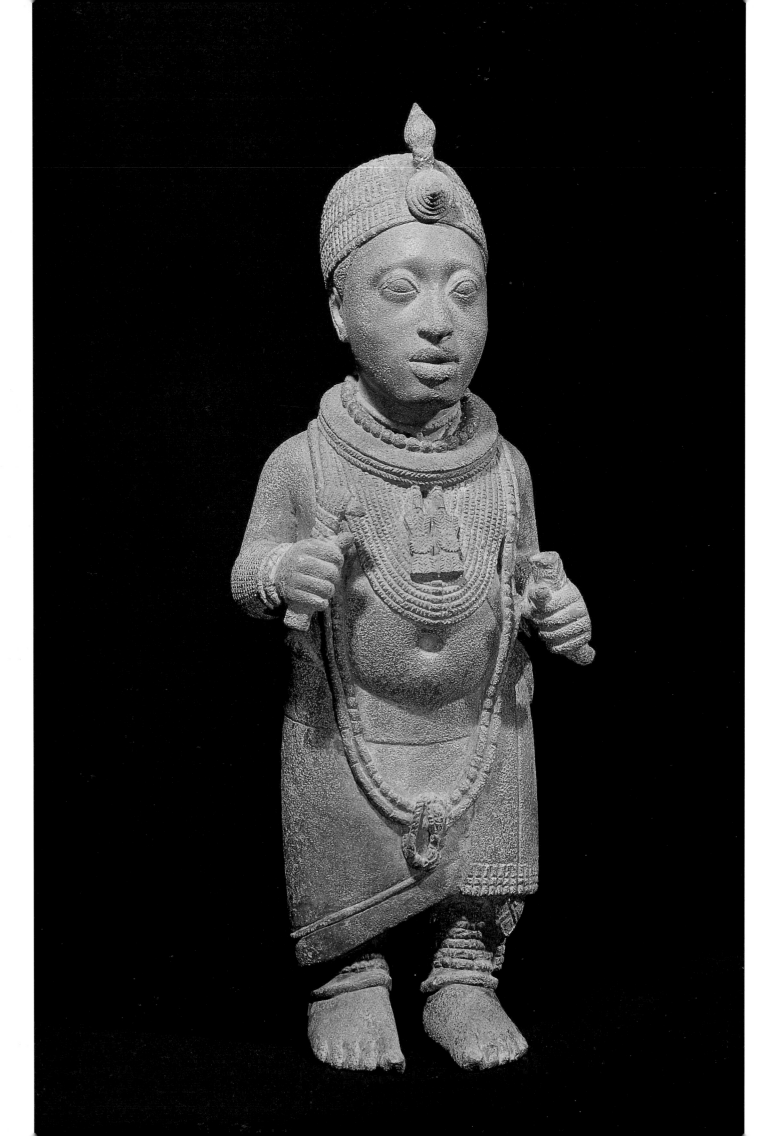

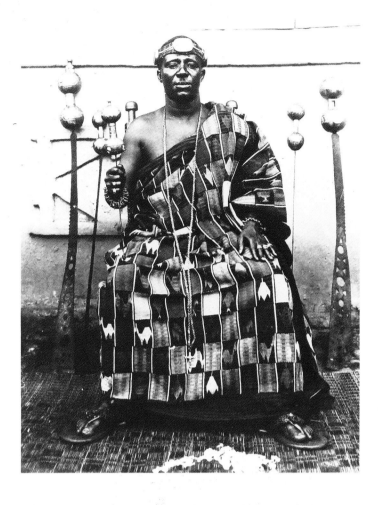

Regalia, privilege of the great chiefs

Of the different types of objects that we have discussed until now, many could be owned by those who were not descended from a noble lineage. It was a matter of respecting the rules fixed by tradition and having enough wealth to hire good craftsmen. Anyone could smoke tobacco, for example, as long as they chose the type of pipe that corresponded to their rank in the social hierarchy. There were chairs and stools for everyone, but only the chiefs had the right and the means to avail themselves of the most prestigious and lavishly decorated models. The same went for fabrics, weapons, musical instruments, jewellery, adornments, and even spoons. In these various categories, the royal object could be distinguished from the common object by the superior degree of refinement that it displayed; yet the distinction between the two was not always so clear cut.

In the pages that follow, we will present objects that were the privileged possessions and prerogative of the chiefs and monarchs alone; objects constituting what is called the *regalia*. No one would have claimed possession of these objects unless they belonged to the royal family or an aristocratic lineage, for these were the tangible symbols of social power.

This was precisely the reason why the regalia were created: to translate into visible form the basis of the chief's

157. Antonin Dioulo (Nampε), King of the Ebrie and the Atye at the age of 40

Photograph taken before WWII.
This king was born in 1889 and died in 1961. During the colonial period, he bore the title of Customary Chief of the Ebrie and Atye. The band on his forehead bears a gold repoussé plaque representing a lion seizing a panther, a royal symbol. Draped in a silk gown like a toga, the king wears gold rings and a long gold chain with a crucifix, because he was Catholic. He also wore a chain (not shown here) with the family emblem, a barracuda. In his right hand, he holds a sceptre. Ritual swords stand on either side of him. Their steel blades are carved with openwork designs; these were not combat weapons.

Opposite

156. Statuette of an oni
Ife. Nigeria. 14th–early 15th cent. Brass with zinc content. H.: 47.1 cm. Museum of Ife Antiquities.

169

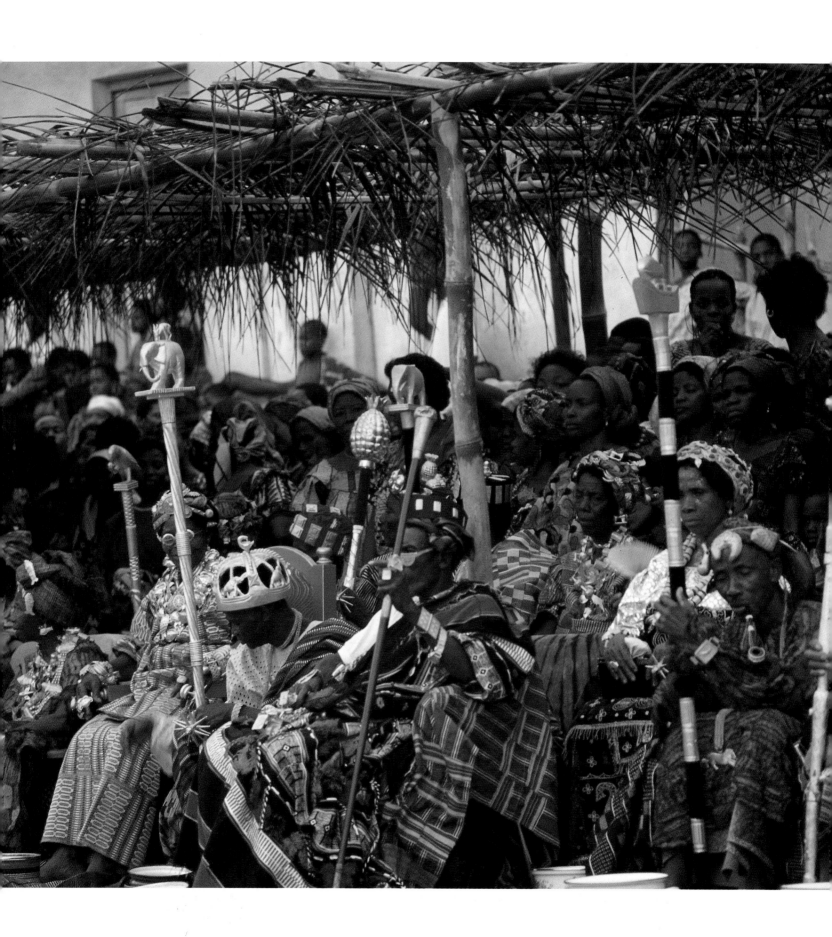

domination. In order to be entitled to possess such an object, one had to be able to justify one's lineage, which could be of divine origin – as was the case in the Kingdom of Benin or among the Yoruba – or through mortal ancestors who could transmit their virtues.

In the second case, one had to assume great powers, including protecting one's subjects from outside enemies, as well as from sickness and death. As the embodiment of the health of his people, the ruler had to display unflagging vigour and invulnerability. He had to appear as a superior being compared with the ordinary run of mortals; a unique and even divine being, who did not have the same physical needs as his subjects. Accordingly, he could neither eat nor drink in public.

Passages from Olfert Dapper's *Description of Africa* (1668)[32] give us a glimpse of some aspects of life at the court of Loango (today's People's Republic of Congo) as it appeared in the seventeenth century. Referring to the king's meal, he wrote:

'Having served, the head butler retires, leaving the King alone, and closes the door; for no man nor beast dare witness the King eating or drinking, under penalty of death. This sentence is so rigorously executed that one day, when a very handsome dog which the Portuguese had offered to the King, and which had become the apple of his eye, broke loose from his keeper and intruded into the chamber while the King was eating .... he was sadly rewarded for his affection: the King, summoning his guards, had the animal seized and killed on the spot .... On another occasion, a small child who happened to fall asleep at the King's side and awaken as he was drinking, was condemned to death.'

When the king wants to drink, 'an attendant presents with him the cup with his back turned, and likewise takes it back'. Generally speaking, the king lived hidden from the curious gazes of the public.

'The King leaves his palace only on the days when solemn occasions are celebrated .... A large space in the middle of the town is chosen for this pomp and the throne is raised. It is a black and white wicker chair .... Seven or eight fans are held around the King .... People are hired to keep these fans moving in circles, and this motion provides a great deal of coolness.'

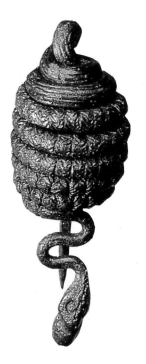

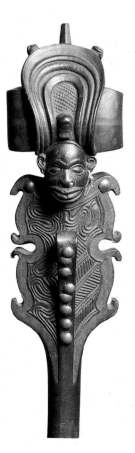

Opposite

158. Feast of Generation
Adiukru. Ivory Coast. Photo Library of the Barbier-Mueller Museum, Geneva.

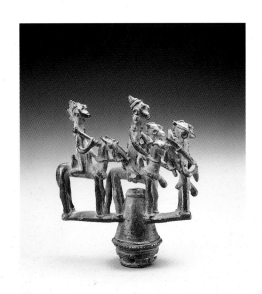

161. Staff ornament
Soninke. Guinea-Bissau.
Bronze with dark
grey-green patina.
The staff was made
of steel. Overall
H.: 135 cm. Height
of the figures: 17 cm.
Barbier-Mueller Museum,
Geneva.

Opposite

162. Sceptre
Luba. Zaïre. Workshop
of the Lukuga. Wood,
copper. H.: 116 cm.
(with top). Private
collection.

Page 171

159. Staff ornament
Igbo-Ukwu. Nigeria.
9th–10th cent. Bronze
with lead content.
National Museum, Lagos.

160. Sceptre
Tshokwe. Angola. 19th
cent. Wood, brass studs.
H.: 32 cm. Museum für
Völkerkunde, Berlin.

The court of the Kingdom of Loango referred to here is a typical example. The major African states were formed to the north and south of the great equatorial jungle, that is, in West Africa and in the Zaïre River basin.

In the region around present-day Mali, between the ninth and the fifteenth centuries, the great empires of Ghana, Mali and Songhaï came and went. In what is today called Nigeria, the Ife Kingdom prospered from the twelfth century onwards, and was relayed by the Benin empire between the fifteenth and nineteenth centuries. In Ghana, the Akan kingdoms established a courtly culture in the eighteenth and nineteenth centuries which attached a great deal of importance to gold regalia. During this same period, the neighbouring Kingdom of Dahomey also maintained a powerful court.

South of the Equator, in Zaïre, as early as the fifteenth century, the Kingdom of Kongo and then the Kingdom of the Kuba rose to eminence and sustained a thriving court art. The nineteenth-century kingdoms of the Luba, Tshokwe and Mangbetu also left vestiges of a highly refined lifestyle.

In between these two great cultural centres to the north and south, the jungles of the Equatorial zone seriously hindered the communication necessary for the creation of vast states. The jungle also had a dispersive effect on political power. In the grasslands of Cameroon, on the other hand, the conditions were optimal for concentrating the power of many chiefdoms in a royal court, as did King Njoya of the Bamum, and also the Bamileke chieftains.

All of these kings and mighty chiefs disposed of a treasury which provided the means to attract the most qualified artisans to the court, where they were handsomely remunerated. The objects which they crafted further enhanced the prestige of the rulers by their beauty. The Africans, who are very sensitive to aesthetic beauty, immediately got the message. The specialized artisans who worked at the court, or in the service of a chief, more often than not belonged to a guild or caste from which they had learned the techniques and traditions of their craft.

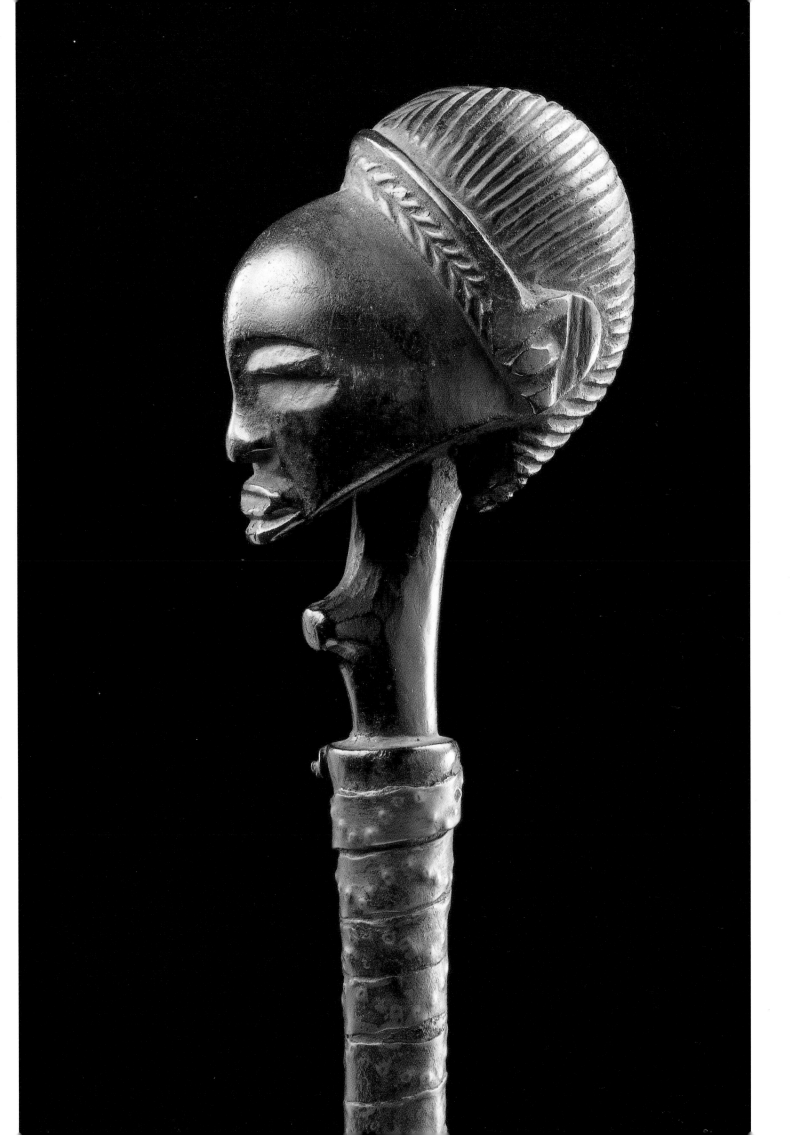

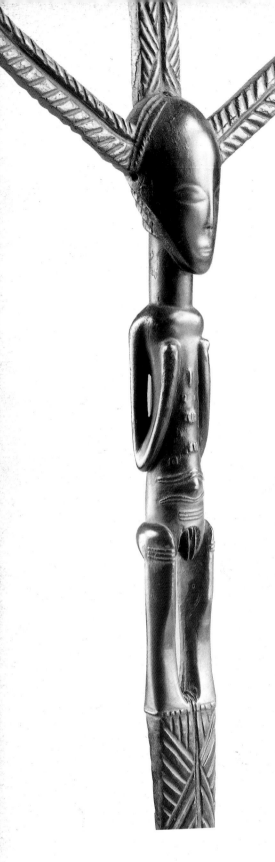

164. Arrow-holder
Luba. Zaïre. Workshop
near Malemba-Nkulu.
Wood. H.: 89 cm.
Private collection.

Opposite

163. Sceptre
Luba. Zaïre. Workshop near
Mwanza. Wood, steel,
glass beads. H.: 151 cm.
Private collection.

What counted as regalia?

Notwithstanding the variations due to differences in time and space, a certain coherence may be observed. A small fourteenth-century statue from the Kingdom of Ife (fig. 156) shows the king, or *oni*, arrayed with the traditional symbols of royalty: on his head, a crown topped by a flame; around his neck, a heavy bead necklace, an additional and even heavier bead necklace around his torso, and smaller rows of beads on his chest. The double-knot pendant in the middle of his chest has been observed on other figures and may also have been a royal insignia. The ram's horn held in the left hand was filled with magic substances, while the beaded sceptre in his right hand symbolized his royal authority.

This statuette presents analogies with two photographs from modern times. The first (fig. 157) shows the king of the Ebrie, who lived in the Ivory Coast from 1889 to 1961; the second (fig. 158) is a contemporary version of the Feast of Generation in the Ivory Coast. These documents demonstrate the continuity of certain attributes of kings and other officials: the sceptre or staff of office (which took a variety of forms elsewhere), the pectoral hung from a chain or necklace, and the crown.

The basic attributes could be accompanied by such accessories as parasols, whips, fly whisks, and fans. These traditional objects today seem to be losing ground, but, as the picture of the Feast of Generation shows, the staffs of office are still very much in vogue.

Batons and staffs of office

These staffs, whether in the form of an actual staff, baton or sceptre, have always been an attribute of African kings. In some cases, they are phallic symbols alluding to the potency and fertility which is associated with royalty. Some very fine specimens from the tenth century were found in excavations at Igbo-Ukwu in Nigeria (fig. 159). Made of a bronze and lead alloy, they were fixed to the top of iron or wooden staffs. The figure of the snake, which probably had a ritual significance, appears on a number of these batons and

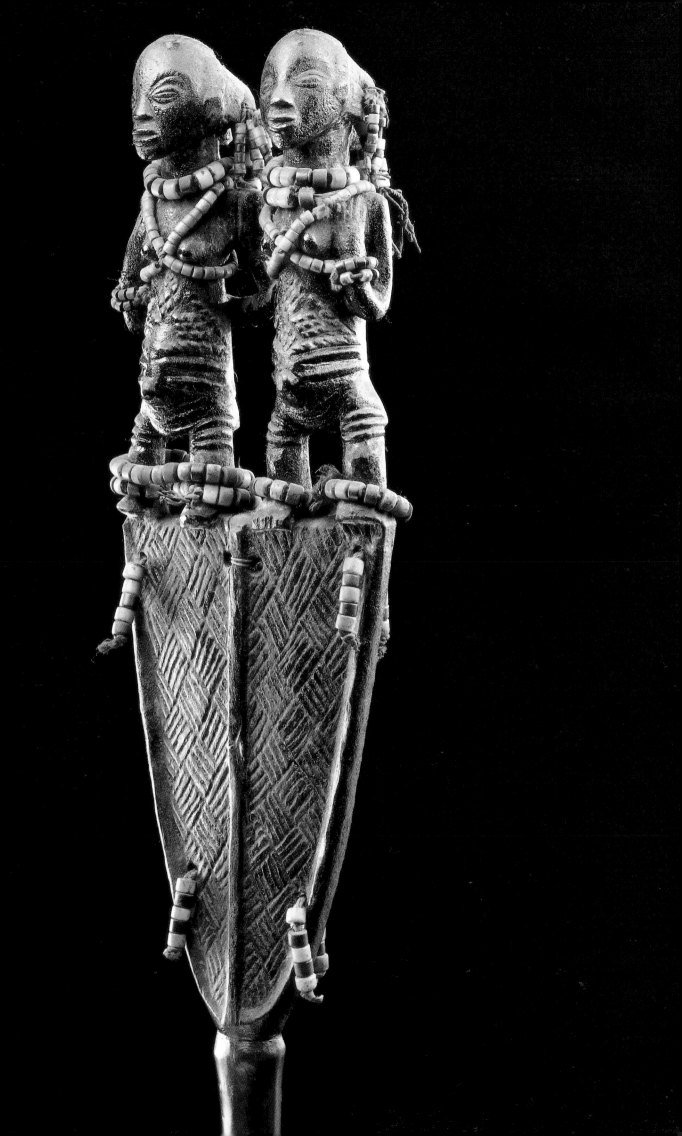

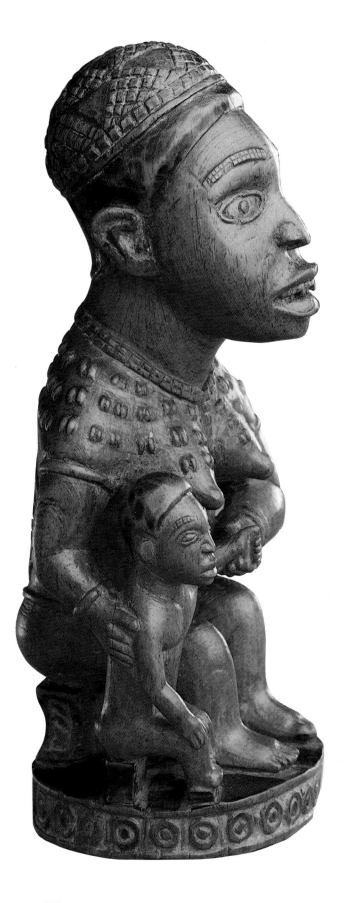

enhances them with its graceful curves. On other specimens, glass-bead incrustations lend a colourful accent to the bronze.

The staff ornament once owned by a Soninke chief from Guinea-Brissau (fig. 161) displays a more warlike aspect. Made with the lost-wax process, it is composed of a group of bronze figures on top of an iron rod decorated at regular intervals with bronze rings. According to one tradition, this object belonged to King Mamedi Pate, who ruled around 1870–80, but it could be one or two centuries older, for the lost-wax technique is no longer used in Guinea-Bissau. It permitted a very stylized rendering that perfectly depicts the attitudes and expressions of the figures, as well as a detailed rendering of the soldiers' weapons and of the horses with all their trappings – all of which signified their prestige. The artist skilfully represented their movement and energy.

The sceptre was such an important symbol of royal power that, even when it was not in the hands of the ruler, it was treated with the respect due to the personage of the king. This was the case among the Dan of the Ivory Coast, and even more so among the tribes of Zaïre: the Tshokwe, the Pende, the Lunda, the Luba, and the Songye. These sceptres were usually crowned by a figure representing the founder of the clan.

Thus, the likeness of the famous hunter Tshibinda Ilunga may be seen at the top of a Tshokwe sceptre from Angola (fig. 160). He is easily recognizable by the round headdress which frames his forehead and expresses his authority. This figure on the sceptre alludes to the noble Lunda ancestors who established their domination over the Tshokwe in the seventeenth century. The most admirable feature of this work is the ease with which the artist succeeded in harmonizing its figurative elements with its abstract ornamentation.

The sceptre also had a great importance for the Luba of Zaïre: it was kept hidden most of the time and displayed only on special occasions. To celebrate a military victory, the chief's first wife would plant it amid the bodies of the fallen enemy. This gesture both asserted and represented the identity of the community. In times of war, the people were prepared to defend the sceptre with their lives. It was a symbol of the king's power, but he could also authorize certain vassals to own one.

The Luba sceptres were composed of cylindrical staffs wrapped with strips of copper, and they could be planted into the ground. They were sometimes crowned by one or more female figures, and in some cases, only by a carved head (fig. 162), which thus took on great significance. The founding and protecting mother illustrated here radiates an admirably rendered strength and austerity.

Other Luba sceptres of more complex construction featured a palette of geometric patterns imitated from basketwork. These palettes often take on the form of an oar-blade, an allusion to the remote past, when the ancestors of the Luba were fishermen. Above this flat surface there were one or two free-standing female figures (fig. 163), always endowed with the serene harmony which characterizes the Luba sculptures.

Before taking leave of the Luba, we should mention a variation of the sceptre that was specific to this tribe and that was together with the spear, another royal attribute: this was the arrow-holder,* which probably developed out of a hunting accessory that permitted a bow and arrows to be always ready at hand. On top of a long carved staff, we see a female figurine from whose head radiate three branches carved out of the same piece of wood and covered with metal (fig. 164). A metal point permitted the arrow-holder to be stuck in the ground. It could be placed outside the king's dwelling at night but could never be entrusted to a messenger for it had a sacred significance. Only a woman of very high rank could have the privilege of its safekeeping. The arrow-holder refers to the bow and arrow attributes of the famous hunter, Kalala Ilunga, the hero of a mythological epic. The female statuette personifies the mother of the clan. The object as a whole therefore symbolizes the power of the king and the supreme authority conferred on him by his ancestors. The female statuette associated with the Luba arrow-holder is always of a high aesthetic quality. Being the link between the sacred realm and secular power, it expresses the serenity of the spirit with its flowing and harmonious forms.

The Yombe tribe at the mouth of the Zaïre River had similar insignia of rank, often crowned by a female figure (fig. 165). The meaning of the carved wooden figure

Opposite

165. Staff ornament
Yombe. Lower Zaïre.
Hardwood. Red patina.
H.: 23 cm.
Barbier-Mueller Museum,
Geneva.

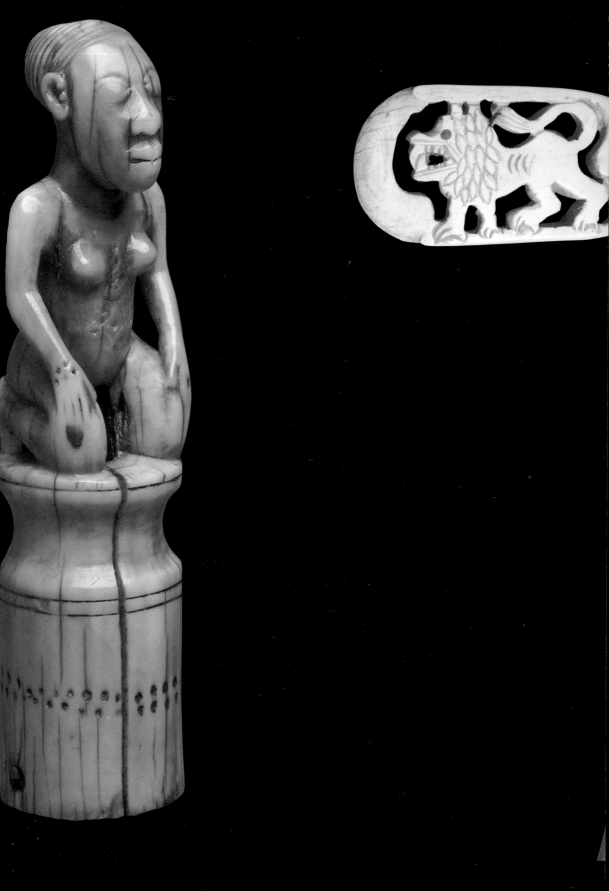

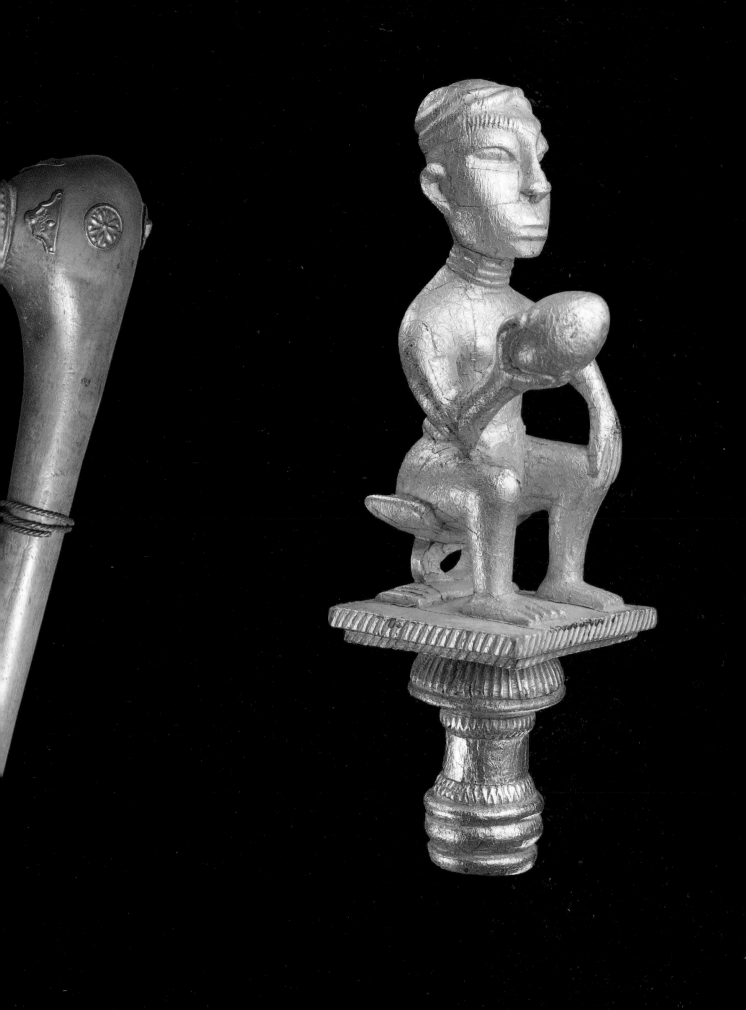

166. Staff or whip ornament
Yombe. Lower-Zaïre.
Ivory with brown patina.
H.: 15 cm. Barbier-
Mueller Museum, Geneva.

167. Recado of King Glele
Fon. Formerly Dahomey.
Republic of Benin. Ivory
and wood. H.: 38 cm.
Length of ivory plaque:
13.5 cm. Musée de
l'Homme, Paris.

168. Ornament from messenger's staff
Seated male figure
holding an egg.
Akan/Ashanti. Ghana.
Carved wood covered
with gold leaf.
H.: 30.7 cm.
Barbier-Mueller Museum,
Geneva.

This staff ornament was
probably carved around
1960–70 by Kojo Bonsu
from Kumasi, who is still
active today. He is
the son of the famous
Ashanti sculptor Osei
Bonsu. The carved egg
illustrates a proverb
which says in essence:
'I am like power: hold
me too tightly, and I will
break; but let me go,
and I will break into
pieces on the ground.'

illustrated here is obvious: the woman depicted is the mythical female founder of the clan lineage, and she is shown in the company of a descendant placed under her protection. This explains why this figure is depicted wearing masculine insignia like the crown, symbol of sovereignty. Despite her authoritative role, her face shows the smiling, almost affectionate expression of a mother with her children. Her shoulders and chest display the ritual scars proper to her clan, rendered with as much care as all the other details.

Another Yombe female figurine (fig. 166) which probably formed the end of a staff or whip must also be included among the regalia. The attitude of this statuette is quite different from the previous one. She personifies the wife and evokes a mythic figure, but was not intended to be read as a portrait. The status of wife is visible by the ritual scars on her breast and her submissive attitude. There are no jewels to relieve the austerity of this image carved in a deeply patinated piece of ivory.

Substitutes for the sceptre

The great prestige attached to the sceptre, even in the absence of the king, helps to explain the significance of the batons or staffs of office held by the various representatives of the monarch and his messengers.

One of the best-known objects in this connexion is the *recado* (a word of Portuguese origin) from former Dahomey. It symbolized the transmission of authority delegated by the king upon the appointment of a chief. Originally, it was a staff with a curved top, not unlike a hoe. The recado, first carried by warriors, later became a royal emblem, and the curved end was progressively decorated with motifs carved out of wood, and later of metal or ivory. These staffs represented the qualities that the respective kings wanted to have associated with their names, or what in Europe would be called 'mottoes'. Thus the recado belonging to Glele, the next-to-last king of independent Dahomey, featured a lion with coral eyes (fig. 167), for it was said: 'The lion's teeth have grown and he is feared by all.' King Ghezo, a despotic ruler of the nineteenth century, used the blacksmith's anvil as his emblem. However, not all leaders wanted to communicate so fearsome an image: a seventeenth-century king who had waited a long time for his accession to the throne chose the chameleon as his device, for 'it advances slowly, but reaches the top of the tree.'

The recado could be borne by the king, who held it in his hand or let it hang from his shoulder, or allowed it to be held by one of his representative chiefs. The chiefs also received attributes upon their appointment to office: a parasol and a stool similar to the kind made by the Ashanti. Under certain circumstances, the recado was carried by a messenger to authenticate the order to be transmitted.

This last function was also ascribed to the herald's batons (or linguist's batons) which have been used in Ghana among the Ashanti since the seventeenth century. Garrard, in his essay in *Gold of Africa*, writes that the use of herald's batons was of European origin; they were brought to the Gold Coast by merchants and given to the chiefs and dignitaries. Their purpose was, and still is, to serve as the accreditation of a messenger. Originally crowned with silver-plated figurines, at the end of the nineteenth century these staffs began to be decorated with fine wooden carvings covered with gold leaf. The figures often represent animals endowed with symbolic meanings or associated with a proverb. One of these figures (fig. 168) represents a man holding up an egg; an allusion to the tact that a ruler must demonstrate in the conduct of his office, for the use of excessive force can have dire consequences.

The technique of covering wooden sculptures with gold leaf was also used to create a variety of other regalia specific to the courts of the Akan and Baule rulers (Ghana and Ivory Coast).

Parasols, fly-whisks and fans

These picturesque accessories have greatly contributed to the pageantry and colourful appearance of the African courts.

Parasols were very often used in the courts of West Africa, where they were introduced as early as the fourteenth century through contacts with Egypt. Their use is documented among

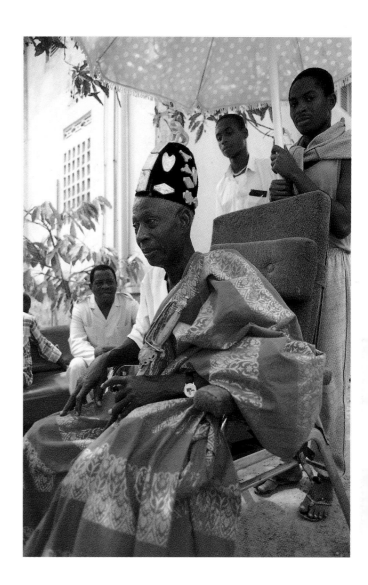

169. Nana Osei Bonzou II, Anyi king of Indenie
Ivory Coast. Photo Library of the Barbier-Mueller Museum, Geneva.

The ruler sits in his palace at Abengourou, under a silk parasol. His crown is decorated with gold motifs. Draped across his shoulder is a sumptuous fabric with brocade designs.

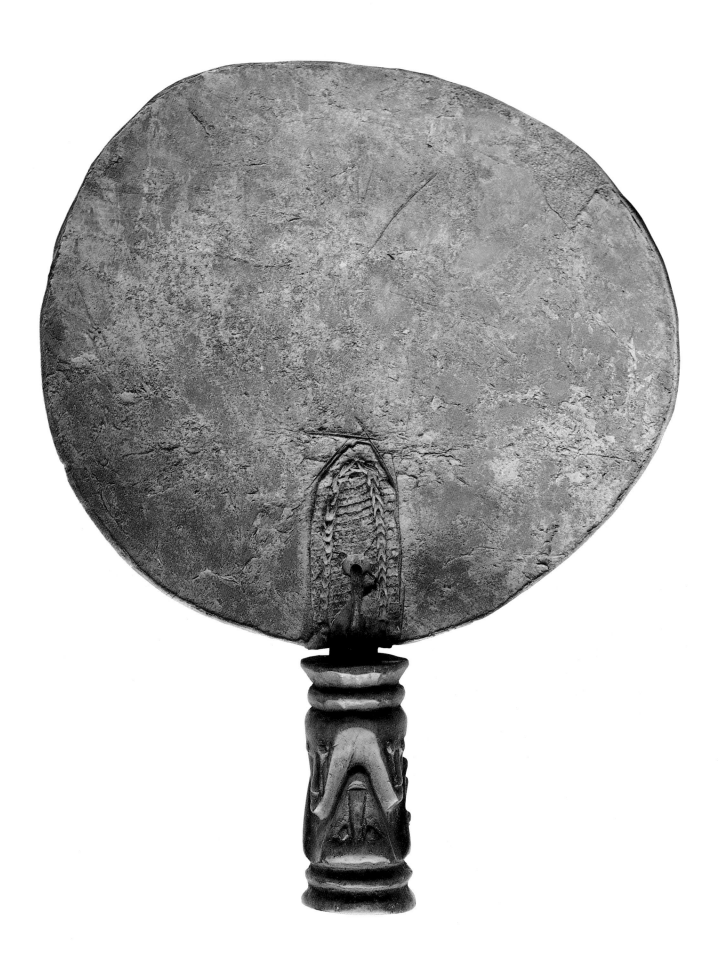

the Akan starting in the seventeenth century. Like the messengers' batons, these brightly coloured silk domes were surmounted by a wooden sculpture covered with gold leaf that invariably had an emblematic significance (fig. 169). Often, the same craftsmen carved the parasol tops and the messengers' batons.

The fly-whisk, like the parasol, was intended to protect the king from environmental nuisances and was fairly often to be found in African courts. Its use was the sole privilege of the ruler. More often than not, these fly-whisks were made with a wooden, metal or ivory handle, from which hung a long tuft of animal hair. At Igbo-Ukwu, a bronze fly-whisk handle decorated with the figure of a mounted horseman was unearthed; it probably dates from the tenth century and the original animal-hair has been lost. The rider's face, with its sombre expression and deeply etched ritual scars, makes this object a remarkable work of art in its own right.

This type of fly-whisk continued to be produced through the nineteenth century, when models of extreme luxury were made – with hair from an elephant's tail attached to a gold-leaf handle.

Also in the nineteenth century also, another type of fly-whisk was made with a leather plate replacing the animal hairs. This type of fly-whisk was fairly common among the Fang of Gabon. The handle could be carved with geometric designs or in the shape of a human figure (fig. 170). In the specimen reproduced here, the figure represented has four impressively stylized and austere faces. Like the staffs of office, these objects were part of the regalia of kings who, although they did not rule over vast territories, liked to have fine objects at their disposal.

This type of round fly-whisk looks very much like a fan, and in all likelihood had a dual function. It was the duty of a slave standing behind the king to wave this fan during the ruler's public appearances. On these occasions, the king displayed all the attributes of his office, as Olfert Dapper described them at the court of King Loango.

Opposite

179. Fly-whisk
Fang. Gabon.
Hardwood and elephant or hippopotamus hide.
Overall length: 29.3 cm.
Handle: 8.2 cm. Barbier-Mueller Museum, Geneva.

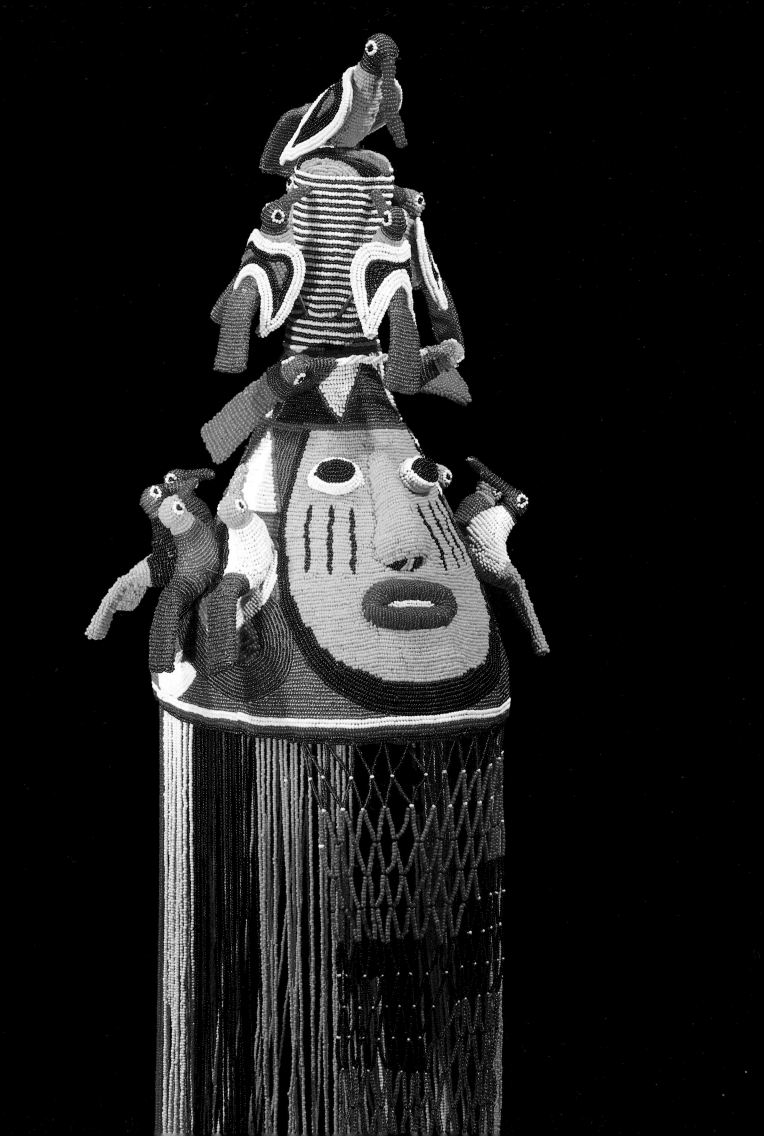

Royal adornments

Like the Ife king mentioned at the beginning of this chapter (fig. 156), and in addition to their many jewels, the African kings and chieftains generally owned property that was the exclusive prerogative of their rank. This consisted mainly of crowns and pendants, and also in some cases special sandals.

The wearing of a crown was by no means a general practice. The crowns worn by the Akan of Ghana were not particulary characteristic, and often reflected European influence. These included headdresses of various shapes made of red or black velvet dotted with gold ornaments. Examples from the Ivory Coast can be seen on the photograph of the Feast of Generation (fig. 158) and on that of the King of Indenie (fig. 169). Velvet bands, like those worn by the king of the Ebrie (fig. 157), were often decorated with symbolic gold ornaments.

Unlike the Akan, the Yoruba of Nigeria used, and still use, crowns of a very typical design (figs. 171 and 172). These are entirely covered with brightly coloured beadwork, surmounted by all sorts of animal figures, and feature a long beadwork veil which completely covers the monarch's face. The staff of office which he held was also covered with beadwork ornaments. Such regalia made for a grandiose spectacle when the king appeared before his subjects.

Sandals were not generally worn outside African towns and cities. They were, however, worn by high officials for purposes of prestige, and the ones decorated with gold may be included among the regalia. This was the case with the Akan, who attributed a talismanic significance to the gold-leaf covered designs with which they decorated their sandals.

Georges Balandier[33] quotes a description written around 1590 by Pigafetta, a traveller in the Kingdom of Congo (Zaïre), to the effect that, under the influence of the Portuguese, 'the worthies of the court began to wear hats and bonnets, leather and velvet sandals, and even short boots in the Portuguese style'. These adopted fashions proved to be a short-lived phenomenon.

Pectoral pendants, a more specifically African accessory, were often among the regalia worn by kings during official ceremonies.

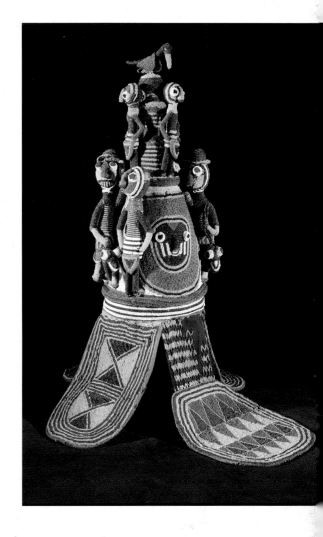

172. Beadwork crown
Yoruba. Nigeria. The
Brooklyn Museum, N.Y.

Opposite

**171. Beadwork crown
with sixteen bird
figures**
Yoruba. Nigeria.
H.: 84 cm.
National Museum, Lagos.

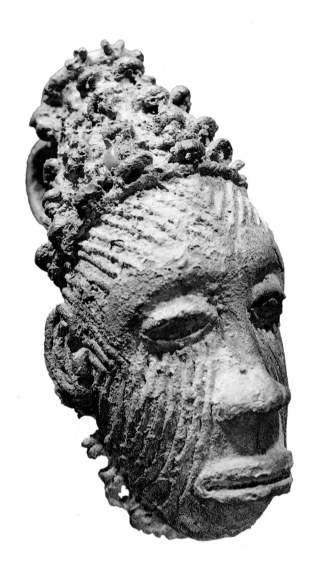

**173. Pendant
in the shape
of a human head**
Igbo-Ukwu. Nigeria.
9th–10th cent. Bronze
with lead content.
H.: 7.6 cm.
National Museum, Lagos.

With its expressionistic
tension and humanity,
this remarkable work
ranks among the
masterpieces of the Ife
arts of Benin. It also
bears favourable
comparison with major
European sculpture.

Opposite

**174. Mask-shaped
pendant**
Kingdom of Edo, Benin.
Nigeria. 16th cent.
Bronze. H.: 17.9 cm.
Barbier-Mueller Museum,
Geneva.

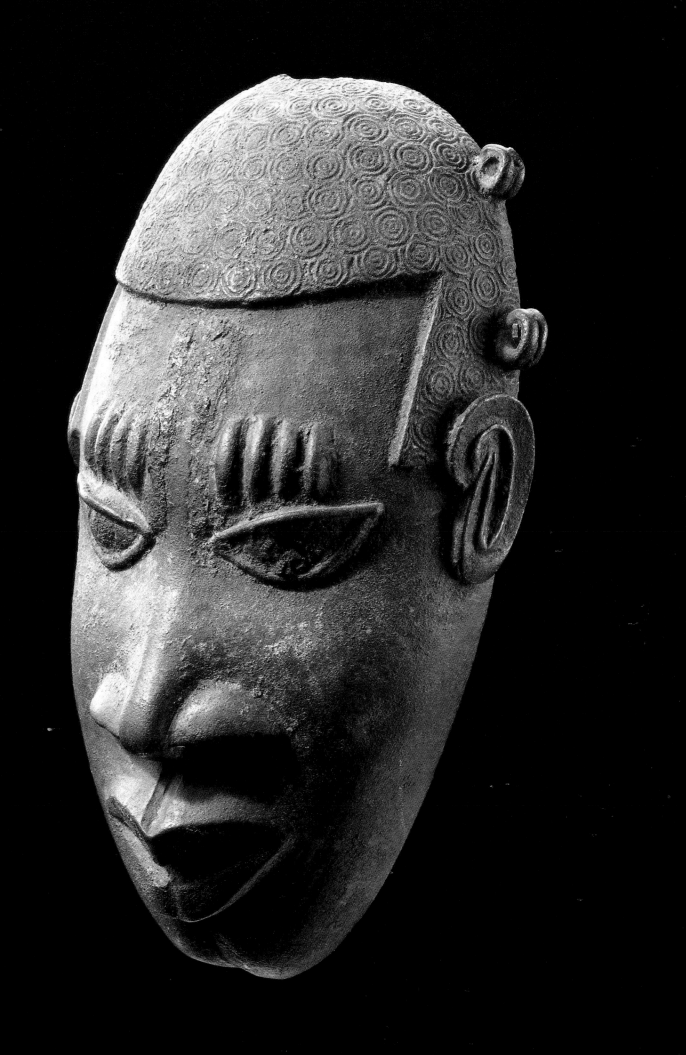

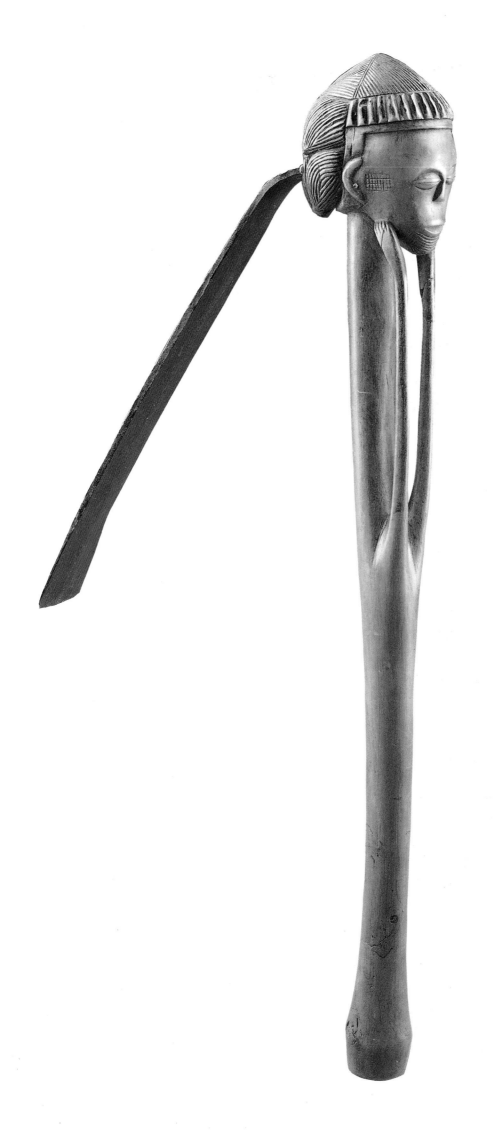

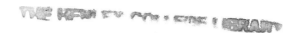

Pectoral pendants

Like the figure of the Ife king represented with a double-knot pendant (fig. 156) as part of his royal insignia, many other African rulers wore metal or ivory pendants hung on their chests or slung on the side as integral parts of their regalia.

A number of highly enigmatic cast-bronze pendants have been found at Igbo-Ukwu among the scores of ritual objects brought to light. They probably date from the tenth century and one of these is in the form of an admirably depicted human head (fig. 173). Professor Willett believes that it was part of an official's ceremonial costume and was worn slung on the hip, like similar objects belonging to the kings of Benin. One such pendant, carved in ivory, is among the highlights of the African collections at the British Museum. There is no evidence to suggest that the mask-shaped pendants from Igbo-Ukwu were primarily intended for religious rituals, as was the case in Benin.

Among the more recent objects, the mask-shaped pendant from the Kingdom of Edo in Benin (fig. 174) has a more clearly identifiable meaning. It dates to the beginnings of the Edo monarchy, around the sixteenth century, a period of great military expansion which saw many neighbouring chiefs become vassals of the King of Benin. To symbolize the new ties, the defeated chieftains were given these head- or mask-shaped pendants. This tradition has continued, and even today, similar mask pendants are worn by the Igala and Yoruba chieftains in the neighbouring areas around Benin. Made of brass that was cast with the lost-wax process, the face displays an elegant stylization which sets off the firm modelling of features that seem to quiver with life. The eyes are lowered, possibly as a gesture of respect for the king, and above them are the four lines which, still today, identify immigrants to Benin. The ears, carved without any concern for realism, have been reduced to ornamental motifs similar to seashells.

The adze

In addition to the prestigious insignia discussed above, African monarchs and chieftains very often bore superbly

Opposite

175. Ceremonial adze
Luba, Kasaï. Zaïre. Made before 1930. Iron, wood.
Length of handle: 47 cm.
Length of blade: 25.7 cm.
Private collection.

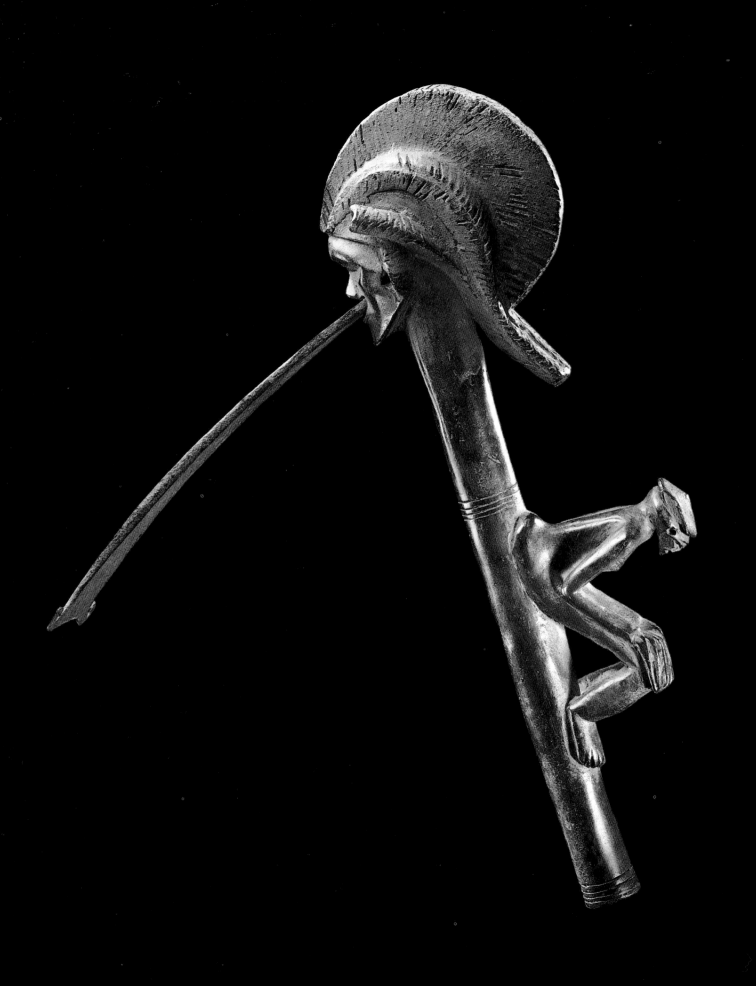

crafted weapons that rivalled jewellery in the beauty of the their design. The tribes of Zaïre distinguished themselves by the use of the *herminette*, or adze, which was neither a tool nor a weapon, but an object permitting the royal rank and status of its bearer to be ascertained. The adze differs from the axe by its elongated blade, which is set perpendicular to the handle. These objects were carried hanging from the shoulder, like the recados of Dahomey, but, unlike the latter, they were not designed to give an emblematic expression of the qualities with which the monarchs wanted to be associated in the minds of the people.

These ceremonial adzes are frequently found among the Luba and the Pende. Those of the Luba from Kasaï (fig. 175) are noteworthy for the wonderful female heads and figures sculpted on the handles. From the heavy-lidded, half-closed eyes and the harmonious composition of the forms, there emanates a feeling of great serenity. Here, once again, the adze represents the Great Mother figure which is so often found in the art of the Luba.

The forms of the adze among the Pende are more accentuated (fig. 176). Male heads are often shown, and the blade very often takes the form of a beard or elongated tongue. The beauty of the figures represented on the handles fulfils the aesthetic standards required of regalia.

Indeed, technical perfection and great formal and ornamental creativity are what all the objects discussed in this chapter have in common. This is also what distinguishes them from those used in the more mundane contexts of tribal life. Artists of recognized ability were very generously rewarded. More often than not, they lived within the immediate environs of the royal precincts. This was the case in Benin and among the Bamum. But even if the artisan remained in his village, he felt himself bound to deliver only a perfectly finished piece, worthy of celebrating the power of his ruler and, through him, the glory of his ancestors. Rich materials like bronze, gold, ivory and beads were provided in ample quantity, and time was not of the essence, so that every detail of the often abundant decoration could be attended to with the necessary care.

Opposite

176. Ceremonial adze
Pende. Zaïre.
Barbier-Mueller Museum,
Geneva.

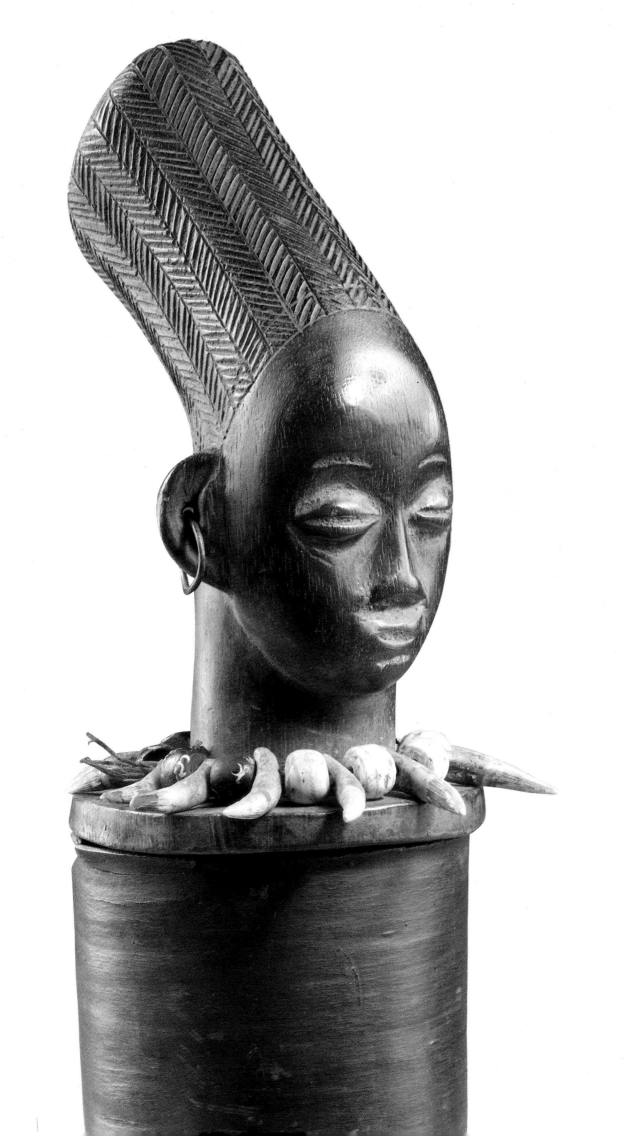

Conclusion

A brief glance through the illustrations in this book suffices to show the extent to which African art cannot be classified according to the traditional Western categories of 'Fine Art' and the 'decorative' or 'applied' arts. Ornamentation on even the finest African objects is not an extraneous element, like some decorative flourish, but an integral part of the overall design, if not its culmination. Material, form and decoration contribute equally to the quality of the work. This is to be seen in countless objects: the two large fish that form the base of the Duala chair (fig. 20, p. 31) are simultaneously form, decoration and a celebration of the wooden material out of which they were made. The same may be said of the Kuba cup with rams' horns (fig. 36, p. 46). Where does the form end and the decoration begin? By an imperceptible transition between the two, the work accedes to the status of art and presents a transfigured vision of reality.

The same unity is displayed in the design of the weapons. Their beauty is not solely the result of the patterns engraved on the blade, or of its other ornamental features. Their aesthetic value is born of the profound complementarity between the formal elements – opposing curves, menacing points – and the properties of the material – the coolness of the iron, the warmth of the copper. The successful

193

integration of these various elements is in effect what satisfies our aesthetic sense when we see these objects.

What may appear as mere decoration to the Western eye, is in fact, an inseparable part of the object for the African. This is surely the case with the Mangbetu harps (fig. 141, p. 153) and the Zande sanzas (fig. 142, p. 152). The woman embodied by the musical instrument is not an element of decoration, but the spirit of music, the poetry to which the musician aspires and ultimately the life principle itself. Without the female form, there is nothing.

These examples, which could be confirmed by countless more, prove that the visual arts in Africa are far from being limited solely to masks and ritual fetishes. The aesthetic sense of the African people can endow the humblest of objects with great beauty, irrespective of its function. The sculptors make no hard and fast distinction between objects intended for ritual purposes and those intended for everyday use. The same artists and artisans carve the religious statues and the utilitarian objects, be they spoons, stools or head-rests. To the mysterious Master of Buli has been attributed a figure with a drinking-cup* as well as a chair with caryatids (fig. 23, p. 33). The technical perfection, the concentrated facial expression and the spiritual intensity are the same in both types of objects, which only the Western mind would assign to different cultural registers.

Not surprisingly, therefore, one finds the distinctive characteristics of African sculpture remain unchanged in both types of objects: there is the same feeling for volume and the same inner density that seems to well up to the surface. This volumetric impulse is counterbalanced by the play of hollow or negative spaces that is such an important feature of African sculpture. Sufficient evidence of this may be found by surveying Bamileke works with this principle in mind. The hollow spaces are at least as important as the dense masses in the definition of the overall form. Last but not least, African objects, like the statues, are always designed according to a fluid vision of forms that avoids discontinuity and keeps the formal energy in motion.

We hope that the many objects reproduced in this book have made it clear that aesthetic sense and the need for beauty are more pervasive in Africa than in the West, for

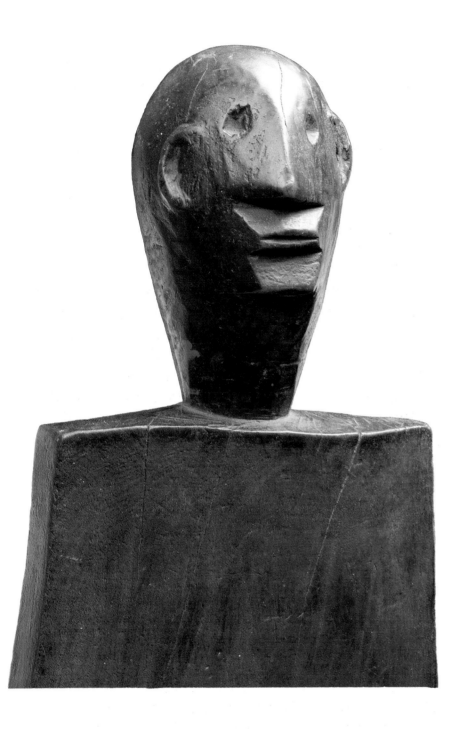

177. Ceremonial chair (detail of back)
Gurunsi. Burkina-Faso. Barbier-Mueller Museum, Geneva. The chair is reproduced in its entirety on pages 28–9.

they are not restricted to a single cultural dimension. They may be encountered anywhere and everywhere, when one expects them the least, independently of luxury and expressed in the most humble materials.

The arts of the African continent are not compartmentalized according to type: statues, masks, objects, etc. They are omnipresent, and the simple objects of everyday life, no less than the most refined accessories, have earned them an enviable place in the cultural heritage of humanity.

Map of Africa

Tribes mentioned in the text

1	Akan	50	Kwele	101	Tellem
2	Akye	52	Lega	102	Thonga
3	Anyi	53	Lobala	103	Tikar
4	Ashanti	55	Luba	104	Toposa
6	Baga	56	Lunda	105	Tuareg
7	Bambara	58	Mande	106	Tukulor
8	Bamileke	59	Mangbetu	107	Tshokwe
9	Bamum	60	Manyema	108	Turkana
10	Banziri	61	Marka	109	Tutsi
11	Baule	62	Masaï	111	Vili
12	Binja	63	Matakam	113	We
13	Biyanda	64	Moors	114	Wongo
14	Bobo	65	Mbuti	116	Xhosa
15	Boni	66	Mossi	117	Yakpa
16	Bushoong	69	Mumuye	118	Yohure
17	Bwaka	71	Ndebele	119	Yombe
19	Dakakari	72	Ngata	120	Yoruba
20	Dan	73	Ngiri	122	Zande
21	Dengese	74	Ngombe	123	Zulu
22	Dinka	75	Nguni		
23	Dogon	76	Nkutshu		
24	Doko	77	Nzakara		
25	Duala	78	Nzombo		
27	Ebrie	79	Nuer		
28	Edo	80	Nuna		
29	Efe	81	Nupe		
31	Fang	83	Pende		
32	Fon	84	Peul		
33	Fulani	85	Pokot		
35	Gbaya	86	Pygmy		
36	Gurunsi	88	Rendille		
38	Hausa	90	Sapi		
40	Ibibio	91	Sarakolle		
41	Ibo	92	Senufo		
42	Igala	93	Shilluk		
44	Karamojong	94	Shoowa		
45	Kele	95	Somba		
46	Konda	96	Songo Meno		
47	Kongo	97	Soninke		
48	Kota	98	Songye		
49	Kuba	100	Teke		

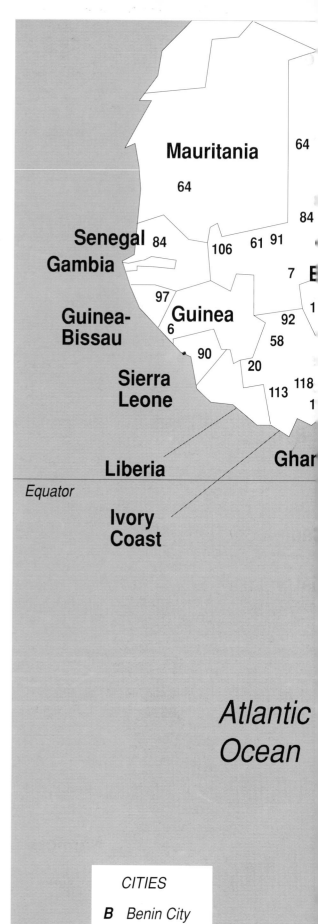

CITIES

B Benin City
I Ife
D Djenne
T Timbuktu

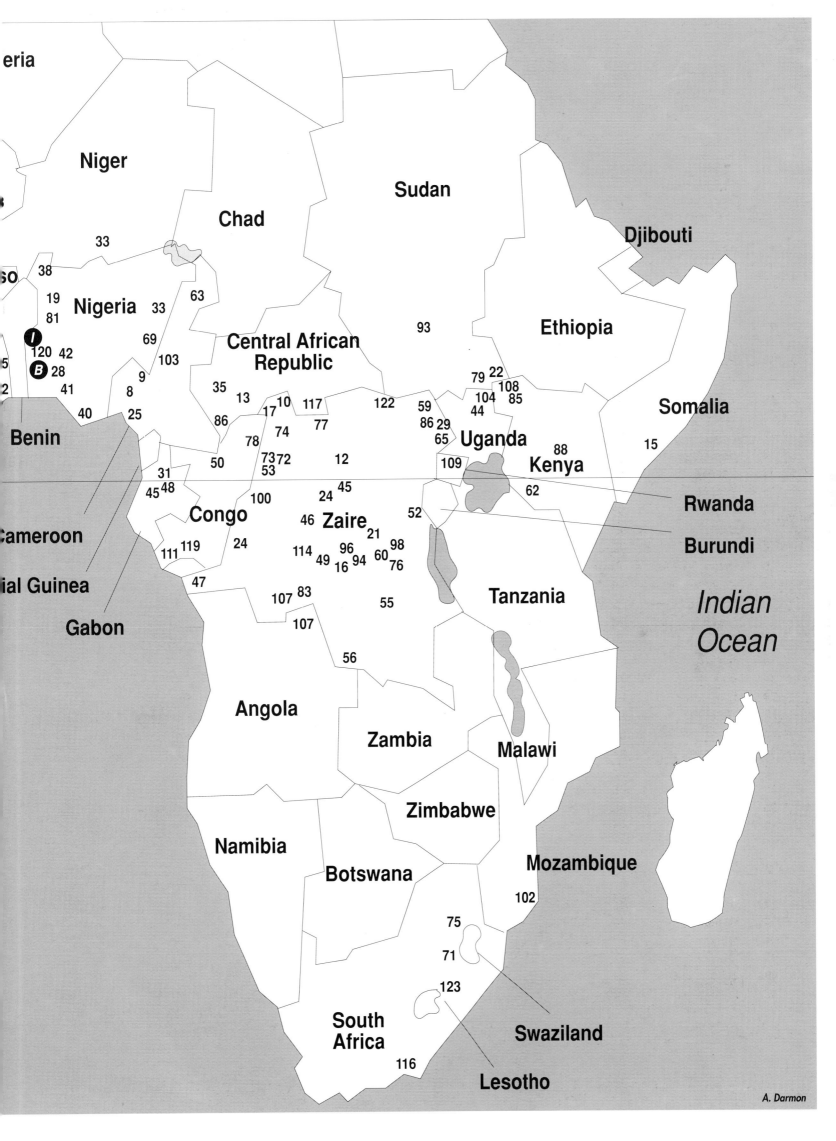

Notes

Chapter I

1. Long excerpts from Tessmann's writings are quoted (in French translation) in the book on the Fang published by the Dapper Museum, Paris, 1992.
2. Marcel Griaule, *Dieu d'eau*, Le livre de poche, Paris, 1966, p. 19.
3. On Herbert Lang, see *African Reflections* by Enid Schildkrout and Curtis Keim, University of Washington Press.
4. René Caillié, *Voyage à Tombouctou*, 2 vols, La Découverte, Paris, 1989, p. 103.
5. Esther Dagan, *L'homme au repos*, galerie Amrad d'Art africain, Montreal, 1985.
6. *Arts de la Côte-d'Ivoire*, musée Barbier-Mueller, Geneva, 1993, p. 172.
7. André Blandin, *Fer noir*, Marignane, 1988, p. 28.

Chapter II

8. Amadou Hampâté Bâ, *Amkoullel, l'enfant peul*, Babel, Paris, 1992, p. 248.
9. Georges Balandier, *La vie quotidienne au royaume de Kongo*, Hachette, 1965.
10. Enid Schildkrout and Curtis Keim, *op. cit.*, p. 114.
11. Joseph Cornet, *Art de l'Afrique noire au pays du fleuve Zaïre*, Arcade, Brussels, 1972, p. 123.
12. René Caillié, *op. cit.*, Vol. I, p. 230.
13. *Ibid.*, p. 275.

Chapter III

14. Amadou Hampâté Bâ, *op. cit.*, p. 153.

Chapter IV

15. Louis Perrois, in *Art ancestral au Gabon*, Geneva, 1985, p. 156.

16. *Günter Tessmann* in *Fang*, musée Dapper, Paris, 1992, p. 191.
17. Angela Fisher, *Africa Adorned*, Abrams, New York, 1984, p. 194.
18. Marcel Griaule, *op. cit.*, p. 91.

Chapter V

19. Olfert Dapper, in *Objets interdits*, Musée Dapper, Paris, 1989, p. 232.
20. Mungo Park, *Travels in the Interior of Africa*, Cassell, London, 1887, p. 133.
21. Joseph Cornet, in *Beauté fatale*, Crédit communal, Brussels, 1992, p. 109.
22. Camille Coquilhat, quoted by Christian Grosseau, in *Beauté fatale*, p. 123.
23. Marc Felix, in *Beauté fatale*, p. 26.
24. Mungo Park, *op. cit.*, p. 31.

Chapter VI

25. Amadou Hampâté Bâ, *op. cit.*, p. 282.
26. Gabriel Seligmann, quoted by Bertil Sönderberg in *Afrique, formes sonores*, Paris, 1990, p. 31.
27. *Arts de la Côte-d'Ivoire*, musée Barbier-Mueller, Geneva, 1993, p. 115.
28. Amadou Hampâté Bâ, *op. cit.*, p. 199.
29. M.-N. Verger-Fèvre, in *Arts de l'Afrique noire*, musée Barbier-Mueller, Geneva, 1989, p. 115.
30. René Caillié, *op. cit.*, Vol. I, p. 336.
31. Marcel griaule, *op. cit.*, p. 23.

Chapter VII

32. Olfert Dapper, in *Objets interdits*, pp. 255–6.
33. Georges Balandier, *op. cit.*, p. 162.

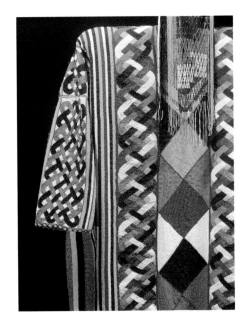 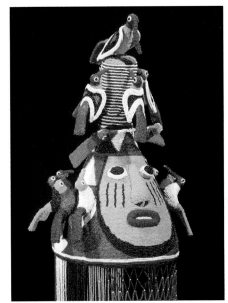

Where to see African objects

In Africa

Museum of the I.F.A.N. (Institut Fondamental d'Afrique Noire), Dakar (Senegal), re-opened in 1994 with a new catalogue.
Musée National d'Abidjan (Ivory Coast).
National Museum, Lagos (Nigeria).
Musée de Fouban (Cameroon).

In France

Musée des Arts d'Afrique et d'Océanie, Paris.
Musée de l'Homme, Paris.
Musée Dapper, Paris.
Musée Municipal, Angoulême.
Musée des Missions Africaines, Lyons.

In Europe

British Museum, London.
Musée Barbier-Mueller, Geneva.
Museum Rietberg, Zurich.
Musée Royal de l'Afrique Centrale, Tervuren (Belgium)
Museum für Völkerkunde, Berlin.
Museum für Völkerkunde, Vienna.

In the United States of America

The Metropolitan Museum of Art, New York.
American Museum of Natural History, New York.
National Museum of African Art, Washington, D.C.

Index

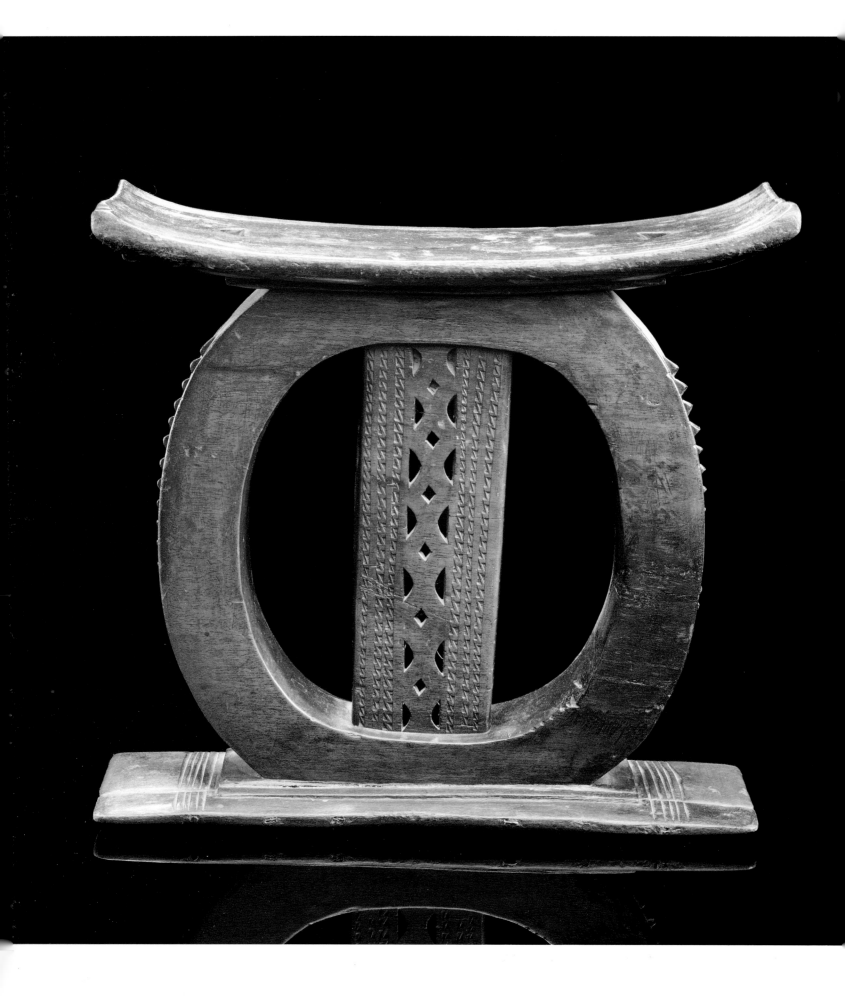

Selected Bibliography

General reference

BALANDIER Georges and coll., *Dictionnaire des civilisations africaines*, Paris, 1968.

BALANDIER Georges, *Afrique ambiguë*, Paris, 1957.

BEN-AMOS Paula, *L'art du Bénin*, Paris, 1979.

CORNET Joseph, *Art de l'Afrique noire au pays du fleuve Zaïre*, Brussels, 1972.

DELANGE Jacqueline, *Arts et peuples de l'Afrique noire*, Paris, 1967.

DESCHAMPS Hubert, *L'Afrique noire précoloniale*, 'Que sais-je' Collection, Paris, 1976.

Geneva, Musée Barbier-Mueller, *Arts de l'Afrique noire*, Paris, 1988.

Geneva, Musée Barbier-Mueller, *Arts de la Côte-d'Ivoire*, 1994.

KERCHACHE J., PAUDRAT J.-L., and STEPHAN L., *L'art africain*, Paris, 1989.

LAUDE Jean, *Les arts de l'Afrique noire*, Paris, 1966.

LEIRIS Michel and DELANGE Jacqueline, *Afrique noire*, Paris, 1962.

LEUZINGER Elsy, *Afrique, l'art des peuples noirs*, Paris, 1981.

MAQUET Jacques, *Les civilisations noires*, Paris, 1981.

NEYT François, *Luba*, Musée Dapper, Paris, 1994.

Ashanti stool
See page 20.

203

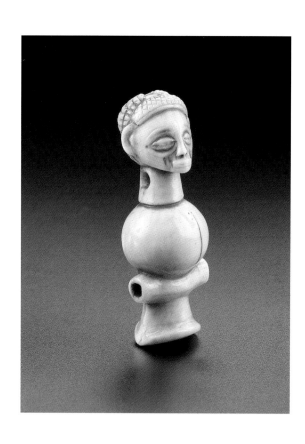

Whistle
Tshokwe. Zaïre. Ivory.
Private collection.

Paris, Galeries Nationales du Grand-Palais, *Trésors de l'ancien Nigéria*, 1984.

Paris, Musée Dapper, *La voie des ancêtres*, 1986.

Paris, Musée Dapper, *Art et mythologie, figures tshokwe*, 1988.

Paris, Musée Dapper, *Fang*, 1991.

Paris, Musée des Arts d'Afrique et d'Océanie, *Les vallées du Niger*, 1993.

PAULME Denise, *Les civilisations africaines*, 'Que sais-je' Collection, Paris, 1980.

PAULME Denise, *Les sculptures de l'Afrique noire*, Paris, 1956.

PERROIS Louis, *Arts royaux du Cameroun*, Musée Barbier-Mueller, Geneva, 1994.

WASSING René, *African art, its background and traditions*, New York, 1988.

WILLETT Frank, *African Art*, London, 1971.

Books by travellers and Africans

BÂ Amadou Hampâté, *Amkoullel, l'enfant peul*, Babel, Paris, 1992.

BARBOT Jean, *Journal d'un voyage de traite en Guinée, à Cayenne et aux Antilles, fait par Jean Barbot en 1678-1679*, Dakar, 1979.

BARBOT Jean, *A Description of the Coasts of North and South Guinea*, London, 1732.

CAILLIÉ René, *Voyage à Tombouctou*, 2 volumes, La Découverte, Paris, 1989.

DAPPER Olfert, *Description de l'Afrique*, long excerpts translated in *Objets interdits*, Musée Dapper, Paris, 1989.

GRIAULE Marcel, *Dieu d'eau*, Le livre de poche, Paris, 1966.

PARK Mungo, *Travels in the interior of Africa*, Cassell, London, 1887.

TESSMANN Günter, long excerpts translated in *Fang*, Musée Dapper, Paris, 1992.

Books on African life

DAGAN Esther, *Man at rest. L'homme au repos*, Montreal, Quebec, 1985.

DAGAN Esther, *Tabourets Asante. Stools,* Galerie Amrad, Montreal, 1988.

Paris, Musée Dapper, *Supports de rêves*, 1989.
RAVENHILL Philip, *The Art of the Personal Object*, National Museum of African Art, Washington D.C., 1991.

On vessels and spoons

DAGAN Esther, *La calebasse africaine*, Galerie Amrad, Montreal, 1989.
Paris, Musée Dapper, *Cuillers sculptures*, 1991.

On textiles

Geneva, Musée Barbier-Mueller, *Art pictural des pygmées*, 1990.
Paris, Musée Dapper, *Pygmées*, 1991.
PICTON John and MACK John, *African Textiles*, British Museum Publications, London, 1991.
SIEBER Roy, *African Textiles and Decorative Arts*, Museum of Modern Art, New York, 1972.
Paris, Musée Dapper, *Au royaume du signe. Appliqués sur toile des Kuba*, 1988.
MEURANT Georges, *Abstractions aux royaumes des Kuba*, Musée Dapper, Paris, 1987.

On jewelry

FISHER Angela, *Africa Adorned*, Abrams, New York 1984.
FALGAYRETTE-LEVEAU, *Corps sublimes*, Musée Dapper, Paris, 1994.
Geneva, Musée Barbier-Mueller, *Gold of Africa*, Munich, 1989.
GAREY Margret, *Beads and Beadwork*, Shires Publications, Aylesbury, 1986.

On weapons

Brussels, Crédit Communal, *Beauté fatale. Armes d'Afrique centrale*, 1992.
FISHER Werner and ZIRNGIBL Manfred, *African weapons*, Passau, 1978 (English and German).

On musical instruments

BRINCARD Marie-Thérèse, *Afrique. Formes sonores*, Paris, 1990.

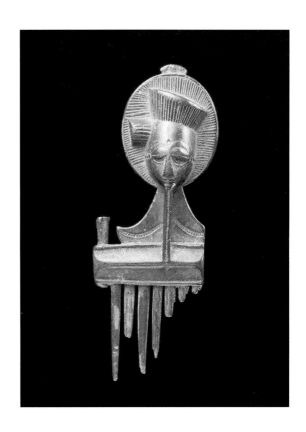

Comb
Lagoons area tribes.
Ivory Coast. Wood.
H.: 16 cm.
Private collection.

Acknowledgements

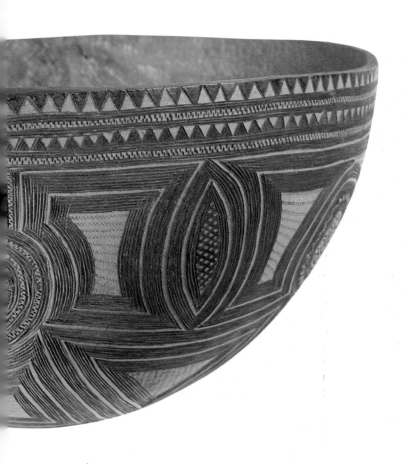

I would like to express my gratitude to all the people who made this book possible through their help and encouragement. Mr Jean-Paul Barbier was extremely generous in lending us photographs of a great many of the objects in his museum, in putting the resources of the Photo Library at our disposal, and in giving us his advice and suggestions. I would also like to thank the many collectors who gave us permission to reproduce some of their finest pieces, yet preferred to remain anonymous.

A great many people also participated in the technical aspects of this publication. It owes much to the skills of Mrs Sibylle de Fischer, who was responsible for the lay-out, and to the talent of the photographers: Hughes Dubois, Pierre-Alain Ferrazzini and François Tissier. Mr Fernando Valmachino mastered the subtleties of coordinating reproduction material from other museums. Mrs Laurence Mattet, from the staff of the Barbier-Mueller Museum, was extremely helpful in smoothing out difficulties during the various phases of this project.

They all receive my heartfelt thanks.

Laure Meyer

Photo credits

Archives Monbrison : p. 8
Basel, musée d'Ethnographie/Artephot/A. Held : p. 79
Berlin, Museum für Völkerkunde/D. Graf : p. 121
(n° 111), 171 (n° 160, inv. : III. C. 778)
Berlin, Museum für Völkerkunde/Schütz : p. 167
(inv. : III. C. 975), 33 (inv. : III. C. 14966)
Brussels, H. Dubois : p. 6, 12, 40, 44, 49, 59 (n° 45 et
n° 46), 65, 71, 74-75, 81, 109, 112, 116, 130, 139
(n° 129), 153, 156, 157, 165, 169, 173, 174, 175, 188,
192, 204, 205
Geneva, archives Barbier-Mueller : p. 67, 83, 114, 117,
137, 147, 148
Geneva, archives Barbier-Mueller/J-P Barbier : p. 25,
181
Geneva, archives Barbier-Mueller/J. Campe : p. 11, 13,
39, 70 (n° 70), 97, 100, 108, 111, 162, 170
Geneva, archives Barbier-Mueller/H. Dubois : p. 78
Geneva, musée Barbier-Mueller : p. 2, 22, 72-73, 90,
92, 93, 95 (n° 80), 105, 163, 176, 187, 195
Geneva, musée Barbier-Mueller/M. Aeschimann : p. 82
Geneva, musée Barbier-Mueller/P.A. Ferrazzini : p. 16-
17, 20 (n° 9), 21, 23 (n° 11, n° 13), 24, 26, 27, 28-29,
31, 35, 38, 43, 54, 58, 62, 63, 64, 84, 85, 87 (n° 72,
n° 73), 88-89, 99, 102, 103, 104, 106 (n° 94), 107, 118,
120, 122-123, 125, 126, 127, 128, 131, 132, 134, 136,
138, 139 (n° 128), 140, 142-143, 144, 146-147, 149,
150, 154-155, 159, 160, 161, 178, 182, 190, 202
Geneva, musée Barbier-Mueller/R. Asselberghs : p. 141,
172
Ife, Museum of Antiquities/Artephot/A. Held : p. 168
Lagos, National Museum : p. 145, 171 (n° 159)
Lagos, National Museum/Artephot/A. Held : p. 5, 50,
51, 52, 106 (n° 93), 184, 186, 199 g d

London, British Museum : p. 19, 20 (n° 8), 47, 69 (n° 57
et n° 58), 110
Los Angeles, Museum of Cultural History, University of
California : p. 42
Marseilles, G. Bonnet : p. 32
Neuchâtel, musée d'Ethnographie : p. 15
New York, The Brooklyn Museum : p. 185
New York, The Metropolitan Museum of Art : p. 30, 53
(inv. : 1991. 17. 126 ab), 119 (inv. : 1977.173)
New York, The American Museum of Natural History /
L. Gardiner : p. 133, 151, 152 (inv. : 90.1 / 3317)
Offenbach (Main), Deutsches Leder-Museum : p. 121
(n° 109)
Paris, musée des Arts d'Afrique et d'Océanie / Artephot /
A. Held : p. 36-37
Paris, musée des Arts d'Afrique et d'Océanie/RMN : p. 98
Paris, musée de l'Homme : p. 41 (inv. : 20 371), 206
(inv. : 20 371), 206 (inv. : 20371)
Paris, musée de l'Homme/D. Destable et Ch. Lemzaouda :
p. 56 (inv. : 11202)
Paris, musée de l'Homme/Artephot/A. Held : p. 178-179
Paris, musée de l'Homme/D. Ponsard : p. 69 (n° 56)
Paris, musée de la Monnaie : p. 70 (n° 62), 96
Paris, musée de la Seita/D. Dado : p. 158
Paris, RMN : p. 80
Paris, F. Tissier : p. 14, 45, 91 (n° 75 et 76), 94 (n° 82 et
83), 94 (n° 79), 115
Rome, musée Luigi Pigorini : p. 155
Vienne, Museum für Völkerkunde : p. 61 (inv. : 91.912)
Washington, National Museum of African Art : p. 76
Washington, National Museum of African Art / Franks
Khoury : p. 18, 46, 164
Zürich, Museum Rietberg/Wettstein et Kauf : p. 34

Printed in Italy
by Grafiche Zanini - Bologna